Walter Robson

British History 1066 - 1900

Oxford University Press 1995

Oxford University Press, Walton Street, Oxford OX2 6DP

Oxford   New York
Athens   Auckland   Bangkok   Bombay
Calcutta   Cape Town   Dar es Salaam   Delhi
Florence   Hong Kong   Istanbul   Karachi
Kuala Lumpur   Madras   Madrid   Melbourne
Mexico City   Nairobi   Paris   Singapore
Taipei   Tokyo   Toronto

and associated companies in
Berlin   Ibadan

Oxford is a trade mark of Oxford University Press

© Oxford University Press 1995

First published 1995

ISBN 0 19 917256 0

Typeset by AFS Image Setters, Glasgow
Printed in Italy by G. Canale & C. S.p.A. - Borgaro T.se - TURIN

Acknowledgements

Ashmolean Museum, Oxford: p137; Bibliothèque Nationale, Paris: p86 (right); Bibliteek van de Rijksuniversiteit te Gent: p126; The Bodleian Library, Oxford: p25, p55 (bottom), p78 (roll 172B), p79 (bottom) (Ms Bodley 764 f44), p84 (top left) (Ms 285 f6v)/Courtesy of the President and Fellows of Corpus Christi College, Oxford, p85 (bottom right), p89 (Ms Bodley 270b f129vd), p90 (bottom) (Ms Bodley 264 f105), p91 (Ms Douce 6 f22), p99; The Bridgeman Art Library: p65/Bibliothèque Nationale, Paris, p105 (left)/Guildhall Library, London, (right)/Ecole des Beaux Arts, p106 (top left)/Rafael Valls Gallery, London, p120 (centre)/V & A, p151 (bottom left)/Blenheim Palace, Oxfordshire, p195/V & A , p196 (centre left), p205, p210/Ackeman & Johnson Ltd., London, p215 (top)/Museum of British Transport, p215 (bottom), p216/Science Museum, p221/Giraudon, p234 (top)/Guildhall Library London, p254 (bottom), p260/British Library, p272 (top right)/Wallington Hall; Brighton Borough Council: p271 (centre); The British Library: p21, p23 (Harl Roll Y 6 (3)), p26 (Sloane 2435 f44v), p27 (Roy 2a XXii f220), p34 (left) Add 4838), pp52 -53 (Add 42130, f158, f173, f171, f172v, f170, f170v), p54 (Cott Tib B V f5 ptl), p58, p61 (left) (Roy 18 Elf175), p62 (left) (Cott Jul E IV f7v), p62 (right) (Add 42130f202v), p70 (Add 40742f10), p74 (bottom) (Roy 15 E 11 f265), p75 (right) (Roy 15E III f259)), p77 (Egerton 1894 f5v)), p79 (top), 84 (top right) (Harl 4431 f81), p85 (bottom left) (Add 28162 f10v), p86 (left) (Harl 3745 fl), p97 (bottom) (Cott Tib A IV f9v); British Library: p98 (topleft), p100, p117 (top), p119 (top right), p125 (top left and bottom), p140, p153 , p176, p190, p193, p194 (bottom), p196 (bottom right), p207 (top), p212, p214, p235, p262 (top); Reproduced by courtesy of the Trustees of the British Museum p42, p124 (centre and bottom right), p222 (centre left and bottom right), pp226-227, p233 (top), p265, p277; British Waterways: p211 (bottom); By permission of the Duke of Buccleugh & Queensberry KT and with the approval of the Keeper of the Records of Scotland , ref no GD 55/174: p44 (top); The Burrell Collection, Glasgow Museums and Art Galleries: p13; Cambridge University Collection of Air Photographs: p52 (top), p57, p191/Crown Copyright ; Reproduced by permission of the Archbishopof Canterbury and the Trustees of Lambeth Palace Library: p64, p68 (topright); Chipchase Castle: p183 (topand bottom); John Cleare: p172 (top right); Charles D Cobb: p218 (bottom left)/National Maritime Museum, London; Courtesy of the Master and Fellows of Corpus Christi College, Cambridge: p14 (top), p39 (top left); Edinburgh Photograph Library: p154; Edinburgh University Library: p45; English Heritage: p24 (bottom); E T Archive: p31/Keir Collection, p93/Honourable Society of the Inner Temple, p98 (bottom left), p119 (bottom left)/Victoria & Albert Museum, p135, p156 (bottom right), p157 (bottom), p171 (top left), p201 (top)/Ironbridge Gorge Museum, p247/Bibliothèque des Arts Decoratifs, Paris, p250, p252 (bottom), p264 (top)/National Maritime Museum, p278 (bottom); Fine Art Photographs: p96/Gavin Graham Gallery; Fotomas Index: p162 (centre right); Giraudon: p186 (bottom)/Bridgeman; Glasgow Museums and Art Galleries: p63 (left) (Reg no 39-65-e); Sonia Halliday Photographs: p19 (top), p28 (top), p28 (bottom right)/Bibliothèque Nationale, Paris, p41, p61 (right), p69; Reproduced by gracious permission of Her Majesty the Queen: p34 (right); HMSO: p134 (top left); Michael Holford: p181, p184 (top); Hulton Deutsch Collection: p160, p228, p237 (bottom), p246 (bottom), p259, p266, p267, p269; Illustrated London News: p194 (centre), p233 (bottom), p242; Manchester City Art Gallery: p206 - p207 (bottom); Mansell Collection: p103, p111 (left and right), p115 (centre right), p119 (centre), p133, p139 (bottom right), p143, p161 (centre left), p164 (bottom left), p166, p174, , p177, p178, p180 (top left), p182, p188, p189 (top), p198, p199 (top), p208, p211 (top), p217, p220 (top and bottom), p222, p223 (top), p229, p230, p232, p234 (bottom), p237 (centre), p241, p251, p252 (top), p254 (top), p256, p257, p258, p262 (bottom), p268, p271 (top), p275, p276, p280; Mary Evans Picture Library: p80, p95,p102 (right), p107, p131 (top), p145 (top left), p171 (top right), p173, 180 (bottom left), p201 (bottom), p202, p218 (centre, p219, p238, p245, p246 (top right), p248 (bottom); Metropolitan Museum, New York: p199 (bottom); Michael Holford: p7, pp10 - 11, p12, p14 (bottom), p17, p19 (bottom), p35, p75 (left), p85 (top); Museum of English Rural Life, Reading: p192 (top right and centre right); The Museum of London: p20, p74 (top), p170, p271 (bottom); The National Gallery of Ireland, Dublin: p50, p255 (top and bottom); National Gallery of Scotland: p120 (top); National Library of Ireland: p125 (top right); National Library of Wales: p129, p130 (bottom right), p131 (bottom); National Maritime Museum: p163; National Museums & Galleries on Merseyside (Walker Art Gallery): p204; The National Museum of Wales: p39 (top right); National Portrait Gallery, London: p71 (left), p108 (bottom left), p109, p112, p113 (bottom left and bottom right), p117 (bottom), p128, p134 (bottom), p138 (left), p139 (bottom left), p146, p149 (top centre and top right), p150 (bottom), p152 (top and bottom), p169 (top, centre and bottom), p187 (top), p279; National Trust: p102 (left)/Upton House (Bearsted Coll.)/Angelo Hornak, p158/Ron Fox, p184 (bottom), p185 (top)/R C Wylie, (bottom)/J Whittaker, p186 (top)/Rob Matheson , p187 (centre left)/Ray Hallett, (centre right)/Mike Williams, p270; Oxford City Council: p150 (top)/Thomas Photos; The Pierpont Morgan Library, New York: p28 (bottom left); Punch: p246 (top left), p278 (top); Royal Commission on the Historical Monuments of England: p55 (top); Royal Commission on Ancient & Historical Monuments in Wales: p131 (bottom left); Royal Geographical Society: p264 (bottom); Royal Society: p145 (topright); Science Museum, London: p203; Historic Buildings and Monuments of Scotland: Crown Copyright: p44 (bottom); Scottish National Portrait Gallery: p122 (bottom), p138 (right); Slide File: p124 (bottom left), p161 (cenre right), p162 (bottom left); Edwin Smith: p71 (right); Sir John Soane's Museum: p225; Stiftsbibliothek St Galien, Switzerland: p51; Tate Gallery, London: p272 (bottom left); Courtesy of the Master and Fellows of Trinity College, Cambridge : p84 (bottom), p87, p88; The Board of Trinity College, Dublin: p48 (topand bottom); Victoria & Albert Museum: p243, p244 (top and bottom); Wales Scene: p131 (top left); Wales Tourist Board: p37; Reproduced by permission of the Trustees of the Wallace Collection: p63 (right); Weidenfeld & Nicholson Archives: p24 (top right)/Trinity College, Cambridge, p29/Bibliothèque Nationale, Paris, p36, p92/Victoria & Albert Museum, p94/Public Record Office, London, p141; The Welsh Folk Museum: p60 (left and right); Woodmansterne Picture Library: p18 (left and right), p24 (top left), p82, p83; Zefa: p39 (bottom), p47; In a private collection: p46.

The illustrations are by Juliet Breese, John James, Peter Kent, Anthony Knill, Miller Craig and Cocking, Martin Sanders, Duncan Storr and Brian Walker.

Cover Photographs: Michael Holford (Bayeux Tapestry) and National Portrait Gallery.

Contents

Contents continued

Preface

The title of this series is *Access to History*, and accessibility is its keynote – accessibility to National Curriculum History, in terms of both the Programme of Study and the Attainment Target.

The exercises which refer to the text, sources, and illustrations, are intended to extend factual knowledge, promote comprehension, and develop a range of skills, all consistent with the National Curriculum Key Elements. The 'criteria grid' (at the end of the book) shows how the individual exercises relate to the Key Elements.

It is not expected that pupils will work through the book unaided. Teachers will wish to omit some exercises and amend others. They will probably decide that some exercises which are set for individual work would be tackled more successfully by using a group or class approach, with the teacher him/herself as leader. The book's aim is to provide teachers with a useful set of resources, not to usurp their role.

The exercises with the fill-in blanks may be either photocopied to provide answer sheets and homework assignments, or copied out by the pupils and filled in as they go along.

The Norman Conquest

A The Battle of Hastings

A south wind blew in the English Channel on 28 September 1066. It took a fleet of little ships across the sea from France to England. They were packed with knights, archers, and horses. **Duke William of Normandy** was on his way to England.

King Harold of England was waiting with his army in Sussex (look at the map). But he heard that the king of Norway, had invaded the north of England. Harold marched his men north at once, and beat the Norwegians in a battle near York.

While Harold was in the north, Duke William and his army landed in Sussex. As soon as Harold heard the news, he rushed south again. But he moved too fast for some of his men. He reached Sussex with only half the army.

The English and Normans met in battle near Hastings, on 14 October 1066. It was a long, hard fight, which the Normans won. By the end of the day, Harold and all his bodyguard lay dead. Just two months later, William was crowned king of England. We now call him **William the Conqueror**.

Now try Exercise 1.1.

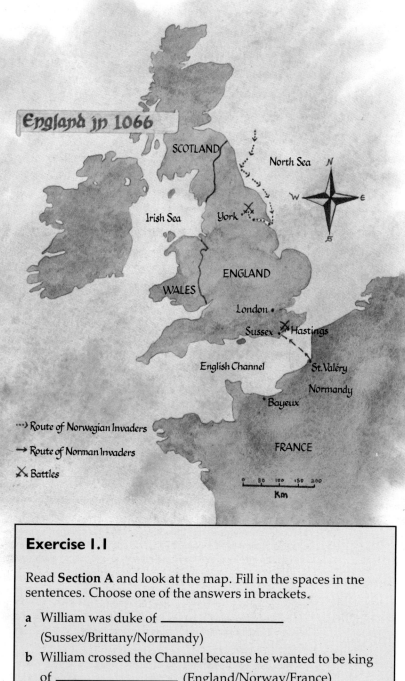

England in 1066

- ···▷ Route of Norwegian Invaders
- ─▶ Route of Norman Invaders
- ✗ Battles

Exercise 1.1

Read **Section A** and look at the map. Fill in the spaces in the sentences. Choose one of the answers in brackets.

a William was duke of _____
(Sussex/Brittany/Normandy)

b William crossed the Channel because he wanted to be king of _____ (England/Norway/France)

c The king of England was called _____
(Harold/Edward/Henry)

d Harold marched north to fight _____
(the king of Scotland/the king of Norway/some Yorkshire rebels)

e The English and Normans fought a battle near _____
_____ (London/Hastings/York)

B The Normans take control

The English did not want a Norman king. There were revolts, but William crushed them. Men who fought against the Normans were killed, and so were their wives and children. The Normans pulled down their homes and set fire to their crops.

The Normans built castles in all the main towns and in many villages. Castles were places where the new Norman lords could live in safety. And it was from the castles that Norman knights rode out to punish the English when there was trouble.

At first, they built **motte-and-bailey** castles. The bailey was a mound of earth, protected by a ditch and a wooden stockade, with wooden huts inside. This is where the Normans normally lived. If the English attacked, and broke into the bailey, they would retreat to the motte, a higher mound, with a wooden tower on top. (Look at the drawing below.)

After a few years, the Normans began to build stone castles. Instead of a wooden tower, they built a keep. This was a high stone tower with thick walls – so strong that many keeps are still standing. (Look at the photograph below.)

Now try Exercise 1.2.

A Norman motte-and-bailey castle

Rochester Castle in Kent. The stone keep was built in 1130. The walls are nearly 4 metres thick.

Exercise 1.2

Read **Section B**. Copy the drawing of a motte-and-bailey castle. Add labels, using words from this list:

bailey stockade ditch bridge tower motte huts.

C Who owns the land?

William the Conqueror said that all the land in England belonged to him. He kept some of it for himself and he gave some to his lords. They became William's **barons** (another word for lords). The most important barons were called **earls**.

The barons and earls were the leaders of the king's army. They had helped him to conquer England, and now they helped him to rule it. The chief men in the church – the bishops and abbots – were just as important as the barons and earls. They too were given land by the king.

Each baron, earl, bishop and abbot paid rent for his land, not with money, but with help in time of war. He promised to lead his **knights** into battle on the king's side whenever there was a war. The more land he had, the more knights he had to bring. We call this the **feudal system**.

The lords and bishops who paid their rent to the king are known as **tenants-in-chief**. When they got their land, they had to kneel before their king and promise to serve him. This was called **doing homage** to the king. A man who did homage to the king was the king's **vassal**.

William did not always trust his great lords. He knew that if the king was not strong, they might rebel. So in 1086 he decided to find out how much land each of them had. He sent his men to each county in England. They had to find out who owned the land, and how much it was worth. They wrote their report in what we call **Domesday Book**.

Now try Exercise 1.3.

THE FEUDAL SYSTEM IN ENGLAND

THE KING

TENANTS-IN-CHIEF
(VASSALS OF THE KING)

EARL OF DERBY
(Paid rent for his land
with 80 knights)

ABBOT OF WESTMINSTER
(Paid rent for his land
with 15 knights)

MANY OTHER
TENANTS-IN-CHIEF

THE MORE LAND A TENANT-IN-CHIEF HAD, THE MORE KNIGHTS HE HAD TO SEND TO SERVE THE KING

Sources

We find out about the past from **sources**. Books and papers are **written sources**. Books written by monks soon after 1066 tell the story of the Norman Conquest. The monks were not present at the battle of Hastings, but some of them may have talked to men who were there. **Source 1b** and **Source 1c** are from books written by these monks.

Old coins, buildings, weapons, and pictures are also **sources**. The Bayeux Tapestry (**Sources 1d** to **1i**) tells the story of the Norman invasion in pictures.

Source 1a

King William sent his men to all parts of England. They had to find out how much land the king had. They also found out how much land the churches and his barons held. This was done so well that every scrap of land, and every ox, cow, and pig was put into the report.

Written by a monk at Worcester soon after the year 1100.

Exercise 1.3

Read **Section** C, then answer the questions in sentences.

a What were barons?
b What were earls?
c In the feudal system, great men paid rent for their land with what?
d What were tenants-in-chief?
e What did doing homage mean?
f What was a vassal?
g What was Domesday Book? (Read **Source 1a**.)

Source 1b

William built three thousand ships, and filled them with mighty horses and brave men. He crossed the sea and landed at Pevensey. He left some of his troops there, and hurried on to Hastings with the rest. He built a castle there. Harold rode all night to reach the enemy. The battle began at nine o'clock, and went on all day. Harold fought in the front rank of the army, and he fell, covered with wounds.

Written by a monk called Robert at a monastery in Normandy, about four years after the Battle of Hastings.

Source 1c

The Normans attacked before Harold's army was ready. The English fought hard, and many men were killed on both sides. King Harold was killed, and so were his brothers Leofwine and Gyrth.

Taken from an old book called the *Anglo-Saxon Chronicle*. This part was possibly written by a monk in York shortly after 1066.

Exercise 1.4

Read the notes on **Sources**. Read **Sources 1b** and **1c**, and look at **Sources 1d** to **1i** on pages 8–9. Now try the questions.

a Who wrote **Source 1b**, and when?
b **Source 1c** comes from which old book?
c Who wrote **Source 1c**, and when?
d Were the authors of **Sources 1b** and **1c** at the battle of Hastings?
e What are **Sources 1d** to **1i** taken from?
f Who made the Bayeux Tapestry, and when?

Sources 1d – 1i The Bayeux Tapestry

The Bayeux Tapestry is a piece of embroidered linen, about 70 metres long. It tells a story in pictures, with words in Latin. It was probably made by some ladies in Canterbury not long after 1066. You can still see the tapestry in a museum in Bayeux in Normandy. Six scenes are printed for you here.

Source 1d

The Normans prepare to invade England.

Source 1e

The Normans cross the English Channel.

Source 1h

The Latin words say 'The brothers Leofwine and Gyrth are killed'.

Source 1i

The death of King Harold

Source 1f

The Normans build a castle at Hastings.

Source 1g

The battle of Hastings – English on the left, Normans on the right.

Exercise 1.5

Read the written sources (**Sources 1b** and **1c**) and look at the pictures in **Sources 1d** to **1i**. Read the notes with **Sources 1d** to **1i** too. Now try the questions. Answer them in sentences.

a What are the men doing in **Source 1d**?
b One of the written sources tells us about William getting ready to cross the English Channel.
  i Which source?
  ii What does it say?
c **i** How big were the ships in **Source 1e**?
  ii How many masts and sails did they have?
  iii How were they steered?
d Which written source says the same as **Source 1f**?
e Look at **Source 1g**. How were the English and the Norman soldiers:
  i the same?
  ii different?
f **Source 1h** tells us something that is mentioned by one of the written sources.
  i What is that?
  ii Which written source does not mention it?
g **i** Which of the soldiers in **Source 1i** do you think is King Harold?
  ii Does **Source 1i** tell us how Harold was killed?
  iii Do the written sources tell us how Harold was killed?

Exercise 1.6

Look again at **Sources 1d** to **1i**, then tell the story in your own words. Put some of the details from the pictures into your story. (You could write out your story, or put it onto tape, or tell it to the rest of your group.)

2 Knights, Lords, and Kings

A Knights

War took up a great deal of a king's time in the Middle Ages. Earls and barons were soldiers above all. Even bishops and abbots sometimes led their knights into battle.

Knights were soldiers who fought on horseback. They were the main fighting force in every army. A knight's main weapons were the **lance** (a long, thin spear) and the sword. (Look at **Sources 1g, 1h** and **1i** on pages 10 and 11.) It took many years of training to become a skilled knight.

A knight went into battle dressed in armour made from lots of iron rings (sometimes called **chain-mail**). He had an iron helmet, and he carried a long, narrow shield. A knight had to be strong to carry all that weight. So had his horse! War-horses were big, heavy animals. They could trot, but not gallop.

At first, Norman knights lived in the great lords' castles. But not long after 1066, the lords began to give away pieces of land to their knights. A knight paid rent for his land by doing guard duty at his lord's castle, and serving with his lord in the army.

Now try Exercise 2.1.

Source 2a

This scene from the Bayeux Tapestry shows the Normans getting ready to invade England. The Latin words say: 'These men are carrying arms'.

Exercise 2.1

Read **Section A**, and look at **Sources 2a** and **2b**. Answer questions **a** to **e** in sentences.

a Which weapons can you see in **Source 2a**?
b How are the men in **Source 2a** carrying the suits of armour? Why do you think they are carrying them like that?
c Describe the helmets worn by the knights in **Source 2b**.
d Describe the shields carried by the knights in **Source 2b**.
e What does **Source 2b** tell us about what knights wore under their armour?
f Draw a picture of a Norman knight. Put labels on your drawing to show the names of his weapons and pieces of equipment.

Source **2b**

A bronze carving showing three Norman knights

Here's the pear you asked for.

Idiot! J'ai demandé mon père.

For 200 years after 1066, all of England's rulers spoke French. Kings, earls, barons, and bishops were French. They knew enough English to give orders to their servants, but no more. "Old English", as we call it, was the language of the peasants. But there were far more peasants than lords. In time, English took over, and by the year 1400 everyone spoke it. By then, though, it was a mixture of "Old English" and the French the Normans brought to England.

B Civil war

Like most countries in the Middle Ages, England was a **monarchy** – it was ruled by a king. And the king needed to be strong. But not all kings were strong enough. King **Stephen**, William I's grandson, spent most of his reign fighting a **civil war** against his cousin **Matilda**.

The earls and barons had their own castles and armies of knights and archers. In Stephen's reign, some fought for the king, and some fought for Matilda. Most of the time, they did as they liked. The worst of them robbed and tortured the English peasants and burned their homes.

When Stephen died, **Henry II**, Matilda's son, became king. Henry was only 21 years old. He was good-looking, tough, and fond of sport. He was also a wise and brave ruler. He was not afraid of the great lords, and had made up his mind that there would be no more civil war.

When he was in England, Henry travelled far and wide, making sure that there was peace, law, and order in the land. He sent his judges round the country, so that accused persons would get a proper trial. He made all the lords and knights swear to obey him, their king.

Now try Exercise 2.2.

Attacking a castle: a knight urges on the footsoldiers. The picture was drawn in about 1250.

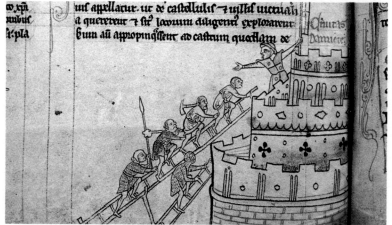

Exercise 2.2

Read **Section B**. Some passages from the *Anglo-Saxon Chronicle* have been printed below, in the wrong order. Write them out in the proper order (earliest first).

1100 William II was killed by an arrow fired by one of his men when he was out hunting.

1137 All the great men built castles and refused to obey King Stephen.

1068 William I built a castle at Nottingham and two castles at York.

1120 Henry I's son was drowned when his ship was wrecked in the Channel.

1154 Stephen died. Henry II arrived from France and was crowned king.

1131 There was a terrible outbreak of disease among cattle and pigs.

1092 King William II made many peasants take their wives and animals and go and live in Cumberland.

The castle of Angers, one of Henry II's strongholds in France

C Henry II's empire

Before he became king of England in 1154, Henry II already ruled part of France. Henry's father was Geoffrey, the count of **Anjou** and **Maine**. (Look at the map on page 15.) Like most great lords, he spent much of his time at war. In 1150, Geoffrey conquered **Normandy**, and gave it to Henry. When Geoffrey died in 1151, Henry got Anjou and Maine.

Henry's wife, **Eleanor**, brought him **Aquitaine** as well. Eleanor was the **heiress** of the duke of Aquitaine. This meant that she was the only daughter of the last duke, and that he had no sons. When he died, all the duke's land (most of south-west France) went to Eleanor's husband.

Later, Henry's third son, another **Geoffrey**, married the heiress of the duke of **Brittany**. So Brittany came under Henry's rule also. By 1171, Henry II was master of half of France. The French king wanted to drive him out. So Henry had to spend most of his time in France, fighting or getting ready for war.

Now try Exercise 2.3.

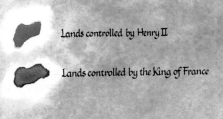

Lands controlled by Henry II

Lands controlled by the King of France

Norman knights won control of parts of South Wales in William the Conqueror's time.

Henry II made himself ruler of part of Ireland in 1171.

Exercise 2.3

Read **Section C**, and look at the map. Complete the following table.

Place	How and when Henry II got control
England	Henry became king in _____ when Stephen died.
Normandy	Henry's father conquered Normandy. Henry became duke in _____.
Anjou and Maine	Henry got these counties when his _____ died in 1151.
Aquitaine	Henry's wife, _____, was the heiress. She was the _____ of the last _____ of Aquitaine.
Brittany	Henry's son _____ married the _____ of the duke of Brittany.
Wales	Part of _____ Wales was conquered by the _____ _____.
Ireland	Henry became ruler of part of Ireland in _____.

Source 2c

When Stephen was king, the great lords built castles everywhere, without the king's permission. Then they seized the men and women who had some money. They tortured them to make them hand over their gold and silver. Some were hung up by their thumbs, and others were put in pits full of snakes. The lords made the peasants pay them taxes as well. When the peasants had no more to give, the lords burned their homes.

From the *Anglo-Saxon Chronicle*. This part was written by a monk at Peterborough in about 1155.

Source 2d

When Stephen died, Henry II became king. Straight away, he said that lords who had built castles in Stephen's reign had to pull them down. Henry was keen on law and order. He sent judges round England to keep the wicked lords in check, and to see that all men got justice. For this, Henry won the praise and thanks of his people.

From *The History of England*, written by a monk called William of Newburgh at a monastery in Yorkshire in about 1190.

Exercise 2.4

Read **Sources 2c** and **2d** and read the note on fact and opinion.

a Write down *three* facts from **Source 2c**.
b What were the opinions of the author of **Source 2c** on:
i King Stephen?
ii the great lords?
c Write down *three* facts from **Source 2d**.
d What was the author's opinion of Henry II?
e What was the common people's opinion of Henry II?
f What would be the great lords' opinion of Henry II?
g Why would the common people and the great lords have different opinions?

Fact and opinion

A **fact** is something which is, or was, true. It is a **fact** that the Normans conquered England.

An **opinion** is what someone thinks or thought. The English people's **opinion** was that the Normans were cruel and greedy.

Exercise 2.5

Look at the cartoon on page 13 and read the caption. Some of the words we now use come from Old English and some from French.
These words are from Old English:

Bloom, Bowman, Folk, Hunt, Leave, Old, Pretty, Right, Teach.

These words come from French:

Archer, Ancient, Beautiful, Chase, Correct, Depart, Flower, Instruct, People.

Find the pairs of words, one English, one French, with the same meanings. Write them out in a chart.

3 The Church in the Middle Ages

A The village church

Most people in western Europe belonged to the **Roman Catholic** church in the Middle Ages. The church was at the centre of everything that went on. Babies were baptised by the priest in the church. Young couples were married at the church door. The dead were buried in the church yard. People were supposed to go to **Mass** (the church service) on Sundays and the main "holy days". These were the only days off work that they got.

All men and women believed in Heaven and Hell. Rich people left land and money to the church in their wills because they hoped it would help them get into Heaven. The church used the money to look after the old and sick.

Village priests were simple men. They could usually just manage to read, and knew enough **Latin** to say the Mass. Priests were not supposed to marry, but a lot of them did have wives. Most priests must have looked and talked like the peasants around them.

Now try Exercise 3.1.

The front of the twelfth-century church at Iffley in Oxfordshire

Source 3a

He has been a parish priest for more than 30 years, but he can neither sing the Mass properly, nor read the Bible. He can't explain the psalms to the people. But he's good at hunting hares in the fields.

From *Piers Ploughman*, a poem written by William Langland in about 1380.

Source 3b

The parson was a poor man. But he knew the Bible and could preach it to the people. He did not like taking money from poor men, and would often give away his own money.

From *The Canterbury Tales* by Geoffrey Chaucer – see Source 3f.

Fact or fiction?

Sources 3a and **3b** are **fiction**, not fact – these are **not about real** priests. But there must have been a lot of priests just like these two in the Middle Ages.

Exercise 3.1

Read **Section A** and **Sources 3a** and **3b**. Answer the questions in sentences.

a Who wrote **Source 3a**, and when?
b Who wrote **Source 3b**, and when?
c Are **Sources 3a** and **3b** fact or fiction?
d Why are **Sources 3a** and **3b** useful to the student of history?
e What were the differences between the priests in **Sources 3a** and **3b**?

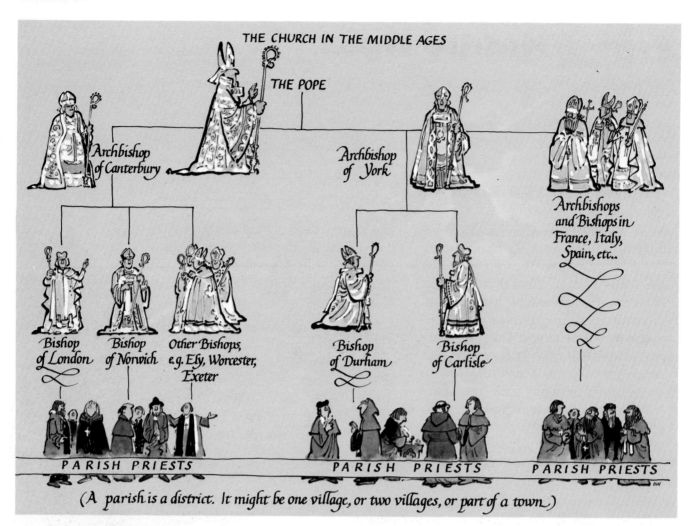

THE CHURCH IN THE MIDDLE AGES

THE POPE

Archbishop of Canterbury

Archbishop of York

Archbishops and Bishops in France, Italy, Spain, etc..

Bishop of London

Bishop of Norwich

Other Bishops, e.g. Ely, Worcester, Exeter

Bishop of Durham

Bishop of Carlisle

PARISH PRIESTS

PARISH PRIESTS

PARISH PRIESTS

(A parish is a district. It might be one village, or two villages, or part of a town.)

Source 3c

Durham Cathedral. This part of the cathedral was built in the twelfth century. (Norman style)

Source 3d

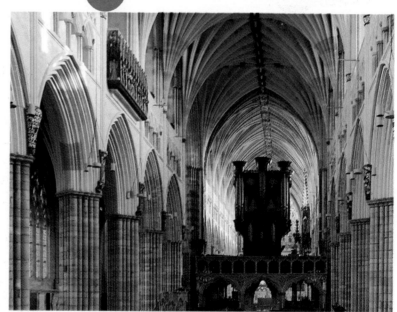

Exeter Cathedral. This part of the cathedral was built in the fourteenth century. (Decorated style)

B Bishops and cathedrals

The head of the Catholic church was the **Pope**, who lived in Rome. Each **see** (or district) was under the control of a **bishop**. Bishops had to make sure that the priests in their sees could read, and that they said Mass at the right times. Bishops took orders from **archbishops**. The Archbishops of Canterbury and York were the top men in the church in England.

The king picked most of the bishops. He often gave the jobs to his own advisers and friends. Many bishops stayed with the king at court. Some never went near their sees.

The chief church in each see was the **cathedral**. The cathedrals built in the Middle Ages are some of the finest buildings in England. The cathedrals were bright and colourful inside. The walls were painted, and there were lots of sculptures, and gold and silver ornaments.

Now try Exercise 3.2.

This stained-glass window in Canterbury Cathedral shows pilgrims at the tomb of St Thomas (page 20).

Centuries

A **century** is a period of a hundred years.
The **first century** A.D. was the hundred years from AD 1 to AD 100.
The **second century** A.D. was the hundred years from AD101 to AD 200.
The **seventh century** was the hundred years from AD 601 to AD 700.
The year AD 410 was in the **fifth century**.
The year AD 1359 was in the **fourteenth century**.

Source 3e

Winchester Cathedral. This part of the cathedral was built in the fifteenth century. (Perpendicular style)

Exercise 3.2

Read the note on **Centuries**, then look at **Sources 3c**, **3d** and **3e**.

a Fill in the gaps in the sentences.

   i **Source 3c** is called the _____ style. It was built in the _____ century (between the years _____ and _____).

   ii **Source 3d** is called the _____ style. It was built in the _____ century (between the years _____ and _____).

   iii **Source 3e** is called the _____ style. It was built in the _____ century (between the years _____ and _____).

b Draw a time-line, from the twelfth century to the fifteenth century. Mark these styles of building against the right centuries: Norman, Decorated, Perpendicular.

C Thomas Becket

In the Middle Ages many people went on **pilgrimages**. A pilgrimage was a journey to a **shrine**. And a shrine was the place where a saint was buried, or where some holy object was kept. **Pilgrims** thought that God would be pleased with them and reward them if they travelled to a shrine and prayed there. He might cure them of their diseases, for example.

The most famous shrine in England was in Canterbury. It was the tomb of **St Thomas Becket**. Thomas was the archbishop who was murdered inside the cathedral in 1170. The pope made him a saint in 1173.

Thomas had been one of Henry II's chief advisers, and his best friend. In 1162, Henry made Thomas his Archbishop of Canterbury. He thought that Archbishop Thomas would make the church obey the king. But he was wrong. Thomas stood up to the king.

A row broke out when the king said that priests who had done wrong must be tried in the king's courts. Thomas said 'No', because the church had its own courts.

Thomas fled from England and lived in France for seven years. When he returned in 1170, the quarrel started again. So four of Henry's knights decided to do their king a good turn and get rid of his enemy. They travelled to Canterbury, and murdered Thomas in his own cathedral.

Henry took all the blame for the murder. On a summer day in 1174, the men and women of Canterbury watched him walk barefoot through their streets. When he reached the cathedral, he made the monks whip his bare back. He spent the night lying on the stone floor near Thomas's tomb.

Now try Exercise 3.3.

Source 3f

Pilgrims bought metal badges to show where they had been. The Canterbury badge, shown here, was supposed to be a flask of St Thomas's blood, which was said to cure the sick.

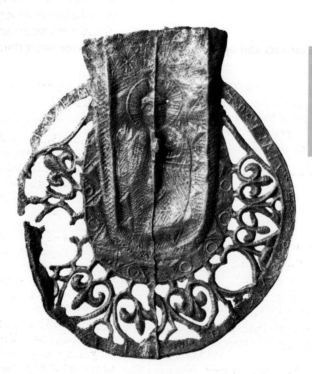

Source 3g

Some pilgrims go to the shrine of saints in far-off lands. In England, crowds go from every county to Canterbury to visit the Holy Martyr. He is famous for helping the sick.

From *The Canterbury Tales*, a long poem written by Geoffrey Chaucer in about 1390. Chaucer pretended that he was one of a group of pilgrims who travelled together from London to Canterbury. To pass the time on the journey, each of the pilgrims had to tell a story.

Exercise 3.3

a Read **Section C**, then make your own notes on the story of Thomas Becket.

   i Who are the *two* most important persons in the story?
   ii Which are the *four* most important events in the story?
b Look at **Sources 3f** and **3h**, and read **Source 3g**.
   i Which *two* facts about pilgrims to Canterbury can we learn from **Source 3g**?
   ii Write down *two* facts about pilgrims that we can learn from Sources **3f** and **3h**.

Source 3i

When the Bishop of Winchester died, King Henry III did not look very sad. He set out to make his own half-brother, Aylmer, the new bishop. Aylmer was not even a priest. In any case, he was too young and was not well educated.

The monks at Winchester have the right to choose the bishop. So the king sent two men there to get them to pick Aylmer. When they failed, the king went to Winchester himself, and made the monks give in.

Written by a monk called Matthew Paris in 1250.

Exercise 3.4

Read **Source 3i**, then read again the notes on **Fact and opinion** on page 14. Write paragraphs for **b** and **c**.

a Write down any *four* **facts** in **Source 3i**.
b What was the author's **opinion** of Aylmer? Did he think that he was the right kind of man to be Bishop of Winchester?
c What do you think was Matthew Paris's **opinion** of the way the new Bishop of Winchester was chosen?

Source 3j

Priests who break the law are tried first by the church courts. The king said that if they are found guilty, they should be sent to the king's court to be punished. Thomas discussed this with the other bishops and abbots. Then he said that what the king wanted was against God's law. The king got angry and told Thomas and the bishops that they had to obey him.

Written by a priest called Henry of Bosham soon after 1170.

Source 3h

Pilgrims leaving Canterbury on their way home.

Causes and reasons

A **cause** is a **reason** for something. It is the answer to the questions '**Why** did it happen?' or '**Why** was it like that?' For example:
   Why did Duke William invade England in 1066?
Often, there is more than one answer to the question **Why**?
   There are a number of **causes** or **reasons** for most things.

Exercise 3.5

Read **Source 3j**. What does **Source 3j** tell us about the **causes** of the quarrel between Henry II and Thomas Becket? Answer questions **a** to **c** in sentences, and question **d** in a paragraph. Use your own words.

a What did King Henry II want to happen to priests who broke the law?
b Why did Thomas disagree?
c Did anyone else agree with Thomas?
d Henry and Thomas had been friends. Do you think this made the king more angry or less? Was it a **cause** of their quarrel?

4 Monks and Friars

Plan of a monastery

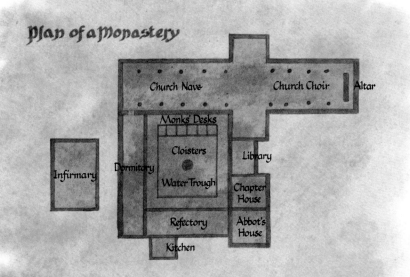

A The life of a monk

Monks were men who gave their lives to God. They spent their time praying and working for their fellow men and women. They lived in **monasteries**, under very strict rules. All monks promised to obey their abbot or prior (the head monk). They had to promise not to marry. And they had to give away all their money and goods. The rules laid down every detail of the monks' lives.

MONKS' DAILY TIMETABLE IN SUMMER (IN WINTER SOME OF THE TIMES WERE DIFFERENT)

Out of bed for the first service at midnight.

Back to bed in the dormitory. Straw mattresses were changed once a year.

Second service at 6 a.m.

Washing in cold water in the cloisters.

Breakfast of bread and ale in the refectory. All meals in silence.

Period of work.

Third service - Chapter Mass at 9 a.m.

Chapter - daily meeting at 10 a.m. in chapter house - to discuss business.

High Mass at 11 a.m.

Dinner - no meat allowed.

Private reading.

Nones (fifth service) at 2 p.m.

Work (e.g. copying books) Monks worked in the cloisters.

Vespers (sixth service) at 4 p.m.

More work.

Supper - bread and ale at 6 p.m.

Last service at 7 p.m.

Bed at 7.30 p.m.

For a large part of each day, the monks were in the **choir**. This was the part of the monastery church where they sang and prayed during the services. The local people were sometimes allowed to stand in the **nave**. (Look at the plan of a monastery.)

Monks also had to work. Some cooked and cleaned. Some worked in the fields. Many studied and taught. Others carefully copied out books by hand (the only way of making new books). But they all had to stop when the bell rang for prayer.

Girls might become **nuns**, but only if their fathers were rich. Convents got gifts from the families of new nuns. Like monks, nuns had to make promises, obey rules, and work. Many of them ran schools for girls.

Now try Exercise 4.1.

B Monks and local life

In most places, the monastery's great stone church was the largest building for miles around. The monks played a big part in local life. They looked after the old and sick. They took in travellers who needed a bed for the night.

Monks not only copied books. They also wrote them. Some of them wrote **chronicles**, which were records of things that happened each year. Monks heard the news from travellers who stayed with them. Chronicles written by monks are useful **sources** for students of history.

People who were accused of crimes could ask for **sanctuary** at a monastery. This meant that they could ask to stay there for 40 days. While they were there, no-one could arrest them. To avoid arrest after the 40 days was up, they had to go straight to the nearest

Exercise 4.1

Read **Section A**. Study the cartoons and the monastery plan. Draw your own plan of a monastery, and write in the names of the buildings. Mark the letters **A**, **B**, **C**, **D**, **E**, **F**, and **G** on your plan to show the following:

A The place where the monks slept.
B The part of the church where the monks prayed.
C The place where the monks washed.
D The place where the monks ate their meals.
E The place where the monks held their daily meetings.
F The place where the monks sat when they were copying books.
G The place where sick people were looked after.

Put a key on your plan to show what the letters stand for.

Source 4a

Monks had the tops of their head shaved. This was called the 'tonsure'.

Source 4b

Source 4c

Durham Cathedral was also a monastery. Anyone wanting sanctuary had to use this knocker on the door.

This picture of a monk comes from a twelfth century book.

port and take the first ship to a foreign country.

Monasteries owned a lot of land. The local peasants worked in their fields. Food from the monasteries' farms fed the monks and their guests. But the monks also sold the spare corn and wool. The money they made paid for the schools and hospitals they ran. What was left paid for extra buildings and decorations for the church.

Now try Exercise 4.2.

Exercise 4.2

Read **Section B**, and study **Sources 4a, 4b, 4c,** and **4d**.
Write your own notes on the following topics. You must use your own words.

a The tonsure
b Sanctuary
c Monks and books
d Monastery farms

Source 4d

Prior's Hall Barn, Widdington, Essex. It was built about 1400. The prior was the prior of St Valéry in Normandy.

C Friars and Lollards

As time went by, some monks forgot their rules. They allowed themselves better food, including meat. They stopped working in the fields. They began to keep servants to cook and clean for them.

Soon after the year 1200, **St Francis** in Italy and **St Dominic** in Spain started groups of **friars**. The friars had to be really poor – they had to live as beggars. It was their job to preach the Christian message to the people. By about 1220, there were friars in England.

Monasteries were often in country places, but friars worked in towns. They wore threadbare clothes, went without shoes, and lived in simple shacks. Their only food was what kind people gave them.

The friars were soon very popular Crowds came to hear them preach. Rich men and women gave them money, which the friars kept for themselves. Before long, they too had fine churches, wore warmer clothes, and were looked after by servants.

Men and women complained about rich and lazy bishops, monks, and friars. A teacher at Oxford called **John Wycliffe** said it was time for reform – putting things right. His followers, who were called **Lollards**, drew big crowds when they preached. The bishops began to worry, and got the kings to take their side. Many Lollards were locked up, and some were put to death.

Now try Exercise 4.3.

Exercise 4.3

Read **Section C**, and read **Sources 4e, 4f,** and **4g.** Now use the sources to find out whether the sentences below are true or false. Write "True" or "False" after each sentence.

Source 4e

a In 1380, the friars still cared only about the poor. _____

d By 1380, the friars had churches of their own. _____

Source 4f

c Some of those who spoke against the church were priests themselves. _____

d People had to pay taxes to the church. _____

e Those who spoke out against the church were popular with ordinary men and women. _____

f You can find nothing written against the church in books written by monks. _____

Source 4g

g At the end of the fourteenth century, monks were still supposed to study and work with their hands. _____

h We do not know whether Chaucer's monk was a rich man. _____

Source **4e**

The friars go after the rich folk. They have no time for the poor. No-one can be buried in one of their graveyards or churches unless he leaves them some money in his will.

From *Piers Ploughman*, written by William Langland in about 1380.

Source 4f

William Swinderby was a priest in Leicester. He said that people should not pay tithes to wicked, lazy, or ignorant priests. The bishop was angry, and banned him from preaching in churches. So he set up a pulpit in the street. Crowds from all over flocked to hear him.

Written by Henry Knighton, a monk in Leicester, in 1390. Tithes were taxes which people had to pay to the church.

Source 4g

The monk was keen on hunting. His stable was full of good horses. He found the monastery rules too strict, and let things slide. He said, 'Why should I study in the cloister or work with my hands?'. Riding and hunting the hare were more in his line.

From Geoffrey Chaucer's *Canterbury Tales*, written in about 1390.

A friar preaching.

A monk drinking in secret.

Source 4h

The Scots soldiers had no respect for God or man. They caused ruin to the whole district. Men and women, lords and peasants, were put to death. Towns, churches, and houses were set on fire. The Scots spared no-one, not even the children.

Our abbey stood right in the path of these madmen. So the local people rushed there for refuge. It is a very holy place, with more than one saint buried there. Not even the savage Scots dared to touch it.

Written by a monk called Richard, who lived at Hexham Abbey in 1138, at the time of the Scots invasion.

Primary and secondary sources

Letters and chronicles written by people who were present, and saw the things they wrote about, are called **primary sources**.

Papers and books written by people who were **not present** are called **secondary sources**. The authors of **secondary sources** must have heard about the events from someone else, or read about them in books.

Points of view

Not every word in the sources is true. A lot of authors had their own **point of view**. If they took part in the events, they might belong to one side or the other. Often, they had opinions, or feelings, about what had happened. Some writers might be pleased, or proud. Others could be sad, or afraid. Their points of view sometimes made them **exaggerate** (say things were better or worse than they really were).

Exercise 4.4

Read **Source 4h**. Answer the questions in sentences.

a What is a primary source?
b Who wrote **Source 4h**?
c When did the Scots invasion described in **Source 4h** happen?
d Where was the author of **Source 4h** at the time of the invasion?
e Which words tell us that the Scots did not damage Richard's abbey?
f Is **Source 4h** a primary source? (Give a reason for your answer.)

Exercise 4.5

Read **Source 4h** again. Write a paragraph giving *your* opinions about the following questions.

What do you think was Richard's point of view?
What were Richard's opinions or feelings about the events?
Which parts of **Source 4h** do you think may be exaggerations?
Why do you think Richard may have exaggerated?

Exercise 4.6

Look again at the cartoons on page 22.
Tell the story of a monk's day. (You do not have to include every scene.)

Either (a) write an essay, **or** (b) make a tape

5 The Crusades

A knight 'taking the cross'. He kneels before a priest and promises to serve God. He is wearing the sign of the cross on his surcoat over his chain-mail armour.

A The Kingdom of Jerusalem

Jesus was put to death in **Jerusalem** in Palestine. (Palestine was called **The Holy Land**). So Jerusalem was a holy place for pilgrims. The long journey there was full of danger – from bandits, disease, and shipwreck. But in 1071 the **Turks**, who were Moslems, conquered the Holy Land, and shut the Christian pilgrims out. The pilgrim route was closed.

The Pope was shocked. He urged Christian knights to go and fight a **Crusade** (or holy war) to win back Jerusalem from the Turks. He said that all who took part were sure to go to Heaven.

The Route to the Holy Land

ENGLAND
GERMANY
Durnstein
Atlantic Ocean
FRANCE
AUSTRIA
Black Sea
Constantinople
SPAIN
ITALY
ASIA MINOR
SICILY
CYPRUS
Antioch
THE HOLY LAND
Mediterranean Sea
Acre
Damietta
Jerusalem
EGYPT

→ Richard I's route to the Holy Land
→ Richard I's journey home

On his journey home, Richard I was held prisoner by Duke Leopold at Durnstein.

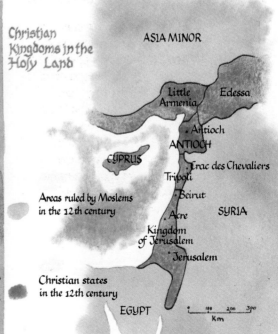

Christian Kingdoms in the Holy Land

ASIA MINOR
Little Armenia
Edessa
Antioch
ANTIOCH
CYPRUS
Crac des Chevaliers
Tripoli
Beirut

Areas ruled by Moslems in the 12th century

SYRIA
Acre
Kingdom of Jerusalem
Jerusalem

Christian states in the 12th century

EGYPT

Crac des Chevaliers, the great fortress of the Knights Hospitaller (see map on page 27). The Knights Hospitaller were like monks in armour. They were knights who gave their lives to God, and promised to obey their Grand Master. 'Hospitallers' came from all over Europe to the Holy Land.

Hundreds of knights 'took the cross'. (Look at Source 5a). They made a big sacrifice. They had to leave their wives and families for at least two years. Many of them borrowed money to buy arms and horses, and to pay the wages of the foot-soldiers who came with them.

The knights met at **Constantinople**, then set out in 1097 across Asia Minor. (Look at the maps.) The roads were bad and the food was poor. Most of the men were ill, and many died. But the Crusaders reached **Antioch**, and took it after a siege. Then they headed for Jerusalem.

The Turks fought hard to keep Jerusalem. (It is a holy city for Moslems too.) But in July 1099 the Crusaders broke in. They killed the Turks and destroyed the **mosques** (Moslem temples). Then some Crusaders went home. But others stayed in the Holy Land. They built churches and castles, and chose one of their leaders to be **King of Jerusalem**.

Now try Exercise 5.1.

Exercise 5.1

Read **Section A**, then write sentences to show that you know what the following words and phrases mean:

a Pilgrims (Look back to page 20 if you are not sure.)
b The Holy Land
c Crusade
d Taking the cross
e Sacrifice
f Mosque

Source 5b

Crusaders attack a Moslem city. The crusaders are using a catapult to try to break down the city walls.

Source 5c

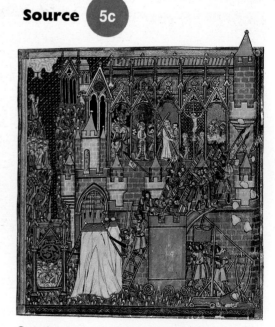

Crusaders using a siege-tower to attack Jerusalem in 1099.

B Richard the Lion Heart

In 1187, Turks led by **Saladin** took Jerusalem and Acre from the Christians. This made the pope call for a new Crusade. **King Richard I** of England took the cross. (He was so brave that men called him **the Lion Heart**.)

Richard reached the Holy Land in 1191. He, King Philip of France, and Duke Leopold of Austria joined the army trying to take **Acre**. Their **catapults** (see Sources 5b and 5d) threw huge stones at the city walls. The miners dug tunnels underneath. Soldiers fought from **siege-towers** (see Source 5c). Both kings, and most of their men, were ill with fever.

At last, the Turks in Acre gave in. Richard and Philip put their flags on the city walls. But when Leopold did the same, Richard threw the Austrian flag into the moat. Leopold was deeply hurt, and left for home. A short while later, Philip of France set sail too.

Richard stayed, and nearly reached Jerusalem. But he had too few men to take it, and had to turn back. He and Saladin made peace. The Turks kept Jerusalem, but Christian pilgrims could visit it.

Richard set out for England. On his way, he was seized in Austria by Duke Leopold. He was held captive for more than a year. The English had to pay a **ransom** of £100,000 to buy freedom for their king.

Now try Exercises 5.2 and 5.3.

Source 5d

When the crusaders attacked the city of Nicaea in Asia Minor, they used the heads of captured Turks, instead of stones, in their catapults.

Exercise 5.2

Look at **Sources 5b, 5c**, and **5d**. Answer questions **a** to **d** in sentences.

a Which different weapons can you see being used in **Source 5b**?
b What did a catapult do? (Look at **Source 5b**.)
c How do you think Crusaders used siege towers? (Look at **Source 5c**.)
d What are the Crusaders doing in **Source 5d**? Can you think why they are doing this?
e Draw a picture of either a catapult or a siege tower.

Causes and results

Causes come before events. Causes are the reasons why the events happen. The conquest of Jerusalem by the Turks was a cause of the Crusades.

Results come after events. One result of the first Crusade was that Baldwin of Flanders became King of Jerusalem.

Exercise 5.3

Read Source 5e. Then read the following sentences. Some are true and some are false. Write 'True' or 'False' after each sentence.

a King Philip went home to France. _____ The result was that the duke of Burgundy was put in charge of the French knights in Acre. _____

b There was a war between two sultans. _____ Source 5e tells us the cause of the war. _____ One result of the war was that there were not many Turks left in Jerusalem. _____

c The duke of Burgundy turned back. _____ The cause was that he was ill with fever. _____ The result was that the Crusaders did not reach Jerusalem. _____

d Richard threw his tunic over his head. _____ The result was that he did not reach Jerusalem. _____

Source 5e

King Philip of France went home in 1191. But he let his knights remain at Acre. Their leader was the duke of Burgundy. King Richard of England was in charge of the rest of the Crusaders.

Richard and the duke heard that there was war between two sultans, and that very few Turks would be left in Jerusalem. So they set off at once. But they had not gone far when the duke said he was turning back. His reason was that he did not want Richard to get the credit for taking Jerusalem. Richard now had too few knights. When one of them said that he could see Jerusalem ahead, Richard threw his tunic over his head. If he could not capture it, he did not want to see it.

From the *Life of St. Louis*, written by Jean de Joinville in about 1290. Jean de Joinville was born in 1225.

C The failure of the Crusades

Popes kept on urging kings, lords, and knights to go on Crusades. Many answered the call. In English churches you can still see carvings of knights who took the cross.

Why did they go? Some just liked fighting. Some wanted a chance to win fame and glory. But faith in God was the most important thing. Men who had done wrong hoped that their sins would be forgiven. They all believed that Crusaders went to Heaven.

Not only soldiers went on Crusades. Monks, priests, and nuns joined them.

Some kings and lords took their wives. There was even a 'Peasants' Crusade' and a 'Children's Crusade'. Most of the peasants were killed, and a lot of the children were sold as slaves by the Turks.

In the end, the Crusaders failed. They were too few in number, and they were fighting far from home. Too often, they quarrelled among themselves. After 1250, the Turks grew stronger. When Acre fell in 1291, the 'Kingdom of Jerusalem' was at an end.

Now attempt Exercise 5.4.

Motives

Students of history often try to work out the **motives** of the people in the past. **Motives** mean their **reasons** for acting as they did. William the Conqueror's **motive** for invading England was that he wanted to be king.

Turkish mounted archers practising. The Turks wore less armour than the crusaders, so their armies could move quickly.

Source 5f

King Louis jumped into the sea, where the water came up to his armpits. He waded to the shore with his shield hung round his neck. When he reached land, he looked at the enemy and asked who they were. He was told they were Turks. At that, he put his lance under his arm and got ready to charge them. But the Turks fled. We all got onto our horses, and rode with the king to Damietta.

From the *Life of St. Louis*, by Jean de Joinville. This piece describes how St. Louis [King Louis IX of France] arrived in Egypt in 1248.

Exercise 5.4

Read **Section C**, and the notes on **Motives**.
What were the **motives** of the Crusaders?
Read the sentences below. Write out the ones which you think describe the motives of **some** Crusaders.

a Some knights just liked war.
b Crusaders knew that it would be easy to beat the Turks in battle.
c Some knights wanted to win fame for themselves.
d Each Crusader got a sum of money from the king.
e Everyone thought that Crusaders went straight to Heaven when they died.
f The peasants and children probably thought that God would protect them.
g A Crusade was just like a holiday.
h Some queens and ladies went to keep their husbands company.
i Crusaders wanted a change from the boring life at home.

Exercise 5.5

Read **Sources 5e** and **5f**, then answer the questions in sentences.

a Who wrote **Source 5e**, and when was he born?
b When did the events described in **Source 5e** happen?
c Could the author of **Source 5e** have been present when King Richard tried to take Jerusalem?
d Is **Source 5e** a primary or a secondary source?
e Who was the author of **Source 5f**?
f When did the events described in **Source 5f** happen?
g What makes you think that the author of **Source 5f** was present when King Louis landed in Egypt?
h Is **Source 5f** a primary or a secondary source?

Exercise 5.6

Read **Source 5e** again.

Either

a Draw a set of cartoons to tell the story

or

b Say what you think was the duke of Burgundy's opinion of Richard, and Richard's opinion of the duke of Burgundy. (Write two paragraphs.)

The English Empire in France at the End of King John's Reign

ENGLAND
English Channel
Normandy
Brittany   Maine   • Paris
Anjou
N
W   E
S
Atlantic Ocean   FRANCE
Gascony

0   100   200
Km

Land ruled by   Land ruled by the
King John   king of France

A Magna Carta

After Richard I returned to England, he was soon at war again. This time it was in France. King Philip of France was trying to take back the land in France which belonged to the king of England.

Richard died in 1199, and his brother John became king. But the war in France went on. By 1204, Philip had conquered all of Normandy. (Look at the map.) King John was not the only loser. Many barons had owned land in France as well as England. When Philip drove John out, they lost their French land too.

John kept trying to win Normandy back. He ordered his barons to serve in

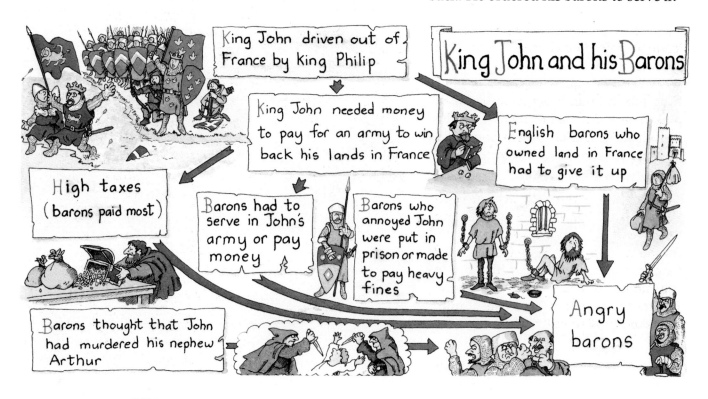

King John driven out of France by king Philip

King John and his Barons

King John needed money to pay for an army to win back his lands in France

English barons who owned land in France had to give it up

High taxes (barons paid most)

Barons had to serve in John's army or pay money

Barons who annoyed John were put in prison or made to pay heavy fines

Angry barons

Barons thought that John had murdered his nephew Arthur

his army, or send him money instead. He made the people pay heavy taxes. Men found guilty of crimes were given big fines in court. John spent the money he raised on hiring soldiers to fight in France.

In the end, some of the barons rebelled. John gave in and met their leaders in June 1215 at Runnymede, a meadow near Windsor. The king agreed to put his seal to **Magna Carta** (Latin for 'the great charter').

Magna Carta said that all **free** men had rights. The law of England would protect them. And the king had to obey the law. He could not take free men's money or put free men in prison just as he liked. (This was all right for **free** men, but most people were peasants, and not free.)

Now try Exercise 6.1.

B The beginning of parliament

King John promised to speak to his 'council' before he charged taxes. This council was a meeting of the bishops, abbots, earls, and barons. Soon after King John's time, it began to be called **parliament**. The name comes from the French word 'parler', to speak or talk. So a parliament was where the king talked to the great lords.

John's son, Henry III, also quarrelled with his barons. He too put up taxes without asking their advice. **Simon de Montfort**, who led the rebel barons, was on top for a while, but in the end he lost and was killed in battle. But Henry learned a lesson. In future, he asked parliament to agree to new taxes.

Henry III sometimes asked **knights**

Source 6a

1 *Before I make the people pay taxes, I will ask the advice of the lords in my council.*
2 *No free man may be arrested or put in prison unless other free men decide that he is guilty, and unless he has a proper trial.*
3 *Judges will not be allowed to take bribes.*
4 *People found guilty in court will not have to pay bigger fines than they can afford.*
5 *Barons will be fined only if the other barons say they are guilty.*

(Some of the promises made by King John in Magna Carta.)

Exercise 6.1

Read **Section A** and **Source 6a**, and look at the cartoon.

a Write down *four* things that made the barons angry with King John.
b Which *two* promises in Magna Carta (**Source 6a**) would most please the barons?
c Which *three* promises in Magna Carta (**Source 6a**) made sure that free men were treated properly by the courts?

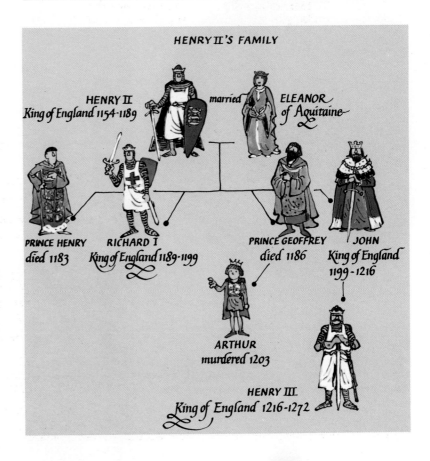

HENRY II'S FAMILY

HENRY II
King of England 1154-1189 — married — ELEANOR of Aquitaine

PRINCE HENRY died 1183

RICHARD I King of England 1189-1199

PRINCE GEOFFREY died 1186

JOHN King of England 1199-1216

ARTHUR murdered 1203

HENRY III King of England 1216-1272

of the shire to come to his parliaments. These knights owned land, but were not as rich as the barons. Later, the **boroughs**, or main towns, were told to send **burgesses**. Burgess just means townsman, but the burgesses who came to parliament were always rich merchants. These knights and burgesses were the first 'common' men, or **commons**, to sit in parliament.

By the end of the thirteenth century, parliament met quite often. It contained both great lords and commons. It had the right to say 'Yes' or 'No' to taxes. And it had the power to make **statutes**, or new laws.

Now try Exercise 6.2.

Exercise 6.2

Read **Section B**, then fill in the blank spaces in the following sentences. Use words or dates from the list below. (You will not need all of them.)

treaties   knights   taxes   1400   burgesses   bishops
kings   law   villages   1300   statutes   lords   peasants
1200   towns

a Parliament at first was a meeting between the king and his great _____.

b _____ of the shire were landowners who were not as rich as the barons.

c Boroughs were the main _____.

d _____ were the men who were sent by the towns to parliament.

e The commons were the _____ of the shire and the _____.

f By the end of the thirteenth century, parliament had the power to charge _____ and make _____.

g A statute was a new _____.

Above: King John's seal, which he fixed to Magna Carta to show that he had agreed to accept it.

Right: King Edward I with his parliament. King Alexander III of Scotland is on Edward's right, and Llyewelyn II, Prince of Wales, is on his left.

C Lords and commons

England's kings were always short of money to pay for their wars. So they often had to ask parliament for new taxes. They found that they could not manage without parliament's help.

The most important men in parliament were still the lords. Wise kings listened to their advice. Two kings, Edward II and Richard II, were **deposed** (thrown out) in the fourteenth century because they would not listen to the lords. By 1450, when Henry VI was king, the great lords were stronger than the king.

At the same time, the commons had won some rights. After 1327, they *always* took part in parliaments. By the fifteenth century, new taxes and statutes *had* to be passed by the commons as well as the lords. But there was still no 'House of Commons' or 'House of Lords'. Parliament did not always meet in London, and there were no 'Houses of Parliament'.

Now try Exercise 6.3.

The Abbey of Bury St. Edmunds in Suffolk – the lords and commons were told to join King Edward I here in 1296. Parliament did not always meet in London.

How useful are the sources?

We should not always believe the sources. It is a good idea to ask questions about them, for example:

● Who wrote this source and when?
● Was this person there when the event happened?
● Did this person have a reason to be biased (tell a one-sided story)?
● Could this person have got hold of false information?

Exercise 6.3

Read **Section C**, and read **Section A** again.
How did things change between the time of King John (early thirteenth century) and the time of King Henry VI (mid-fifteenth century)?

Fill in the spaces in the chart. Under **John** and **Henry VI**, write **Yes** or **No**. Under **Change**, write **Change** or **No Change**.

	John	Henry VI	Change?
Was the king often at war?		Yes	
Did the king need money?		Yes	
Did they use the word "parliament"?	No		
Were the lords important?			
Did the commons take part in parliament?			
Were there any "Houses of Parliament"?			

Source 6b

The devil has stirred up the barons of England against you. They have dared to make war on you. They have forced you to agree to a charter which is illegal and unfair. I completely condemn this charter. I order you not to keep it.

Letter from the pope to King John in 1216.

35

Source 6c

In the year 1215, in a place called Runnymede, King John put his great seal on Magna Carta. It was a great event in English history. It meant that from that time on, kings must obey the law. The law gave rights to all men, and kings could not take them away.

Adapted from comments by Professor W. S. McKechnie in 1915.

Source 6d

My next parliament will be held at Easter 1275 in London. All the bishops, abbots, and nobles will be there. I order you to send four knights from your county to the parliament. You must also send four or six good men from each town.

Letter from Edward I [written by one of his clerks] to the sheriff of Middlesex in 1275. Each sheriff would get the same kind of letter.

Source 6e

The nobles gathered at Oxford for the parliament. They ordered their knights to come with them, to defend them from their enemies. They were afraid that the king and his half-brothers from France would attack them. When parliament opened, the nobles told King Henry III that he must keep his promise to obey Magna Carta.

Written by a monk called Matthew Paris at St. Albans Abbey in 1259. Matthew did not go to the Oxford parliament himself.

Exercise 6.4

Not everyone thinks the same about the events of the past. For example, there have been many different opinions about Magna Carta. Read **Sources 6b** and **6c**, then answer the questions in sentences.

a Who wrote **Source 6b**, and when?
b The author of **Source 6b** said that the barons had done two things which were wrong. What were they?
c Did the author of **Source 6b** think that the king could do as he liked?
d Who wrote **Source 6c**, and when?
e **Source 6c** was written how many years after **Source 6b**?
f Did the author of **Source 6c** think that the barons were wicked?
g Why did the author of **Source 6c** think that Magna Carta was important?

Exercise 6.5

Read **Sources 6d** and **6e**. Then answer questions **a** to **g** in sentences and question **h** in a paragraph.

a Who wrote **Source 6d**, and when?
b On whose orders was **Source 6d** written?
c What does **Source 6d** tell us about the parliament of 1275?
d Should we believe what **Source 6d** tells us about the parliament of 1275?
e Who wrote **Source 6e**, and when?
f Was the author of **Source 6e** present at the Oxford parliament?
g How might the author of **Source 6e** have got to know what happened?
h Can you think of any reasons why the author of **Source 6e** might have got things wrong?

The tomb of King John in Worcester Cathedral.

7 Wales in the Middle Ages

A Wales and the marcher earls

Wales is a land of hills and mountains. In the Middle Ages, its people lived mostly by rearing cattle and hunting. They spent much of their time fighting each other, or the English. But they were also fond of music and poetry. And they were proud of their ancient Welsh language.

There was never a king of Wales. Each district had its chief, who fought wars with his neighbours. Sometimes, one man made himself master of a large part of Wales. But when he died, his land was split up among his sons.

William I did not try to conquer the whole of Wales. He gave land on the Welsh border to his most trusted lords. We call them **marcher earls** or **lords of the marches**. (March means border.) They were allowed to build castles, raise armies, and fight as much as they liked with the Welsh.

The marcher earls conquered part of south Wales. They built castles (such as Cardiff and Pembroke) and brought in English peasants to farm the land. But strong Welsh chiefs, such as the **Lord Rhys**, could get the better of the marcher earls and trouble their king. Henry II made peace with Rhys in 1171, leaving him in charge of most of Wales.

Now try Exercise 7.1.

A Welsh chief's castle at Dolbadarn in north Wales.

Source 7a

The Welsh are good horsemen. They are quick on their feet, and not fussy about what they eat. They are very different from Norman knights. In Normandy, they fight on flat land, but here all battles are on rough ground. In Normandy, there are open fields, but here there is forest. In Normandy, captured knights are ransomed, but here they are put to death. Norman knights wear heavy iron armour. The Welsh wear light armour, so that they can move easily, and fight on foot if they have to.

From a book about Wales, written by a priest called Gerald in 1188.

Wales in the Middle Ages

ANGLESEY
Degannwy
Beaumaris
Conwy
Flint
Rhuddlan
Caernarfon
Dolbadarn
Chester
GWYNEDD

Harlech

Shrewsbury

N
W — E
S

Irish Sea

Ludlow

St. Davids

Milford Haven
Pembroke

Caerffili
Chepstow

Cardiff

0   20   40   60
Km

Land more than 500 metres above sea level.
Land between 200 and 500 metres above sea level.
Land less than 200 metres above sea level.
Border with England

Exercise 7.1

Read **Section A** and **Source 7a**.

a Write down *three* important facts about the country of Wales.
b Write down *three* important facts about Welsh fighting men.
c Write down *three* facts about the marcher earls.

B The Llywelyns and Edward I

The greatest Welsh princes were the two **Llywelyns**, grandfather and grandson. Like Rhys, they were leaders of bands of archers and spearmen who could face and beat the famous Norman knights. But also like Rhys, they were wise judges and fair rulers as well.

In the time of King John, **Llywelyn I** was a prince of **Gwynedd**. (Look at the map.) He conquered his neighbours, and became the ruler of most of Wales. King Henry III of England kept on good terms with him.

When Llywelyn I died in 1240, his kingdom fell apart. His grandson, **Llywelyn II**, had to fight his way back to power. But by 1258 he was strong enough to call himself 'Prince of Wales'. And when Edward I became king in 1272, Llywelyn II refused to do homage. This was Llywelyn's way of saying, 'Keep out! The king of England has no rights in Wales'.

That meant war. Edward I invaded north Wales. He used his navy to seize Anglesey, where the corn that fed Llywelyn's men grew. The prince made peace, but it did not last. A new revolt began in 1282, but the outcome was bad for Wales. Llywelyn was killed in battle. His brother Dafydd (David) was captured and hanged. The two brothers' heads were stuck on lances and put on show in London.

Edward wanted no more trouble from Wales. He carved it up into counties, like England, with a sheriff in charge of each. He gave Wales English courts, which used English law. Thousands of English workmen were sent to build a string of castles round Gwynedd. (Look at the map.)

Now try Exercise 7.2.

Exercise 7.2

Read **Section B**, then answer the questions.
Write your answers in sentences.

a What do you think was Henry III's **motive**, or **reason**, for staying friendly with Llywelyn I?
b What do you think was Llywelyn II's **motive** for refusing to do homage to Edward I?
c What do you think was Edward I's **motive** for putting Llywelyn's and Dafydd's heads on show?
d What do you think was Edward I's **motive** for building a ring of castles round Gwynedd?

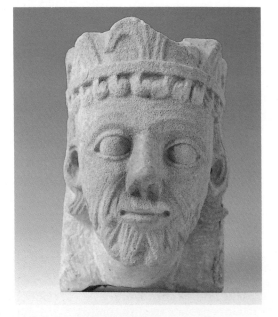

Far left: A thirteenth-century drawing showing Llywelyn I on his deathbed.

Left: A carved stone head from Deganwy, said to show Llywelyn II.

Caerffili Castle in south Wales. It was built by a great marcher earl called Gilbert de Clare.

C Glyn Dŵr and Tudor

In 1301, Edward I made his own son 'Prince of Wales'. He thought that this would bring the English and Welsh together. Since then, 'Prince of Wales' has always been the title of the king or queen of England's eldest son. Not many of them have learned to speak Welsh.

For a few years after the conquest of Wales, the Welsh stopped fighting each other and the English. But they did not all live in peace. English kings were glad to have Welsh archers in their armies. And young Welshmen were keen to earn money by fighting for the English against the Scots and French (see Chapter 10).

Some Welshmen still dreamed of a free Wales. **Owain Glyn Dŵr** (Owen Glendower) was the son of a Welsh chief. He studied law in London, and served in the English army. But when some English earls rebelled against King Henry IV in 1400, Owain joined in. He raised an army of Welshmen

A Welsh archer

and captured the king's Welsh castles. His men made him Prince of Wales.

All went well for a time. Then Henry hit back. He beat the English earls, invaded Wales, and won back his castles. Owain was killed in battle. Henry passed harsh laws which said that Welshmen could not carry arms or hold meetings. Wales was as good as part of England.

In a way, though, the Welsh were the winners in the end. **Henry Tudor**, who was a quarter Welsh, grabbed the throne of England in 1485 (see Chapter 12). Henry came by ship from France to Milford Haven in Wales. As he marched through Wales, a lot of Welshmen joined his army. They carried with them the red dragon flag of Wales. When Henry became king of England, he kept Welsh poets and singers at his court.

Now try Exercises 7.3 and 7.4.

Exercise 7.3

Read **Sections A, B and C**.
We call the years 1101 to 1130 the **early twelfth century**.
The years 1131 to 1170 are the **mid-twelfth century**.
The years from 1171 to 1200 are the **late twelfth century**.
Complete the sentences below.

a William the Conqueror invaded south Wales in 1081 (in the _____ eleventh century.)

b Owain Gwynedd ruled most of north Wales between 1137 and 1170 (in the _____ twelfth century.)

c Llywelyn I died in 1240 (in the mid-_____ century).

d Llywelyn II called himself 'Prince of Wales' in 1258 (in the _____ _____ century).

e Edward I made his son 'Prince of Wales' in 1301 (in the _____ _____ century).

f Henry Tudor landed at Milford Haven in 1485 (in the _____ _____ century).

Exercise 7.4

Historians have different **opinions** about the past.
You have to use the **facts** to decide which opinions you agree with and which ones you are against. You often find some facts on one side, and some on the other.
Think about this opinion:
'After 1301, the Welsh were quite happy to be ruled by the English. And the English expected no trouble from the Welsh.'

a Write down any facts in Section C which might make you **agree with** the opinion.

b Write down any facts which might make you **disagree with** the opinion.

Source 7b

Last Sunday I came to the town of Flint, with its great double walls and huge gates. I would like to see it on fire! There was a wedding feast going on there. But there wasn't much to drink – it was an English feast.

I tried to earn a few pence by singing some songs and playing my harp. But the guests just mocked me and jeered at me. Those simple farmers know nothing about music. They chattered about peas and manure as I sang. They sent me away with nothing, not even a bowl of bean soup. I won't go near Flint or its English people again.

From a fifteenth-century Welsh poem.

Exercise 7.5

Read **Source 7b**, then answer the questions in sentences.

a Write down as many **facts** as you can find about the *town* of Flint.
b Write down as many **facts** as you can find about the *people* of Flint.
c What was the wedding guests' **opinion** of Welsh music?
d What was the author's **opinion** of the wedding guests?
e What was the author's **opinion** of Flint?

Source 7c

Harlech Castle from the south. The houses on the hillside were not there when Edward I built the castle to keep the Welsh under control.

Source 7d

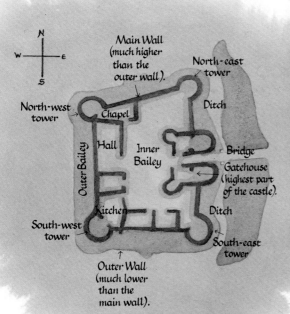

N
W   E
S

Main Wall (much higher than the outer wall).

North-east tower

North-west tower

Chapel

Ditch

Hall

Inner Bailey

Outer Bailey

Bridge

Gatehouse (highest part of the castle).

Kitchen

Ditch

South-west tower

South-east tower

Outer Wall (much lower than the main wall).

Exercise 7.6

Look at **Sources 7c** and **7d**.

a Draw a copy of the plan of Harlech Castle (**Source 7d**).
b Compare **Sources 7c** and **7d**.
  i Which parts of the castle can you see in **Source 7c**?
  ii Which parts can you not see?
c Harlech Castle was strong and difficult to attack.
  Either
  i Describe in writing how the Welsh might have attacked it. Say which would be the hardest parts of the castle to capture.
  Or
  ii Draw a set of cartoons to show an attack on Harlech Castle.

8 Scotland in the Middle Ages

A The King of England's vassal?

The peasants of Scotland were poor. They kept cattle, and grew some oats and barley. They lived in wood and earth shacks, which they shared with the animals. At first, most people spoke **Gaelic**, but English slowly spread from the south and east.

In the Middle Ages, Scotland had its own king. He was often at war. He fought the king of **Norway**, who owned the islands of the west and north. He fought the king of England,

his neighbour to the south. And he fought his own chiefs and lords. (Each chief had a band of fierce peasant soldiers.)

There was no Norman Conquest of Scotland. But **David I**, who was king from 1124 to 1153, invited some Norman knights to settle in Scotland. The knights did **homage** to the king, and became his **vassals**, or servants. With Norman knights in his army, David was a much stronger king.

These chess pieces, carved from walrus ivory, were found on the Isle of Lewis in the Hebrides. They were made in the early thirteenth century. At that time, the Hebrides belonged to Norway.

Scotland in the Middle Ages

Shetland Islands

Belonged to Norway until 1469

Orkney Islands

0   100   200
Km

Land more than 500 metres above sea level.

Land between 200 and 500 metres above sea level.

Land less than 200 metres above sea level.

Hebrides

N
W   E
S

Belonged to Norway until 1265

Aberdeen

St. Andrews
Stirling   Bannockburn
Glasgow   Edinburgh   Berwick
Norham
Alnwick
ENGLAND

IRELAND

Carlisle   Newcastle

William 'the Lion' was so-named because he was the first Scottish king to use a lion on his banner.

King **William the Lion**, David's grandson, led his knights against the Highland chiefs and forced them to obey him. But in a war with England in 1174, he was captured. Henry II of England did not set him free until William did homage and became **his** vassal.

Now try Exercise 8.1

Dates

Dates are useful things. They tell us which order events happened in. They tell us how old people were at certain points in their lives. They tell us how much time passed between events.

For example, King David I of Scotland was born in 1084, and became king in 1124. If we take away 1084 from 1124, we get the answer 40. So David I was 40 years old when he became king.

B The War of Independence

For a time there was peace, but trouble began again in 1286 when King Alexander III died. The next in line to the throne was a girl of three, Margaret, the **Maid of Norway**. (Look at the family tree.) And in 1290 Margaret herself died on her way from Norway to Scotland.

Thirteen men now claimed the right to be king. The Scots asked **Edward I** of England to choose a king for them. Edward picked **John Balliol**, and John did **homage** to Edward. This made Edward think that he could treat the king of Scotland as one of his **vassals**. When John Balliol and the Scots objected, there was war. The Scots were beaten, John gave up the throne, and Edward took control of Scotland.

Exercise 8.1

Read **Section A**, and read the notes on **Dates**.
Look at the list of dates, which are all to do with Scottish history.

1141 Malcolm IV was born.
1143 William the Lion was born.
1153 Malcolm IV became king.
1165 Malcolm IV died and William the Lion became king.
1174 William the Lion was captured at Alnwick in Northumberland.
1214 William the Lion died.

Now answer the questions.

a Malcolm IV and William the Lion were brothers. Which of them was the elder? _____

b How old was Malcolm IV when he became king? _____

c For how long was Malcolm IV king of Scotland? _____

d How old was William the Lion when he became king? _____

e How old was William the Lion when he was captured? _____

f For how long was William the Lion king? _____

g How old was William the Lion when he died? _____

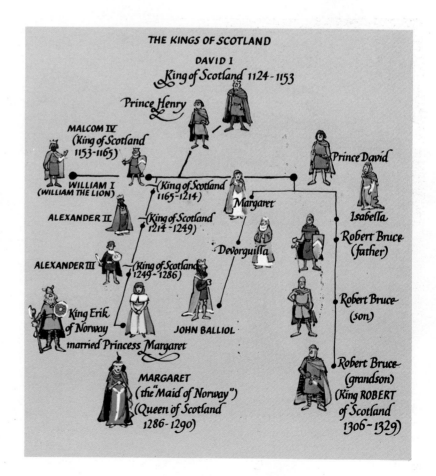

THE KINGS OF SCOTLAND

DAVID I
King of Scotland 1124-1153

Prince Henry

MALCOM IV
(*King of Scotland 1153-1165*)

WILLIAM I
(WILLIAM THE LION)
(*King of Scotland 1165-1214*)

ALEXANDER II
(*King of Scotland 1214-1249*)

ALEXANDER III
(*King of Scotland 1249-1286*)

King Erik of Norway *married Princess Margaret*

Margaret

Devorguilla

JOHN BALLIOL

MARGARET (the "*Maid of Norway*") (*Queen of Scotland 1286-1290*)

Prince David

Isabella

Robert Bruce (father)

Robert Bruce (son)

Robert Bruce (grandson) (King ROBERT of Scotland 1306-1329)

Some Scots, led by **William Wallace**, rebelled. They beat an English army in 1297. Scots **national feeling** was on their side. But when Edward came north again they fled to the hills and forests. At last, in 1305 Wallace was captured. He was taken to London, tried, and put to death as a **traitor**.

The Scots took heart when Edward himself died in 1307. His son, **Edward** II, was a poor leader. And the Scots now had **Robert Bruce** as their general and king. Bruce's army won battles and took castles from the English in a war that lasted from 1307 to 1314. It ended in a great Scots victory at **Bannockburn**, near Stirling, in June 1314. The English left Scotland – the Scots had won their **War of Independence**.

Now try Exercise 8.2.

The two sides of King Alexander II's seal show him as a judge and a soldier.

> ### Exercise 8.2
>
> Read **Section B**, and look at the family tree.
>
> **a** Who do you think are the three most important people in the story? Write a sentence about each, saying why he or she is important.)
> **b** What do you think are the four most important events in the story?

C The 'Auld Alliance'

After Bannockburn, England and Scotland were often at war. They quarrelled about land – the town of Berwick changed hands thirteen times. Both sides complained about thieves who crossed the border to steal their cattle.

For all this time, Scotland's kings kept on good terms with France, England's other enemy. The French kings were pleased if the English had to fight the Scots – it meant they had fewer troops to send to France. The Scots called this friendship the '**Auld Alliance**'.

After Robert Bruce, though, the Scots did badly in their wars. England had more men, and it was a richer country. So its king could afford bigger armies and more modern weapons. Also, the Scots lords were always fighting with each other, and with

The Scots did not have as many guns as the English. 'Mons Meg' was one of their few cannon. It was made in Flanders in about 1450. You can still see it in Edinburgh Castle.

their king. They made Scotland much weaker than it should have been.

Things improved in the time of **James IV**, who became king in 1488. James was a bright young man, keen on all kinds of art and science. He made the Scots lords obey the law, and gave his country peace for a while. But then the French talked him into invading England. He and most of his lords were killed at the battle of **Flodden** in 1513.

Now try Exercise 8.3.

Exercise 8.3

Read **Section C**.

a What were the causes of the wars between England and Scotland?
b Why was the king of France glad to have Scotland as an ally?
c Write down three reasons why the Scots did badly in the wars.

An extract from the Aberdeen Breviary – one of the first books printed in Scotland during the reign of James IV. The first printing press in England was set up by William Caxton in 1477.

Source 8a

You seized my castles and land without any excuse. You robbed me and my subjects. You took Scotsmen off to England to be prisoners in your castles. Things just go from bad to worse. Now you have crossed the border with a great army and have started killing and burning.

Part of a letter from John Balliol to Edward I, written in 1296.

Source 8b

John Balliol, the king of Scotland, promised to obey me. Then he and some of his nobles began to plot against me. English ships that were in Scottish ports were burned, and the sailors were killed. An army of Scots invaded England. They burned villages, monasteries, and churches. In one place, they set fire to a school with the children still in it. I could stand it no more. So I declared war and invaded Scotland.

Part of a letter from Edward I to the Pope, written in 1301.

Exercise 8.4

Read **Sources 8a** and **8b**. They are both about the beginning of war between England and Scotland in 1296. Answer questions **a** to **e** in sentences.

a **Source 8a** says that the war was whose fault?
b What complaints does John Balliol make? (Use your own words.)
c **Source 8b** says that the war was whose fault?
d What complaints does Edward I make? (Use your own words.)
e Which fact is mentioned in both sources?
f Why do you think the sources are so different? (Write a paragraph.)

Source 8c Scotland in the Middle Ages

45

...lace lived by robbery in the forests and hills. King Edward said he would give £200 to any man who killed Wallace. At last, Sir John Menteith captured him. He was taken to London, and tried for treason, theft, and murder. They cut off his head and cut his body into four parts to show people what happens to traitors and thieves.

Written by a monk in Bridlington in Yorkshire in the early fourteenth century.

Source 8d

Wallace led the 'common folk' of Scotland. This was why Edward I hated him so much. Edward knew that if the people were against him he would never rule Scotland in peace. So he called Wallace a traitor. And when he caught him, he had him put to death. Edward hoped that this savage act would make all Scots people fear him, and obey. But the murder of their hero just made the 'common folk' of Scotland hate the English more.

Written by a Scottish historian called E. M. Barrow in 1934. (Adapted.)

Source 8e

King James IV of Scotland. This portrait was painted in the seventeenth century by Daniel Mytens. He probably saw an earlier picture of James IV, painted by an artist who knew the king.

Exercise 8.5

Read **Sources 8c** and **8d**, then discuss these questions in a group.

a Who wrote the sources? When and where did they live?
b What did the two authors think of William Wallace?
c Did the two authors think that Edward I treated Wallace fairly?
d Can you think of any reasons why the two authors had different opinions of Wallace and Edward I?

One person should give a talk to the rest of the class (or make a tape) saying what your answers to the questions are.

Exercise 8.6

Look at **Source 8e**, then answer the questions in sentences.

a **Source 8e** is a portrait of which king of Scotland? When did he live?
b What does **Source 8e** tell us about the appearance of the king?
c **Source 8e** tells us that the king was keen on which sport?
d When was the portrait painted? Could it have been painted from life?
e How did the painter know what the king looked like?
f Should we trust what **Source 8e** tells us about the king? (Write two or three sentences.)

9 Ireland in th[e] Middle Ages

Ireland in the Middle Ages

ULSTER
Carrick-fergus
CONNAUGHT
R.Shannon + Kells
Atlantic Ocean
Clonmacnoise + Durrow . Dublin
Clonfort + The Pale
LEINSTER Irish Sea
Limerick . Clara
Jerpoint +
Waterford .Wexford
MUNSTER

N / W E / S

Land more than 500 metres above sea level.

Land between 200 and 500 metres above sea level.

Land less than 200 metres above sea level.

+ Important monasteries

0   100   200 Kms
0   62   124 miles

A Dermot and Strongbow

In the Middle Ages the Irish were mainly cattle-farmers. They used cows, not coins, as money. But they were not backward. They had been Christians for hundreds of years. Irish priests took the Christian message to many parts of Europe. Irish monks ran schools, and they were very fine artists.

The only towns in Ireland had been built by the **Vikings**. These raiders from Norway had come to rob and burn, but had stayed to trade. **Dublin** was their chief base.

Each part of Ireland had its own king, and they spent a lot of time fighting each other. A 'high king of Ireland' was supposed to rule over

When the Vikings raided Ireland, the monks in many monasteries built tall round-towers. These were look-out posts and strong places where the monks could take refuge.

Irish monks were famous all over Europe as scholars and artists. This page from the *Book of Kells* is an example of their work. It was written in about AD 800, long before the Normans came to England.

them all, but most high kings were weak. **Brian Boru** was different. He made the Irish combine to fight the Vikings in 1014. The Irish won, but Brian was killed in the battle.

Rory O'Connor, who was high king in 1166, fell out with **Dermot**, the king of Leinster. Dermot was banished (forced to leave Ireland). He made his way to the court of King Henry II of England, to ask for help.

Henry said that his lords and knights could go with Dermot to Ireland if they wished. One of those who went was **Richard of Clare**, whose nickname was 'Strongbow'. He won back Leinster for Dermot, and married Dermot's daughter. When Dermot died, Strongbow became King of Leinster.

Now try Exercise 9.1.

Exercise 9.1

Look back at Exercise 7.3 on page 40 before you begin.
Read **Section A**. Complete the sentences.

a In about 450, St. Patrick came to Ireland to preach the Christian religion (mid-_____ century).

b The Book of Durrow (picture to the right) was written in the late seventh century (between _____ and _____).

c The Vikings raided the coasts of Ireland in the early ninth century (between _____ and _____).

d In 1014, Brian Boru beat the Vikings in the battle of Contarf (_____ _____ century).

e Strongbow crossed to Ireland in 1169 (_____ _____ century).

f In 1175, Rory O'Connor did homage to Henry II (_____ _____ century).

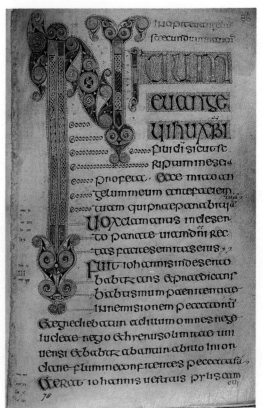

A page from the *Book of Durrow* – it was written before AD 700.

B Ireland nearly conquered

Henry II did not want Strongbow to be a king. In 1171 he himself crossed to Ireland with his army. He did not need to do much fighting. Strongbow **did homage** to him. The Irish kings and chiefs did the same. Each of them promised to pay Henry so many cows' hides each year.

Henry left Ireland after six months. But some of his lords and knights stayed to fight and conquer. Soon there were castles (wood and earth at first, stone later) all over the eastern half of Ireland.

Henry gave his youngest son, John, the title **lord of Ireland**, and sent him there on a visit in 1185. The Irish chiefs, in their long robes, came to Dublin to do homage to him. But John and his young friends were foolish.

They laughed at the chiefs and pulled their beards. The Irish went home in disgust.

When John himself was king, he came back to Ireland. He acted more wisely this time, and showed respect to the Irish. He built castles and appointed judges, and brought law and order to at least part of the land.

English rule spread westwards in the thirteenth century. Irish peasants tilled the fields, and English lords lived in the castles. Some towns grew up, but the men and women in them were English, or Welsh, or French. They used money in the towns, but most Irishmen still counted in cows or cows' skins.

Now try Exercise 9.2.

Source 9a

From north to south, Ireland stretches a distance of eight days at 40 miles a day. From east to west, it stretches for four days. The country is low-lying round the coast. Inland it rises up to hills and mountains. The Shannon is the biggest river. Its source is in a lake that lies between Connaught and Munster. From there, part of it flows south to Limerick and the sea. The other part flows north between Ulster and Connaught. It reaches the sea in the north.

From a book written by a Welsh priest called Gerald in about 1190.

Exercise 9.2

Read **Section B** and **Source 9a**, and look at the map of Ireland on page 47. Was Gerald (the author of **Source 9a**) right about Ireland? Fill in the blank spaces.

a Gerald said that Ireland stretches _____ miles from north to south. He said that it stretches _____ miles from east to west.

b The map shows that Ireland is _____ miles long from north to south, and _____ miles wide from east to west.

c Gerald was _____ when he said that there are hills and mountains in Ireland. But he was _____ when he said they were not near the coast.

d In some ways, Gerald was right about the River Shannon:
   i It is Ireland's _____ river.
   ii It does flow south to _____ and the sea.

e In some ways, Gerald was wrong about the Shannon:
   i Its source is not in a _____ between Connaught and Munster.
   ii Part of it does not flow _____.

C The Irish strike back

The Irish did not give in to the English. After the year 1250, they began to get on top. The English had to fall back to the east coast of Ireland. By 1400, they ruled only the **Pale**, the district round Dublin.

One reason for the change was that the Irish got help from Scotland. The Scots soldiers could stand up to and beat the English knights. A second reason was that the English kings had no soldiers to spare for Ireland. They were too busy with wars in Wales, Scotland, and France.

A third reason for the Irish success had nothing to do with war. Most English (and French) lords and knights who stayed in Ireland married Irish girls. Their sons, and *their* sons, also took Irish wives. In time, they became completely Irish.

The great lords were vassals of the English king. But they and their families spoke the Irish language. They kept Irish poets in their homes. They were keen on stories of Irish heroes, giants, and magic. They had no time for English laws and taxes.

Now try Exercise 9.3.

Source 9b

You are not proper Irishmen. You cut your hair short in the English style. You should leave it long and curling as the Irish do. No Irish hero ever wore English breeches, or jewelled spurs, or a fancy cloak. They didn't wear ruffs round their necks or gold rings on their fingers. They lived in wattle houses, not stone castles.

From a sixteenth-century Irish poem.

Source 9c

A group of soldiers and peasants in Ireland, drawn in 1521.

Exercise 9.3

Read **Section C**. Then read **Source 9b** and look at **Source 9c**.

a How were the Irish and English different, according to **Source 9b**? Make your own notes about the following
  i Hair-style
  ii Clothes
  iii Jewellery
  iv Houses
b Which are the peasants in **Source 9c**? What makes you think they are poor? (Write two or three sentences.)

Source 9d

The monks of Clonmacnoise were having a meeting. Suddenly, they looked up and saw a ship. It was sailing over them in the air, as if it were on the sea. When the crew of the ship saw the monks, they dropped an anchor. A man came out of the ship, swimming as if he were in the water. The monks tried to reach him, but he said, 'Let me go, you are drowning me'.

This story was told by a fourteenth century Irish poet. Another poet told the same story a hundred years earlier.

Two Irish pilgrim monks, St Columbanus and St Gallus, being rowed across Lake Constance, Switzerland, while travelling in Europe.

Exercise 9.5

Read the notes on 'different kinds of evidence'. How would *you* go about discovering more about Ireland in the Middle Ages? What kinds of evidence would be useful? Study the list below.

 i Reading books that were written in the Middle Ages.
 ii Talking to people who lived in the Middle Ages.
 iii Looking at drawings and pictures made in the Middle Ages.
 iv Visiting old houses, castles, and churches.
 v Looking at photographs taken in the Middle Ages.
 vi Looking at carvings in churches or on gravestones.
 vii Visiting museums where they have articles from the Middle Ages.

a Write down all the things in the list which would be useful ways of finding out more about Medieval Ireland.
  Write a sentence about each, saying what you might learn from it.
b Which things have you left out? Write a sentence about each, saying why you have left it out.

Exercise 9.4

Read **Source 9d**.
Which of these statements do you think is true?

a The story is pure fiction. Probably no-one ever believed it.
b The story can not be true, but at the time the Irish people probably believed it.
c There are some true things in the story. (Look at the map.) Most of it is fiction, but some people may have believed it.
d The story may be true.

Write out the statement which you think is true. Write a paragraph giving your reasons.

Different kinds of evidence

The **sources** help us in different ways. For example, old books give us the names of people in the past, and tell us what they did. Old pictures show us how they dressed.

A student of history must know **what kind of evidence** he or she is looking for. And he or she must know where to look for it.

Exercise 9.6

In your own words, tell the story of Dermot and Strongbow (see **Sections A and B**). Begin with the quarrel between Dermot and Rory O'Connor, and end with the Irish kings doing homage to Henry II.
(Write the story out, or make a tape, or tell the story in pictures.)

10 Life on the Land in the Middle Ages

From the air, you can still see signs of the strips in Padbury's open fields.

A Open-field villages

Nine out of ten people in the Middle Ages worked on the land. In Wales, Scotland, Ireland, and the north-west of England, the peasants (country people) kept sheep and cattle, and grew only a few crops. They lived on farms or in small hamlets. But in the Midlands and the east of England, the peasants tilled the land and lived in villages.

In the time of the Normans, a lot of English villages had two large **open fields**. The fields were divided into long, narrow **strips**. Each peasant would have some strips in one field, and some in the other.

Source 10a

Taking the grain to the mill.

Above, stacking the crop.   *Below,* harrowing to cover the seed.

Each year, the peasants grew crops in **one** of the two fields. All of them worked together to plough, sow the seed, and harrow the land to cover the seed with soil. When the wheat or barley or beans had grown, everyone joined in the work of harvest. Each man kept the crops which grew on his strips.

The other open field was left **fallow**. This meant that nothing but grass grew there. Animals were allowed to graze there, and their manure made the soil richer. The next year, the fallow field would be used to grow crops, and the first field would be left fallow.

As well as the open fields, each village had a meadow for hay. And there was some **common** land, where the peasants' sheep and cattle could graze. In the winter there was not enough food for the animals. So the peasants had to kill most of the animals in the autumn. They salted the meat to preserve it. They ate some, and sold the rest.

Now try Exercises 10.1 and 10.2.

Exercise 10.1

Read **Section A**.
Write six sentences to show that you know what each of the words below means. Use your own words if you can.

a peasant
b open fields
c strips
d fallow
e meadow
f common

Exercise 10.2

The pictures in **Source 10A** show peasants in the Middle Ages doing farm work – milling, stacking, harrowing, reaping (or harvesting), ploughing and sowing. Each of these jobs had to be done at the right time of the year.

a Put the six jobs into the right order and write them in a list.
b Copy one of the pictures. Add labels to explain what is happening.

Above, reaping (harvesting) the crop.

Below, ploughing the field.

Sowing the seed.

B The lord of the manor and the peasants

The most important man in the village was the **lord of the manor**. (Manor is another word for village.) The land belonged to the lord, and the peasants had to pay him rent.

Most peasants were **villeins**. Villeins were not free, nor were their wives and children. They could not leave the village unless the lord of the manor said so. They paid rent to the lord by working two or three days a week on his land. Many of them paid money as well, and they had to give him hens at Christmas and eggs at Easter. At harvest time, they did extra work, called 'boon days'. (Where does the modern word 'villain' come from?)

A villein's corn was milled in the lord's mill, and the lord got a share of the flour. If a villein's daughter got married, the villein paid money to the lord. And when a villein died, his son had to give the lord the family's best ox or cow.

The village **reeve** made sure that each man did the right amount of work for the lord. If there was a quarrel between two peasants, it was settled in the lord of the manor's court. Men, or women, who had done wrong ended up in the village stocks. The same happened to reeves who did not do their jobs properly.

Freemen were better-off peasants. (There were a lot of freemen in the south-east of England.) They paid rent in money to the lord of the manor, but had to do little or no work on the lord's land. And they could leave the village if they wished.

Cottars and **bordars**, on the other hand, were worse off than villeins. They had far less land in the open fields, and earned money by working for wages on the lord's land. Like villeins and freemen, they could keep cattle and sheep on the common.

Now try Exercise 10.3.

Shepherds looking after the sheep on the common land.

Source 10b

In Boldon, there are 22 villeins. Each villein has 60 acres. He has to pay four shillings (20 pence) a year, and work three days a week for the lord. He does four extra 'boon days' at reaping time. He must give the lord two hens and ten eggs each year.

There are twelve cottars. Each of them has twelve acres. A cottar works two days a week.

From the records of the Bishops of Durham. This extract tells us about the manor of Boldon in Durham in the year 1183.

Source 10c

In Kettering there are 40 villeins. Each villein has about 30 acres of land. He has to work three days a week for the lord, and must plough four acres for the lord in the spring. He has to pay two shillings (10 pence) to the lord each year. And he must give the lord a hen at Christmas and 16 eggs at Easter.

There are eight cottars, and they have five acres of land each. A cottar works one day a week for the lord.

From the records of Peterborough Abbey. This extract tells us about the manor of Kettering in Northants in the year 1125.

This stone manor house was built at Boothby Pagnell in Lincolnshire in about 1200. Wooden manor houses, with thatched roofs were more common.

A reeve watching over the harvesting.

Exercise 10.3

Read **Section B** and **Sources 10b** and **10c**.
We can find out a lot from the sources if we ask the right questions. Try asking 'How many . . .?' and 'How much . . .?' about **Sources 10b** and **10c**. They are about two different parts of England. They show that the peasants were the same in some ways, and different in others.
Answer the questions. In each case, write one sentence about each manor, starting as shown in **a**.

a How many villeins were there?
  i In Boldon . . . .
  ii In Kettering . . . .
b How much land did a villein have?
c How much work did a villein do for the lord?
d How much money did a villein have to pay to the lord?
e How many hens and eggs did a villein have to give to the lord?
f How many cottars were there?
g How much land did cottars have, and how much work had they to do?

C How did things change?

The population of England rose steadily between 1066 and 1348. The extra people needed more food, and the chief food was bread. So the peasants had to plough more land, and grow more corn.

In some parts of England, they ploughed up part of the common land, and made extra fields. So now many villages had three open fields. The peasants still left one field fallow each year, but they grew crops in the other two. They still worked the fields in strips.

Money began to play a bigger part in the peasants' lives. Some lords stopped making villeins give them two or three days' work a week. They let them pay **rent** instead, like freemen. The lords' land still had to be worked, of course. So the lords paid **wages** to cottars, bordars, and poor villeins to work for them.

Some freemen and villeins became quite rich by selling corn in the market towns. (The more land they had, the more corn they grew.) So they rented extra land from their lords, and became richer still. Like the lords of the manor, they paid the poorer peasants to work for them.

Now try Exercises 10.4 and 10.5.

Exercise 10.4

Read **Section C**.
   How much changed, and how much stayed the same?
Write four short paragraphs about the following. Say which things changed, and which did not change, in the lives of peasants between the eleventh century and the fourteenth century.

a The village, and how the peasants farmed the land.
b Work, rent, and wages.
c Rich peasants.
d Poor peasants.

Exercise 10.5

Write out the sentences below. Instead of the words in **bold print**, write 'In the .... century'. (Add the words 'early', 'mid', or 'late' if they are needed.)

a **In 1066**, the population of England was about two million.
b **Between 1071 and 1100**, a lot of villages had only two open fields.
c **In 1150**, peasants lived in wood and clay huts, with thatched roofs and earth floors.
d **Between 1171 and 1200**, peasants cut down a lot of trees and turned some forests into farm land.
e **Between 1201 and 1300**, many peasants started paying their rents in money.
f **Between 1301 and 1330**, rich peasants rented extra land from their lords.
g **In 1348**, the population of England was about five million.

11th century peasants

11 The Black Death and the Peasants' Revolt

A The Black Death

The 'Black Death' – a kind of plague – reached the ports of southern England in 1348. It swept through the country in the next year. Those who caught it died in a day or two, sometimes less. Between a third and a half of the people in England died. No-one knew what caused the Black Death, or how to cure it.

We know now that the plague was carried by black rats. It was spread to humans by the rats' fleas. The dirt and rubbish which lay in the streets of towns were ideal for the rats, so the towns were hit worst by the plague. London had special 'plague pits' for burying the dead.

When townspeople fled to the country to escape the disease, they took it with them. So many peasants died that there were not enough people left to till the fields. Whole villages were deserted, and the houses began to fall down.

Now try Exercise 11.1.

Exercise 11.1

Read **Section A** and **Sources 11a** and **11b**.

a Which **fact** is mentioned in **both Source 11a** and **Source 11b**?
b Write down *three* facts that are mentioned **only** in **Source 11a**?
c Write down *three* facts that are mentioned **only** in **Source 11b**.

The remains of the deserted village at Olney in Northamptonshire, seen from the air. Can you see where the village street use to be, and signs of the strips in the fields?

Source 11a

In 1349 the great plague spread through the whole world from south to north. It was so bad that hardly half the population remained alive. Towns that were once full of men were left empty. In the end there were not enough men left alive to bury the dead.

Written by Thomas Walsingham in about 1400.

Source 11b

In 1349 there was an outbreak of plague. Those who caught it died suddenly. At least a third of all the people in the world died. Men called penitents flogged themselves with leather whips, spiked with iron. They hoped that this might persuade God to stop the plague.

From Jean Froissart's *Chronicles*, written in about 1400.

B The Peasants' Revolt

The peasants who survived the Black Death asked for higher wages. Lords of the manor had to pay, or leave their land untilled. For a while the peasants were on top. Then the lords hit back. They tried to make the peasants work two or three days a week for them, without wages, as in the past. Then parliament passed a law which banned high wages for peasants.

The peasants did not like any of this. Nor did they like the poll tax which was charged in 1380 to help pay for a war with France. Complaints led to revolt. Angry peasants attacked manor houses and made bonfires with the lords' record books.

Rebels from Essex and Kent reached London in June 1381. They pulled down and burned the houses of the great lords and rich merchants. They killed foreign tradesmen. They even cut off the head of the Archbishop of Canterbury, whom they blamed for the new tax.

King Richard II, who was only fourteen years old, met the rebels at Smithfield, on the edge of London. A fight broke out there between the mayor of London and Wat Tyler, the peasants'

Rebels murder the Archbishop of Canterbury and other advisers of the king.

Source 11c

The revolt broke out because the peasants were so well off. The bad people did not like having to work for their lords. They said that when the world began there were no villeins and lords. A crackbrained priest called John Ball told them that they had a right to proper wages. More than once, the Archbishop of Canterbury arrested John Ball and put him in prison. He should have had him put to death at once.

Also from Jean Froissart's *Chronicles*.

Source 11d

The common people of Kent and Essex revolted. They were against the duke of Lancaster and the other great lords. The main cause was the heavy tax that had been passed. It hit the poor people very hard.

From the *Anonymous Chronicle*.

leader. The mayor drew his sword and cut Tyler down. The peasants might have killed the mayor and the king in revenge. Richard kept cool. He faced the rebels, told them he would see to their complaints, and asked them to go home.

The king broke his promise. As soon as the danger was over, his ministers sent soldiers to deal with the rebels. They put the leaders to death. They burned down the villages where the peasants had revolted. But it was not all loss – the hated poll tax was not charged again.

Now try Exercise 11.2 and 11.3.

Exercise 11.2

Read **Section B**, and **Sources 11c** and **11d**.

a What were the **causes** of the Peasants' Revolt according to **Section B**?

_____

_____

b What were the **causes** of the Peasants' Revolt according to the author of **Source 11c**?

_____

_____

c What were the **causes** of the Peasants' Revolt according to the author of **Source 11d**?

_____

_____

Exercise 11.3

a Write down all the **facts** you can find in **Source 11c**.

_____

_____

_____

b What were the **opinions** of the author of **Source 11c** on

i The peasants? _____

_____

ii John Ball? _____

_____

c Whose side was the author of **Source 11c** on – the lords' or the peasants'?
Which words in **Source 11c** tell us the answer?

_____

_____

d **Source 11d** tells us that the peasants in which counties rebelled?

_____

_____

e Whose side was the author of **Source 11d** on? – the lords' or the peasants'?
Which words in **Source 11d** tell us the answer?

_____

_____

C Peasants in the fifteenth century

The Peasants' Revolt was crushed in 1381. Life did get better, though, for the peasants in the next hundred years. Those who did best were the freemen and the richest villeins, who by now were called **yeomen**. Yeomen added to their own strips in the village fields by buying land from other peasants. Then they rented more land from the lords of the manor.

There were clear signs that the yeomen had money. They built new, bigger houses, sometimes in stone instead of wood and clay. They could afford better clothes and furniture. They kept servants. Some of them even sent their sons to school.

Times were better even for the poor peasants. (People had stopped using the name 'villein' by the year 1450.) They no longer had to do unpaid work for their lords. They had some land of their own, and they earned wages by working for the lords or the yeomen as well. And wages were quite high in the fifteenth century.

But peasants' lives were always hard. Their families were often hungry. The men (and often women as well) worked in the fields, six days a week, from dawn to dusk. The women also milked the cows and sheep, made butter and cheese, looked after the children, and cooked what food there was. Not many peasants lived to be more than fifty.

Now try Exercise 11.4.

This is a Welsh farmhouse from the Middle Ages. The family lived at one end, and the animals were kept at the other.

The interior of the Welsh farmhouse. It has been rebuilt in the Welsh Folk Museum.

Making up your mind

As you know, the sources contain different opinions about the past. And authors of history books do not all say the same thing.
How do you decide who is right?
The best idea always is to look at the **facts**. Ask, 'Do the facts show, or **prove**, that this opinion is right?'
There may be no facts to show that it is right. In that case, the opinion may be wrong.

Exercise 11.4

Read **Section C**, then study the following question.

Were yeomen the only peasants who were better off in the fifteenth century?

Now plan an answer to the question above.

a Write down any facts which show that yeomen were better off.
b Write down any facts which show that poor peasants were better off.
c Is it true that **only** yeomen were better off?

Source 11e

The mayor of London kills Wat Tyler. King Richard II is shown twice. The artist wanted to show that after Wat Tyler was killed, the king rode over to the peasants.

A fifteenth-century scene showing criminals in the stocks.

Source 11f

The mayor drew a great sword, struck at Wat Tyler, and laid him flat. The crowds began to mutter. 'They've killed our leader', they said. Then the king rode alone right up to those crazy people and said: 'What do you want? I am your king. I am your leader. Go home in peace'.

Also written by Jean Froissart.

Exercise 11.5

Look at **Source 11e** and read **Source 11f**.

a Which things can we learn from **both Source 11e** and **Source 11f**?
b Which things can we learn **only** from **Source 11e**?
c Which things can we learn **only** from **Source 11f**?
d What kind of things can we find out best from **picture sources** (paintings, portraits, drawings, tapestries, etc.)? What kind of things can picture sources not normally tell us? Draw a chart to show what we can learn from picture sources (paintings, drawings, tapestries, etc.) and what can we learn **only** from written sources?

12 The Hundred Years' War

A How warfare changed

War was part of normal life for Norman kings and lords. Princes and young nobles had to learn to ride and fight as knights. Barons, earls, and bishops, with their knights, had to fight for the king when he needed them. This was how they paid the rent for their land.

Three hundred years later, kings and lords still went to war. And knights were still the main troops in the army. But there were some changes. Norman knights wore chainmail. By the fourteenth century, though, knights' armour had some solid plates of steel. In the fifteenth, they wore full suits of armour.

The Normans had archers, armed with short bows. From the year 1300, there were always archers with **longbows** in the English army. Longbows were two metres long, and could shoot arrows right through plate armour. By 1350, there were also some guns. But they often did more damage to their own side than the enemy.

In the fourteenth and fifteenth centuries, kings needed a lot of money to fight wars. Each of the great lords had his private army, and soldiers had to be paid wages. So the king gave money to the great lords, and they paid wages to the soldiers.

Now try Exercise 12.1

Source 12a

Knights sometimes fought on foot in the fourteenth and fifteenth centuries. When they did so they were called 'men-at-arms'.

Source 12b

A knight's lady hands him his helmet.

Source 12c

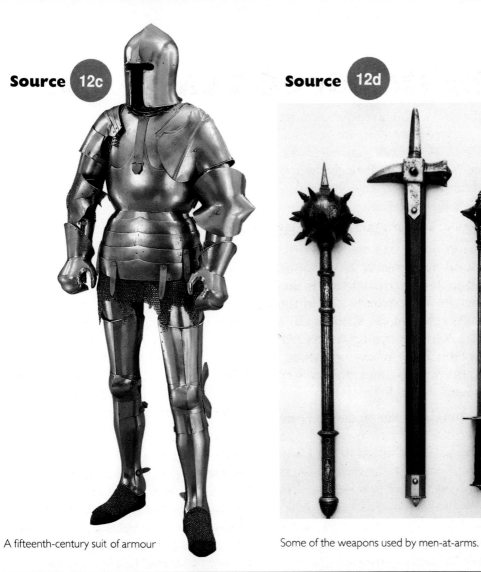

A fifteenth-century suit of armour

Source 12d

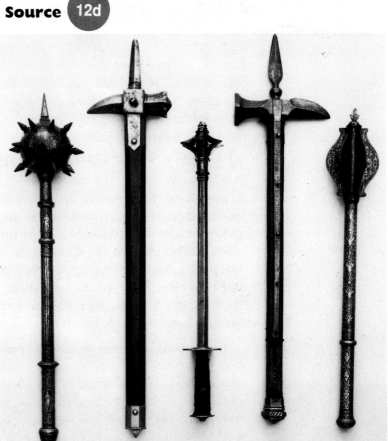

Some of the weapons used by men-at-arms.

Exercise 12.1

Read **Section A**, and look at **Sources 12a**, **12b**, **12c**, and **12d**. Which things changed between the eleventh century and the fourteenth and fifteenth centuries? Fill in the blank spaces in the chart below. In the column headed 'Change?', write either **Change** or **No Change**.

11th Century	14th & 15th Centuries	Change?
Kings led their armies into battle.	_____ led their armies into _____	_____
Knights were the most important soldiers.	_____ were the most important soldiers.	_____
Knights wore armour made of chain-mail.	Knights wore _____ _____	_____
Archers with short bows fought in the army.	Archers with _____ _____	_____
The great lords paid rent for their land by sending knights to help the king.	The king paid _____ _____ _____ _____	_____
There were no guns.	_____	

B The Hundred Years' War

England's longest war was against France. It lasted, with a few breaks, from 1336 to 1453, and was called the 'Hundred Years' War'. It began when King **Edward III** said that he had a right to be king of France.

Edward and his son, the **Black Prince**, won some famous victories. Edward beat the French at **Crécy** in 1346, and took the town of **Calais** the next year. In 1356, the Black Prince beat the French king at **Poitiers**. But when the Black Prince and Edward died, the French began to win battles. By 1400, the English had only a few towns around the French coast.

Henry V began the war again in 1415. He took the town of Harfleur in Normandy, then beat a large French army at **Agincourt**. Henry was a hero to his men and all the people of England.

King **Charles VI** of France made peace in 1420. He said that Henry would become king of France when he, Charles VI, died. Henry married Charles's daughter, and a son was born in 1421. But the prince was only nine months old when Henry V died. Charles VI died six weeks later. The English said that the baby (**Henry VI**) was now king of England and France.

Now try Exercise 12.2.

The 'burghers' of Calais kneel before Edward III.

Source 12e

The siege of Calais lasted for a whole year. The people were so hungry that they ate all the horses, dogs, and cats. At last, the captain and his chief men came out without hats or shoes, and with ropes round their necks. They gave Edward the keys of the town and begged him not to kill them. He said he would spare their lives, and sent them to the Tower of London.

From a book written by a monk in York in the fourteenth century.

Source 12f

Edward agreed that if six men of Calais surrendered to him, he would spare the rest. They had to come out with their heads and feet bare, ropes round their necks, and the keys of the town in their hands. Edward said their heads were to be cut off straight away. But the queen begged him on her knees to spare them. So the king gave way and let them go.

From Jean Froissart's *Chronicles*.

Exercise 12.2

Read **Section B**, then read **Sources 12e** and **12f**.

a Write down *three* facts mentioned in **Source 12e**, but **not** in **Source 12f**.
b Write down *three* facts mentioned in **Source 12f**, but **not** in **Source 12e**.
c Which facts are mentioned by **both** sources?

C Joan of Arc and the end of the war

Charles VI of France had a son (another Charles). Men called him the **Dauphin**, which was always the title of the French kings' eldest son. When Charles VI died, some Frenchmen fought on for the Dauphin. They did not have much hope, for he was a weak and idle youth.

Then **Joan of Arc** appeared. Joan was a peasant girl from Domrémy in eastern France. She said that she had heard voices and seen visions of the saints. The voices told her to go to the Dauphin at the castle of **Chinon** and help him to save **Orléans** from the English.

The courtiers at Chinon laughed at Joan. But the Dauphin gave her arms, and sent her with 4,000 men to relieve Orléans (make the English give up the siege). Joan beat the English in battle, and drove them back to the north. The Dauphin was crowned King Charles VII in Rheims cathedral.

Then Joan was captured by the duke of Burgundy (England's ally), and put on trial by the English. They said she was a **witch** – she had seen and talked to devils. She was found guilty and burned to death in the market-place at **Rouen** in May 1431.

Killing Joan of Arc did not save the English. As Henry VI grew up, it was clear that he was not a soldier. In any case, England could not afford the long war and lost its chief ally, the duke of Burgundy. In 1453, the French took Bordeaux, and the war was over. **Calais** was the only part of France left in English hands.

Now try Exercise 12.3.

The French, commanded by Joan of Arc, attack Paris (which was held by the English).

France in the Time of Henry V and Joan of Arc

Land Controlled by

the Dauphin in 1429

the King of England in 1429

the Duke of Burgundy in 1429

Exercise 12.3

Read **Section C**.
Write sentences to show that you know what these words mean:

a Dauphin   d Siege
b Vision   e Relieve
c Courtiers   f Witch

Source 12g

The French army was crowded together between two small woods. The knights hardly had room to raise their lances. It had rained all night, and the ground was too soft for the horses. The heavy armour worn by the French knights made things worse.

The English knights were on foot and advanced in good order. The archers were at the sides of the field. When they fired, the arrows fell so fast that the French did not dare look up. When the English knights reached them, many of them had already been killed or wounded. The men at the back of the French army saw what was happening and ran away.

Jean de Waurin's account of the Battle of Agincourt in 1415. Jean fought as a knight on the French side in the battle.

Source 12h

The men of Orléans badly needed Joan's help, for they had begun to give up hope. They greeted her well. The troops promised to follow her, and she led them out to attack the English. They won one victory after another. Then men said she had been sent by God, and that nothing could stop them.

Adapted from a book written by Sir Charles Oman in 1895.

Source 12i

The English were short of men and money. They never had much hope of taking Orléans. They only had a weak hold on northern France. Joan did not need to be a great general or to have God's help to relieve Orléans and capture other towns.

Adapted from a book written by Dr. A. R. Myers in 1952.

Exercise 12.4

Read **Source 12g**.

a Is **Source 12g** a primary or a secondary source? (Write a sentence, giving your opinion and your reason.)

b What were the **causes** of the English victory at Agincourt? (Write down a list of causes.)

c Which was the most important cause of the English victory? (Write a paragraph, giving your opinions and your reasons.)

Exercise 12.5

Read **Sources 12h** and **12i**, then answer the questions.
Write at least one sentence in answer to each question.

a The siege of Orléans:
   i What does **Source 12h** say about Orléans before Joan arrived?
   ii What does **Source 12i** say about the siege of Orléans?

b Joan as a general:
   i What does **Source 12h** say to make you think that Joan was a good general?
   ii What does **Source 12i** say about Joan as a general?

c God's help:
   i What does **Source 12h** say about God's help for Joan?
   ii What does **Source 12i** say about God's help for Joan?

Exercise 12.6

Read the story of Joan of Arc in **Section B** again. Which do you think are the three most important events in the story? Write your own notes saying what happened and why the events were important or make a tape.

Lancaster, York, and Tudor

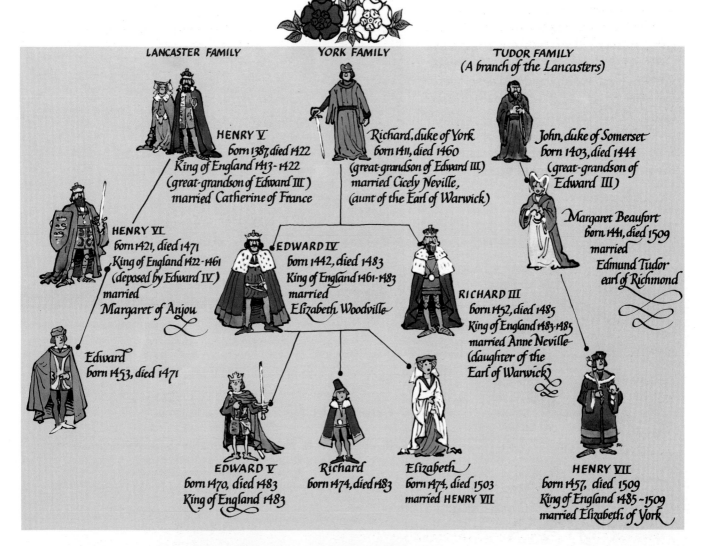

LANCASTER FAMILY   YORK FAMILY   TUDOR FAMILY
(A branch of the Lancasters)

HENRY V
born 1387, died 1422
King of England 1413–1422
(great-grandson of Edward III)
married Catherine of France

Richard, duke of York
born 1411, died 1460
(great-grandson of Edward III)
married Cicely Neville,
(aunt of the Earl of Warwick)

John, duke of Somerset
born 1403, died 1444
(great-grandson of
Edward III)

HENRY VI
born 1421, died 1471
King of England 1422–1461
(deposed by Edward IV)
married
Margaret of Anjou

EDWARD IV
born 1442, died 1483
King of England 1461–1483
married
Elizabeth Woodville

RICHARD III
born 1452, died 1485
King of England 1483–1485
married Anne Neville
(daughter of the
Earl of Warwick)

Margaret Beaufort
born 1441, died 1509
married
Edmund Tudor
earl of Richmond

Edward
born 1453, died 1471

EDWARD V
born 1470, died 1483
King of England 1483

Richard
born 1474, died 1483

Elizabeth
born 1474, died 1503
married HENRY VII

HENRY VII
born 1457, died 1509
King of England 1485–1509
married Elizabeth of York

A The Wars of the Roses

Henry VI could not win the war in France. He could not keep the peace in England either. Each lord had a band of men who wore his badge. They stole from the people, and beat them up if they complained. The courts were no help – the lords' men bullied the judges and juries as well.

The greatest nobles had private armies. When they fell out with each other in the 1450s, there was civil war. One group, led by Henry VI's wife, **Queen Margaret**, fought to keep Henry on the throne, and make sure that their son was the next king. Their enemies thought that England would be better off with **Richard, duke of York**, in charge.

The two sides were called **Lancaster** (the king's family) and **York**. The wars between them are known as the **Wars of the Roses**. (The captions below tell you why.) Most nobles took one side or the other. The greatest lord in England, the **earl of Warwick**, was on the side of York at first.

The York family won the wars, but Duke Richard was killed in battle. His son, **Edward IV**, became king. By 1471, when the wars ended, Henry VI and his son were dead, and so were the earl of Warwick and many other lords. The common people stayed out of the fighting – the wars were not their business. But while they lasted, there was no real law and order.

Now try Exercise 13.1.

King Edward IV (seated), with the queen and their son, the future Edward V, standing on his left. Kneeling before the king is William Caxton, who published the first books to be printed in England.

The Red Rose of Lancaster

The White Rose of York

The Red Rose was the badge of the Lancaster side, and the White Rose was the badge of the York side.

Exercise 13.1

Read **Section A**, and study the family trees. Write your answers to the questions in the spaces.

a How old was Henry VI when he became a king? _____

b Who was Henry VI's wife? _____

c For how many years was Henry VI king of England? _____

d How old was Henry VI's son when he died? _____

e Who was the duke of York's wife? _____

f How old was Edward VI when he became king? _____

g For how many years was Edward IV king of England? _____

B The princes in the Tower

Edward IV died in 1483, aged only forty-one. His two sons were twelve and nine years old. The elder of them was now **King Edward V**, but he was too young to rule. His uncle **Richard, duke of Gloucester,** became 'Protector', to govern England until the boy-king grew up.

In less than three months, the Protector had made himself **King Richard III**. The two 'princes' (Edward V and his brother) were put in the Tower of London 'to be safe'. Rumours soon spread that they were dead. They were never seen again.

Did Richard III have his nephews killed? No-one really knows. Richard had a good reason to get rid of the princes – each of them had more right to be king than he did. Their own mother was sure that they were dead. And if they **were** put to death in the Tower, Richard would have known about it.

A revolt against Richard broke out in October 1483. One of the causes was the rumour that the princes had been killed. Richard could have crushed the rumour and the revolt by letting people see the princes, alive and well. He did not. Does this mean that they were dead?

One last fact came to light nearly 200 years later. In 1674, some workmen found the bones of two children in the Tower of London. Experts who examined the bones in 1933 said that they belonged to two boys, aged about twelve and nine.

Now try Exercises 13.2 and 13.3.

This stained-glass window in Canterbury Cathedral shows the two 'princes in the Tower'. Richard is on the left and Edward is on the right.

Exercise 13.2

Read **Section B**, then answer the questions.

a Do **you** think that the princes were murdered? (Write a sentence.)
b Do **you** think that Richard III ordered someone to murder the princes? (Write a sentence.)
c **Why** might Richard III have ordered someone to murder the princes? (Write one or two sentences.)
d Which of the facts given in **Section B** make Richard III look guilty?
e Did the discovery of the bones **prove** that Richard III was guilty? (Write at least one sentence, giving your reasons.)

Richard III – notes about the sources

a Sources written in Richard III's lifetime did not say that he murdered the princes. They said that there was a **rumour** that they had been killed. No-one ever confessed to the crime.

b Sir Thomas More wrote a book about Richard III in 1520 (35 years after Richard's death). He said that Richard got a man called James Tyrrel to go to the Tower with two murderers. Tyrrel and his men, More said, smothered the princes with their own bedclothes.

c William Shakespeare, who wrote his play *Richard III* in 1593, more than a hundred years after Richard's time, told the same story as Sir Thomas More. In the play, we hear Richard telling Tyrrel to kill the princes.

The badge worn by supporters of the earl of Warwick.

Exercise 13.3

Think again

Sometimes, new facts should make you think again.
Read 'Richard III – notes about the sources'. Some people say that there is no **proof** that Richard III murdered the princes. There were **rumours** that he had done so, but no more. After Richard's death, the rumours were turned into a legend.

Now read again your answers to Exercise 13.2. Do you still think the same? Or do you think you were too hard on Richard III? (There is nothing wrong with changing your mind, or saying that you are not sure.) Write a paragraph, saying how your ideas have changed, and why. If they have not changed, give your reasons.

C Henry VII, the first Tudor king of England

Richard III reigned for only two years. He was popular in the north, where he had lived as a young man. But he was not liked in the south. He made things worse by giving top jobs in the south to his northern friends.

Henry Tudor, earl of Richmond, was now the chief hope of Richard's enemies. Henry's mother was one of the last of the Lancasters. His father was a half-Welsh lord. When Henry landed in Wales from France in August 1485 with a small army, a lot of Welshmen joined him.

Richard met the invaders at **Bosworth** near Leicester on 22 August. Richard had the bigger army, but not all his men were loyal. He lost the battle, and his life. Henry, earl of Richmond, became **Henry VII**, England's first **Tudor** king.

Henry VII knew that England needed peace, law and order. There must be an end to civil war. He put some supporters of Richard III to death, and kept others in prison. But he hoped there would be friendship in the future between York and Lancaster. That is why he married Elizabeth, Richard's niece.

Henry banned private armies. Lords who disobeyed him had to pay big fines. Those who rebelled against him lost their lands. The money and lands made Henry so rich that he did not need to ask the lords for help.

Now try Exercise 13.4.

Exercise 13.4

Read **Section C**, then answer the questions in sentences.

a What was Henry Tudor's **motive** or **reason** when he landed in Wales in 1485?
b What was Henry VII's **motive** for putting some of Richard III's supporters to death?
c What was Henry VII's **motive** for marrying Elizabeth of York?
d What was Henry VII's **motive** for banning private armies?
e What were Henry VII's **motives** for taking money and land from lords who were against him? (Try to think of more than one motive.)

Source 13a

He is more popular with the people than any king was before. As he travels around, he does good to the poor. He refuses gifts of money offered by the cities and towns. God has sent him to help us.

Part of a letter written in the reign of Richard III by Thomas Langton, the bishop of St. David's in Wales.)

Source 13b

A portrait of King Richard III

Source 13c

A wood-carving of King Richard III in Christchurch, Dorset.

Source 13d

Richard was a little man, with a crooked back. His left shoulder was much higher than his right. He had a hard face and a cruel look. He was bad-tempered, envious, and dishonest. He pretended to be friendly to men he was planning to kill. They say that with his own hands he killed King Henry VI when he was a prisoner in the Tower.

From Sir Thomas More's *History of Richard III*, written in about 1520.

Exercise 13.5

Look at **Sources 13b** and **13c**, and read **Sources 13a** and **13d**. Note down the answers to these questions. Then discuss your answers in a group.

a What does **Source 13d** say about Richard III's appearance?
b What does **Source 13c** tell us about Richard III's appearance? Does it tell us the same things as **Source 13d**?
c What does **Source 13b** tell us about Richard III's appearance? Does it tell us the same things as **Source 13d**.
d What does **Source 13d** say about Richard III's character?
e What does **Source 13a** say about Richard III's character?
f Why do you think the sources say different things about Richard III? Do you think that any of them show bias, either against Richard, or in favour of Richard?

14 Towns and Trade in the Middle Ages

A The Main Towns in England in About 1180

SCOTLAND

Newcastle
Carlisle

York

Chester · Lincoln
Stafford
Shrewsbury · Leicester Norwich
Warwick · Thetford
WALES Worcester Northampton · Cambridge
· Ipswich
· Oxford
· Bristol · London
Canterbury
Winchester ·
Lewes ·
· Launceston

0 50 100 150 200
Km

One of London's town gates with town walls beyond

A The towns

Most people lived in villages in the Middle Ages, and did not often leave home. When they did go to town, they had to walk – up to ten miles (16 kilometres) each way.

Every town had a market. Peasants' main reason for going to town was to buy and sell there. They sold the eggs, cheese, wool, or corn they had brought with them. And they spent the few pence they made on the things they could not grow or make – shoes, cloth, pots and pans.

There were no big shops or factories in the towns. The only shops, apart from the market stalls, were the front rooms of craftsmen's houses. Customers stepped straight from the narrow, dirty streets into the workshops.

Most townspeople were part-time farmers. There were fields and common land outside every town, and gardens inside the walls. Some families kept animals in their homes. Hens and pigs searched for food in the heaps of refuse in the streets.

London was the biggest town in England. About 10,000 people lived there in 1066. Like other towns, it grew in the twelfth and thirteenth centuries. Even so, it was just a cluster of streets on the north bank of the Thames, between the Tower of London and Fleet Street. Rich merchants and great lords owned the only stone houses.

Now try Exercise 14.1.

(B) Towns in England in the 14ᵗʰ Century

0   50   100   150   200
Km

SCOTLAND

Newcastle ◉

N
W ✦ E
S

York ◉   Beverley
          • Hull

          Lincoln
Newark ◉
Nottingham •   Boston ◉
Shrewsbury ◉   • Stamford   King's Lynn
          Peterborough •   ◉ Great Yarmouth
WALES   Coventry ◎   Ely   Norwich
     Hereford   Cambridge   • Bury St. Edmunds
Gloucester •   Oxford ◎   • Ipswich
     Bristol ◉   • Luton
          Newbury   ▣ London
Salisbury ◉   • Winchester   • Canterbury
• Exeter   • Southampton
Plymouth •

Key: Population

▣ Over 50,000   ◉ 5,000 to 10,000

◎ 10,000 to 20,000   • 2,500 to 5,000

The population figures are estimates, based on the amount of tax each town paid in 1334

Exercise 14.1

Read **Section A**, and look at **Maps A** and **B**. Answer the questions. Write your answers in the spaces.

a How many people lived in London:

   i in the eleventh century?

   _____

   ii in the fourteenth century?

   _____

b In which part of England were there most towns in 1180 (south-east, south-west, midlands, north)?

   _____

c Which of these towns are shown on **B**, but *not* on **A**? (York, Southampton, Bristol, Newcastle, Boston, King's Lynn, Oxford)

   _____

d Why do you think these towns are not shown on **Map A**? _____

   _____

e Study **Map B** carefully, then complete the chart below by writing in the names of the towns.

Population of towns in the fourteenth century			
Over 50,000 people	10,000 to 20,000 people	5,000 to 10,000 people	2,500 to 5,000 people
....	....	....	....
	....	....	....
		....	....
		....	....
		....	....
			....
			....

B Merchants and craftsmen

This wine jug from France was found in the remains of a 13th century merchant's house in Southampton. It proves that English merchants imported French wine at that time.

The most important persons in a town were the merchants. They fixed the taxes to be paid by people coming into the town to sell goods. They set the laws for the markets. They tried to make sure that no-one cheated or stole.

Merchants were traders who got rich by buying and selling goods. They bought wool, corn, and skins from country people. Then they sold them at a profit, sometimes to traders from abroad at trade **fairs**. These were big markets, where merchants met to buy and sell their goods.

Craftsmen were skilled workers. They made shoes, pots, swords, hats, etc. The most important of them were the men who owned the workshops. They were called the **masters**. But each craftsman began as an **apprentice**, living in the master's house and learning in his shop. When he was old enough and skilled enough, he became a **journeyman**. Now he worked for real wages, paid by the master. Every journeyman hoped one day to be a master.

By the thirteenth century, each town had a **guild** for each of the main trades. And the craftsmen had to belong to the guilds. (All the stocking-makers in York had to belong to the York hosiers' guild. All the leather-makers in Newcastle were in the New-castle tanners' guild.)

A group of masters was in charge of each guild. They said how the goods should be made and what the prices should be. They made rules about what the apprentices had to learn. They gave money to members who were ill, and paid pensions to the widows of members who had died. The masters of most guilds were men, but some (such as the silk-makers of London) were women.

Now try Exercise 14.2.

Two craftsmen being tested by their Guild Master.

Exercise 14.2

Read **Section B**. Write your own notes on **guilds**. Use your own words.

a Say what a guild was.
b Give two examples of guilds.
c Say which men were in charge of guilds.
d Say what kind of rules guilds made.
e Say what guilds did to look after their members and their families.

C The wool and cloth trade

English wool was the best in Europe. Lords and abbots kept huge flocks of sheep, and the wool made them rich. **Wool-merchants**, who bought and sold wool, had big houses and wore fine clothes. The richest men in London were those who sold wool to the cloth-makers of **Flanders** (modern Belgium). Even the king borrowed money from the wool-merchants.

Before the fourteenth century, **woollen cloth** was made in the towns. After that, a lot of the work was done by village people. Rich **clothiers** in the towns bought raw wool from the wool-merchants. Then they sent it by packhorse out to the villages. Peasants spun the yarn and wove the cloth in their homes. The clothiers paid their wages.

Most English people had always dressed in English-made cloth. But not much English cloth was sold abroad – it was not good enough. Then, soon after the year 1300, there was a change. English cloth improved, and clothiers started selling it in Flanders, France, and Spain. Exports of wool fell, and exports of cloth grew.

Cloth-making did not make the peasants rich. But it made the fortunes of the wool-merchants and clothiers. You can still see clothiers' houses in towns like Colchester and Chipping Campden. And in many parts of England there are churches that were rebuilt with wool-merchants' money.

Now try Exercise 14.3.

Lavenham Church – work on the new tower began in 1490. It was paid for by the rich clothiers of the town.

Dyers in the Middle Ages dying cloth.

Exercise 14.3

Read **Section C**. Which things changed, and which things stayed the same? Write your own notes about the following:

a Wool exports.
b Cloth-making.
c Cloth exports.
d The quality of English wool.
e Merchants' profits.

Source 14a

King Henry III takes all the food, drink, and clothing he needs, by force, from the merchants. To save themselves, they have gone into hiding. Foreign merchants will not come to England. So trade has been brought to a stop. The king does not even let the poor fishermen sell their herrings as they want. They dare not come ashore for fear of being robbed.

Written by a monk called Matthew Paris in 1248.

Source 14b

You officers of the law should put dishonest brewers, bakers, butchers, and cooks in your pillories and ducking-stools. These are the men who do most harm to the poor. They poison them with bad food, and over-charge them. They grow rich by robbing the poor. How could they build such tall houses, and buy up land and farms, if they were honest?

From *Piers Ploughman*, a poem written by William Langland in about 1380.

Source 14c

I have been round all the drapers' shops in this town (Norwich), and I can't buy any cloth good enough for a dress. Everything is too simple in colour and quality. Would you please get me three yards and a quarter of something you think would suit me? Choose whatever colour you like.

A letter from Margaret Paston to her husband, who was in London, in 1465. The Pastons were quite rich landowners in Norfolk.

Source 14d

I am giving you five shillings (25 pence) to buy sugar and dates for me. Please send them as soon as you can. Let me know the price per pound of pepper, cloves, mace, ginger, cinnamon, almonds, rice, and raisins. If these things are cheaper in London than they are here, I shall send you the money to buy them.

A letter from Margaret Paston to her son, who was in London, in 1471.

Exercise 14.4

Read **Sources 14a** and **14b**, then answer the questions.

a Write down three **facts** from **Source 14a**.
b What was Matthew Paris's **opinion** of Henry III?
c Which words show that Matthew Paris was sorry for the fishermen?
d **Source 14b** says that 'dishonest' tradesmen have done what?
e **Source 14b** says that the tradesmen have spent their money on what?
f Whose side do you think the author of **Source 14b** was on?

Exercise 14.5

Read **Sources 14c** and **14d**. Answer questions **a** and **b** in sentences, and questions **c** to **e** in paragraphs.

a Who wrote **Sources 14c** and **14d**, and when?
b Are **Sources 14c** and **14d** primary or secondary sources? (Give a reason for your opinion.)
c What do **Sources 14c** and **14d** tell us about the clothes and food that the Pastons liked?
d What do **Sources 14c** and **14d** tell us about the shops in Norwich and London?
e Do you think that most families in the fifteenth century were like the Pastons? Do **Sources 14c** and **14d** tell us how most men and women did their shopping? (Give your reasons.)

15 Technology in the Middle Ages

'**Technology**' means the right tools or equipment to do a job, and knowing how to use them. Technology may be advanced, like the computer. Or it may be simple, like the windmill or the spinning wheel.

A Builders

We can still see the castles, cathedrals, and churches of the Middle Ages. We admire their high stone walls, towers, and huge windows filled with coloured glass. Their carved stone **vaults** carried higher and wider roofs than anyone had built before. The **masons** who built them were skilled craftsmen and artists.

Source 15a shows how masons worked. Their scaffolding was made from wooden poles roped together. Men pulled the heavy stones up with ropes and pulleys. For arches and vaults, they first made a wooden frame, then set the stones in the frame and cemented them together.

The masons were bands of craftsmen who travelled from job to job. Cathedrals took years to build. Some were built and rebuilt more than once. Not all the buildings were perfect – walls sometimes collapsed. Many a mason lost his life in an accident.

Now try Exercise 15.1.

Masons working on a tower.

Exercise 15.1

Read **Section A**, and look at **Source 15a**.
The four building workers in **Source 15a** have been marked with numbers. Write a sentence about each of them, saying what you think the person is doing and what tools are being used (if any)?

B Mills

In 1086, there were more than 5,000 **water-mills** in England. A water-mill used the village stream to turn a great wooden wheel. This turned the stone that milled the flour. But water-mills could do more than grind corn. They were used by cloth-makers and iron-workers (see Sections C and D). Water power even helped to make paper.

The first **windmills** were built in England just before the year 1200. A windmill was useful if there was no stream to drive a water-wheel. It worked only if the sails faced the wind, but the wind does not always blow from the same direction.

Technology's answer was a wind-mill that moved to face the wind. The whole mill turned to and fro on a huge wooden post fixed into the ground. That is why they were called 'post-mills'. Unlike water-mills, windmills were only used for grinding corn.

Now try Exercise 15.2.

Source 15b

Herbert the dean set up a windmill. When the abbot heard about this, he got so angry that he could hardly eat or speak. He ordered his servants to pull the mill down straight away. But the dean said he had a right to have a mill on his own land. He said any man had a right to use the wind. He also said that the mill was to grind his own corn and no-one else's. But the abbot had his way and the mill was pulled down.

Written by a monk at Bury St. Edmunds in 1191.

A windmill

Exercise 15.2

Read **Section B**, and read **Source 15b**.

a Who set up the windmill (**Source 15b**) and who objected?

_____

_____

b What was the abbot's opinion about the windmill?

_____

c The dean's opinion was that he had which two rights?

_____

_____

d What promise did the dean make?

_____

e Can you guess **why** the abbot was so angry? (Write a sentence.)

_____

_____

_____

C Cloth-making

Making woollen cloth was England's main industry in the Middle Ages. Wool from the sheep was **combed**, then **spun** into thread or yarn. (Women used spindle and distaff to pull and twist the wool.) Next, the **weaver**, on a loom, turned the yarn into cloth. After that, the **fullers**, or 'walkers', trod and shrank the cloth in troughs of water to make it thicker and more solid. Finally, the cloth was **dyed** and finished.

There were two big steps forward in the Middle Ages. **Fulling mills** began to do the work that walkers had done. They used water-wheels to drive hammers, which beat the cloth as it lay in the troughs of water. Soon after, the **spinning-wheel** started to take the place of the spindle and distaff. Technology was slowly changing.

Combing, spinning and weaving

Water mills like this were used for fulling from the thirteenth century onwards.

D The iron industry and the printing press

In the Middle Ages, ploughs, knives, spades, and scythes all had iron blades. Horses needed iron shoes, held on by iron nails. Spears and arrows had iron heads. Knights wore iron armour. The best swords were steel, which is made mainly from iron.

Miners dug **iron ore** from the ground, then **smelters** used charcoal-burning furnaces to extract iron from the ore. **Blacksmiths** worked, or wrought, the iron – they heated it to make it soft, then hammered it into the right shapes. Every village had its smith.

After about the year 1300, some smiths used water-wheels to drive the bellows which blew air into their furnaces. A mechanical bellows meant a much hotter furnace, so the iron could be melted and poured into **moulds**. The objects made this way were called cast iron. The guns that were used in the wars after 1350 had cast-iron barrels.

In the Middle Ages, books were written out slowly by hand, often by monks. They were expensive because they took such a long time to make. So monasteries took great care of the books in their libraries.

Books became cheaper when **printing** began. The Chinese invented printing in the eleventh century. But no books were printed in Europe until 1445. **William Caxton**, who learned how to print in Germany and Flanders, published England's first printed books in 1477. After that, more books were on sale, and more people learned to read. One result was that news and ideas spread more quickly.

Now try Exercise 15.3.

An early printing press

pɛelũ Aſcẽſianũ

Exercise 15.3

Change
Read **Sections C** and **D** on pages 79 and 80.
Look at the chart, 'Technology in the Middle Ages', then answer the questions in sentences.

a What change in castle-building happened in the twelfth century?
b When did cathedrals begin to have larger windows, with coloured glass?
c Where were there windmills before they reached England?
d What kind of mills were there in England in the eleventh and twelfth centuries?
e Which job in the cloth-making industry did not change much in the Middle Ages?
f In which century were water-mills first used in the iron industry? What were they used for?
g In which century was the printing press invented?

Technology in the Middle Ages

Date (AD)	1000	1100	1200	1300	1400

Building
Castles

● Normans built wood and earth castles ● Stone castles ● Chimneys instead of open hearths ● Glass windows

Cathedrals & Churces

● Normans built new stone cathedrals and churches with vaults ● Larger windows with coloured glass

Mills

Water mills used throughout the Middle Ages

● Windmills in France ● First windmills in England

Cloth-making
Spinning

Spinners used distaff and spindle ● Spinners began using spinning wheel

Weaving

Weaving done on a handloom throughout the Middle Ages

Fulling

Fulling done by walkers ● Water driven fulling mill

Iron Industry
Wrought iron

Smiths made iron objects by hand ● Some smiths began using mechanical hammer (water power)

Cast iron

No cast iron before 1350 ● Mechanical bellows (cast iron began)

Other Technologies

● Ship's compass ● Mechanical clock ● Water-powered paper mills

● Ship's rudder

● Guns first used ● Printing press

● More coal needed – bigger, deeper coal mines

Exercise 15.4

The invention of the printing press was a very important step forward in technology. What were its results?

The sentences below have been split in half. Join together the halves that fit, and write out the complete sentences.

First half

- Monks could spend their time on other work because . . .
- Books became more plentiful and cheaper because . . .
- More people were able to own books because . . .
- More people wanted to learn to read because . . .
- There were soon more schools because . . .
- Men and women learned more about the outside world because . . .

Second half

- they were cheaper to buy
- parents realised that reading and writing were important.
- they were not needed to copy out books by hand.
- they could read about it in books.
- they could now afford to buy books, and wanted to be able to read them.
- it took much less time to produce them.

Source 15c

The master of the works says that the builders were paid higher wages than they were due. One of them got a fortnight's wages when he was absent and had done no work. The men got too much money for drink. Wood and stone had been taken away, and no-one knew where it went. The workmen often quarrelled, so that the work was delayed or done carelessly. The carpenter is an old man and cannot work in high places.

A report on the work going on at York Minster in 1345.

Source 15d

The nave of York Minster. This is the part of the minster that was being built in 1345, when Source 15c was written.

Exercise 15.5

Read **Source 15c**, and look at **Source 15d**.
Note down the answers to these questions. Then discuss these answers in a group.

a Who wrote **Source 15c**, and when?
b What was the author's **opinion** of the building workers?
c The men mentioned in **Source 15c** were working on which part of York Minster? (Look at the caption to **Source 15d**.)
d Describe what you can see in **Source 15d**.
e Does **Source 15d** make you disbelieve **Source 15c**? Is it possible to believe both sources?
f Why should we not always believe written sources?

The members of the group should tell the rest of the class what they think, either in short talks or by making a tape.

16 Daily Life in the Middle Ages

A Houses and furniture

Peasant families lived in one-room or two-room shacks. The shacks were made of wood, turf, and clay. The roofs were thatched. Fires burned in the centre of the earth floors. There were no chimneys, and there was no glass in the windows. In winter, the animals lived under the same roof as the people.

In the twelfth century, lords' houses were the same as peasants', only bigger. But by the year 1450, the **manor house** had become much grander. It was built of stone, and had tiled floors and glass windows. There were extra rooms for the lord and his family, and there was a separate kitchen, with a stone chimney.

Town houses were built in streets, and they were quite narrow. Rich merchants and master-craftsmen built extra storeys. The shop was on the ground floor, the family lived upstairs, and the servants slept in the attics. Often, the upper floors hung over the street.

Peasants' furniture was as simple as their houses. They had a trestle table, a few stools, and a chest to keep things in. They slept on straw mattresses on the floor. Even manor houses had only one chair. But lords and merchants had wooden beds with curtains, and tapestries to hang on the walls.

Now try Exercise 16.1.

A merchant's house in Exeter, built in the fourteenth century.

Exercise 16.1

Read **Section A**.
   Why do we know so little about peasants' houses in the Middle Ages? Some reasons are printed below.
   Decide which *you* think are the *five* most important reasons.
   Write out your five reasons in order, with the most important first. If you can think of some reasons of your own, write them down as well.

a No-one has looked for remains of peasants' homes.
b Peasants' houses were made of wood and clay, so they soon fell down.
c The sources did not describe peasants' houses.
d Peasants often pulled their own houses down, and built new ones.
e No-one wants to live in peasants' cottages today.
f There are no TV programmes about peasants' houses.
g Cottages had no chimneys, so many of them burned down.
h Peasants lived in the country, and most people now live in the town.

B Clothes

The rich wore smart clothes made from fine wool, linen, velvet, silk, or fur. Both sexes liked bright colours. Lords and ladies had their clothes decorated with gold and silver thread, jewels, and fancy buttons.

Ladies' dresses were always long. (**Sources 16b** and **16c** show you how fashions changed.) Their heads were kept covered, and in the fifteenth century they wore large, heavy head-dresses. Between 1450 and 1500, the well-dressed man wore a very short tunic and bright hose (or tights). Sometimes the hose had different-coloured legs.

Peasants' clothes were made from coarse woollen or linen cloth. Many of them kept warm by wearing sheepskin or leather jackets. They dressed in dull colours – grey, dark brown, or dark green. Some could not afford shoes.

Now try Exercise 16.2.

Source 16a

Peasants' clothing from the fourteenth century

Source 16b

Fifteenth-century men's and women's fashions

Source 16c

Eleventh-century ladies costumes

Exercise 16.2

Read **Section B** and look at **Sources 16a, 16b** and **16c**. Do any *one* of the following:

a Describe the changes in women's costume between the eleventh and fifteenth centuries.
b Describe a fourteenth-century peasant's clothes.
c Describe fifteenth-century men's fashion.

Write a paragraph and draw a picture (coloured if possible).

C Food

The poor were often hungry. They lived mainly on dark rye bread and oat cakes, and porridge made from peas, beans, and oatmeal. There was also home-made cheese, and sometimes a little salted pork. But there was hardly ever any fresh meat. To drink, they had ale or cider.

Kings and lords ate much more, and had more variety. They liked fish, beef, and venison, and drank huge amounts of wine. At a fifteenth century feast there would be dishes like roast peacock, swan, and stork. By that time, there were rich sauces made with spices from the Far East.

No-one had forks in the Middle Ages – they made do with knives, spoons, and their fingers. Peasants ate off wooden plates, and the rich used pewter. Table manners were crude. A fifteenth-century book says that in polite company you should not lick your plate clean, or spit too far!

Now try Exercise 16.3.

Source 16f

A beggar at a feast

Source 16d

A Norman feast

Source 16e

Cooking on a spit

Exercise 16.3

Read **Section C** and look at **Sources 16d**, **16e**, and **16f**.
What was a lord's feast like in the Middle Ages? What do the sources tell you about the following? (Write at least a sentence about each.)

a The food and how it was cooked.
b Plates, cups, knives, forks, spoons, etc.
c Servants.
d Beggars and animals.

D Education

Children were not forced by law to go to school, and most girls did not go at all. **Some** boys went to school with the village priest. For a small fee, he taught them to read, write, and do simple arithmetic. The boys had to sit on benches, often in the church porch, and learn their lessons by heart. (Look at source 16h.) Pupils who were badly behaved or lazy were flogged.

Rich men's sons went on to **grammar schools**, where they learned Latin, and nothing else. By the age of fourteen, they could read, write, and speak it as well as they could English.

Latin was the language of the church. The Mass and the Bible were in Latin. The books which the monks copied were in Latin. So were the chronicles which they wrote. All over Europe, educated men spoke and wrote to each other in Latin. Students travelled a long way to hear learned priests lecturing, in Latin, in the 'schools'. (We would call them universities.) In the twelfth century, English students crossed to the schools of Paris. By the year 1200, there were schools at Oxford, and at Cambridge soon after. (Read source 16g.)

Many rich men sent their daughters to school in nunneries. The nuns taught them to read and write, and to behave like ladies. They might learn a little French and Latin as well. By the year 1500, though, a lot of lords had private tutors for their daughters. At the end of the Middle Ages, many noble women were very fine scholars.

Now try Exercise 16.4.

Source 16g

There was a scholar from Oxford. His horse was as lean as a rake. And he wasn't fat himself. His cheeks were hollow, and he had a sad face. His coat was threadbare, for he had very little money. But he would rather have twenty books, bound in red and black, than any number of fine robes.

From Geoffrey Chaucer's *Canterbury Tales*. The scholar was a teacher in the university.

A schoolroom

Source 16h

A woman teaching reading. Many women in the middle ages could read better than their husbands.

E Health and sickness

For most men and women, life was hard. For many, it was short. A lot of children died young, and at fifty a man or woman was old. Lack of food was often the basic cause of sickness and death. But impure water and dirty houses with no proper drains played their part. When disease struck, death soon followed.

Only the rich could call in a doctor when they were ill. But doctors often did more harm than good. (They used to **bleed** patients to get rid of fever.) Their knowledge came mainly from the ancient **Greeks**. It had been passed on to **Arab** scholars in the Near East and Spain. From them, it reached the west. But this knowledge came only from books. No-one knew much about how the body really worked.

Doctors did know about **infectious** and **contagious** diseases. **Leprosy** was the most feared of them. Lepers were made to live apart, in 'lazar houses'. They had to wear special cloaks, and carry bells or clappers to warn that they were coming. They could not even go to church. In a way, this cruel treatment worked. By 1500, there were only a few lepers in England.

Monasteries and **hospitals** gave clean beds and decent food to some of the sick and old. And monks made medicines from the herbs they grew in their gardens. As a rule, though, fami-

A doctor in the Middle Ages making medicines.

Operating on a patient's head.

Source 16i

Some 'cures' from the Middle Ages

a A cure for leprosy. *Make an ointment from unicorn's liver and the white of an egg.*

b A cure for smallpox. *Wrap the patient in a red cloth. Hang red curtains at the windows and round the bed.*

c A headache cure. *Make a mixture of leaves of green rue, mustard seed, and the white of an egg. Using a feather, smear it on the side of the head that is not sore.*

Source 16j

A stick which once belonged to St Curig is good for getting rid of lumps on the body. You are cured if you kneel before the stick and make a gift of a penny. A man with a lump once gave only a half-penny. The result was that only half his lump went down.

From a book about Wales written by a priest called Gerald in 1188.

lies looked after their own. Women kept 'cures' (part fact, part magic) among their recipes. But they, and most others, had more faith in prayers to the saints than in medicine.

Now try Exercises 16.5 and 16.6.

Exercise 16.5

Read **Section E** and **Sources 16i** and **16j**.
Write at least one sentence in answer to each of the questions.

a What was the doctors' **motive** for bleeding their patients?
b What was the **motive** for forcing lepers to live separate lives?
c What was the monks' **motive** for taking care of the old and sick? (If you are not sure, read the beginning of Chapter 4 again.)
d What do you think were the **motives** of the doctors, monks, and others who said that the 'cures' in **Source 16i** worked?
e What do you think might have been Gerald's **motive** (**Source 16j**) for telling the story about St. Curig's stick?

Exercise 16.6

Discuss in a group:

a the things you would have liked about living in the Middle Ages.
b the things you would have disliked.

Make a chart or wall display divided into two halves – good things and bad things. Draw pictures or cartoons for the display **or** write short pieces in your own words.

17 Women in the Middle Ages

A A woman's place...

It was a man's world. Girls obeyed their fathers before marriage, and their husbands after. If they did not, they were beaten. Even the church said that men had a right to beat their wives. Most villages had a ducking stool for 'scolds' – women who nagged their husbands.

Some women lived without men. Ladies whose husbands were at the wars had to look after the estates. All the servants and tenants – men and women – had to take orders from them. **Widows** had to manage alone. Most widows were poor, and many must have starved. But rich merchants' widows were well off. And craftsmen's widows got help from the guilds.

Many rich men's daughters became **nuns**. (Their fathers had to make a gift of money when they entered the convent.) The abbess was often the daughter of a lord. Nuns' main work was to teach the daughters of good families how to behave like ladies, and how to read and write. The only men allowed in convents were the priests who came to say Mass.

Men were supposed to be the bosses. This did not stop some women from getting their own way. And in the songs and stories of the Middle Ages, women had a very high place. Knights were supposed to fight for their ladies, and defend them from all dangers, such as dragons!

Now try Exercise 17.1.

A woman making her confession to a priest.

Source 17a

When you are walking in the street, keep your head still and look straight ahead. Fix your eyes on the ground about 20 yards in front of you. Do not look up, or glance at any men or women. Do not laugh. Do not stop to speak to anyone in the street.

Instructions for his young wife written by Goodman of Paris in the fourteenth century.

Exercise 17.1

Read **Section A** and **Source 17a**.
Write 'True' or 'False' after each sentence.

a The church said that women were equal to their husbands. _____

b Women who nagged their husbands were punished in public. _____

c All widows were very poor. _____

d Male servants wouldn't take orders from women. _____

e Only rich men's daughters became nuns. _____

f Nuns were able to read and write. _____

g Knights were expected to defend their ladies. _____

h Goodman of Paris (**Source 17a**) expected his wife to appear shy and modest. _____

i Goodman did not mind if his wife chatted to her friends. _____

j Goodman himself probably did not speak to people in the streets. _____

B Marriage

Most girls married young – at fifteen or sixteen, or younger. They married the men their fathers chose. For marriage, at least to the rich, was business. Only the really poor married for love.

It cost a man money to feed and clothe a daughter. When she got married, her husband took on the job of keeping her. So her father paid the bridegroom some money or gave him a present. This was the **dowry**. All but the very poor paid dowries. Tradesmen might give some furniture and cooking pots. Kings and great lords paid vast sums.

A marriage, and the payment of a dowry, was a deal between two families. If the fathers were kings, it might be part of a peace treaty. If they were merchants, it was a piece of business. The young people's wishes had nothing to do with it.

Heiresses were special. They were girls who had no brothers. When their fathers died, they (and their husbands) got the land or money. Many men dreamed of marrying a rich heiress. To a king, marrying an heiress was as good as winning a war. Henry II of England became ruler of all of southwest France when he married Eleanor of Aquitaine.

Now try Exercise 17.2.

The poet Chaucer wrote about the Wealthy Wife of Bath. She had been married five times and was looking for a sixth husband.

Weddings in the Middle Ages took place at the church door, not in the church.

Exercise 17.2

Read **Section B**.
Use your own words to write brief notes about the following:

a The age at which girls married.
b Choice of husband.
c Dowries.
   i What was a dowry?
   ii Which classes of people paid dowries?
   iii Why were dowries paid?
d Marriage was a deal or treaty.
e Heiresses.

C Women's Work

Married women had a lot of children, but about half of them died young. Not even the rich were spared the pain and sadness of bearing children who lived only a year or two. Often the mothers themselves died in childbirth.

Rich ladies had servants to do the housework and look after the children. The ladies gave orders to the servants and kept the accounts. They had time to talk, read, and write letters. Most of them did some weaving or embroidery.

Craftsmen's wives had serving girls to help run the house. But they had to cook and see to the children themselves. They also served in the shop, and made sure the apprentices kept out of mischief. They had no time to spare.

Peasant women had the hardest life of all. They had to cook, clean, care for the children, and help their husbands in the fields. On top of that, they would spin yarn and make cheese to sell in the market. Most of the time they must have been cold, wet, hungry, and tired. Not many lived much beyond the age of thirty.

Now try Exercise 17.3.

A peasant woman cooking a meal for her children.

Source 17b

The poorest folk are the widows with children. The landlords keep putting their rent up. The money they make by spinning has to be spent on rent, or on milk and oatmeal for the hungry children. These women are often miserable with hunger and cold. They get up before dawn to card and comb the wool, to wash and scrub and mend, and wind yarn.

From *Piers Ploughman*, written by William Langland in about 1380.

Source 17c

I saw a poor man and his wife ploughing. She had a short coat, with a sheet on top to keep out the weather. Her feet were bare. At the end of the field was a basket, with a little child in it, wrapped in rags. Two others, about two years old, stood beside it. They were all crying in misery.

From *Pierce the Ploughman's Crede*, written in the 1390s.

Exercise 17.3

Read **Section C** and **Sources 17b** and **17c**.
Write down at least five **reasons** why peasant women had a hard and miserable life.

Source 17d

When I was in Norwich this week, I called at my mother's. While I was there Mr Wrothe came in. He saw our daughter, who was with me, and said she was a fine-looking girl. My mother asked him if he could find her a good husband. He said that he knew a young man from a good family, who has an income of £200 a year. He is eighteen years old. What do you think about the idea? My mother thinks that if we wait any longer we will have to pay a bigger dowry.

A letter from Margaret Paston to her husband in 1462.

Source 17e

This brass engraving from a tomb in Isleham church, Cambridge shows a rich lady dressed in the style of about 1485.

Exercise 17.4

Read **Source 17d**, then answer the questions in sentences.

a Where did Mrs Paston's mother live?
b What was Mr Wrothe's **opinion** of Mrs Paston's daughter?
c Which *three* **facts** about the young man did Mr Wrothe mention?
d What was Mrs Paston's mother's **opinion** about the marriage?
e Did Mrs Paston say what her opinion was?
f Which *two* people were not asked for their opinions?

Source 17f

There once was a merchant, who had so much money that people thought he must be wise. His wife was beautiful and liked company. They were always having visitors at their house. Now the wife loved fine clothes and ornaments. The merchant liked her to be well dressed, for it showed how rich he was. But he had to pay the bills!

From one of the stories in Geoffrey Chaucer's *Canterbury Tales*, written in about 1390.

Exercise 17.5

Look at **Source 17e** and read **Source 17f**.
Answer questions **a** to **f** in sentences, and question **g** in a paragraph.

a Who wrote **Source 17f**, and when?
b Is **Source 17f** fact or fiction? (Look at **Source 3g** on page 20 if you are not sure.)
c What does **Source 17f** tell us about the merchant's wife?
d Where does **Source 17e** come from?
e What does **Source 17e** tell us about the rich lady?
f Could the lady in **Source 17e** have been the same person as the lady in **Source 17f**?
g How much do **Sources 17e** and **17f** tell us about rich ladies in the late Middle Ages? (Which things do they tell us about, and which things do they not tell us about?)

18 Crime and Punishment in the Middle Ages

A Sheriffs, Judges, and Juries

England had no police force in the Middle Ages. Instead, all the peasants had to join a **tithing**. This was a group of men who made sure that their neighbours behaved. If there was a crime, the tithing had to say who had done it. If they did not, they were all punished.

Also, when a crime took place, all the men in a town or village had to join the **hue and cry**. This meant that they were supposed to rush out and chase the suspect. If they caught him, they handed him over to the sheriff. Of course, the suspect often got away.

The **sheriff** was the king's man in each county. One of his jobs was to catch criminals and put them in prison. He kept them there until the king's **judges** arrived on their tour of the country.

The judges were told what crimes had taken place. Then a **jury** said who had committed the crimes, if they knew. If the accused man or woman confessed, he or she was sentenced. If not, he or she went to **trial by ordeal**. (See Section B).

Now try Exercise 18.1.

Source 18a

Hue and Cry

At least four armed men in each village have to keep watch all night. When a stranger passes through, they must arrest him. If they think he is not honest, they have to hand him over to the sheriff. If the stranger runs away, they must raise the hue and cry. All the men of the village should then join in the chase until the suspect is caught.

A law passed by King Henry III in 1242.

The court of king's bench in the fifteenth century. Try to find the five judges, the clerks, the ushers with their sticks, the lawyers, and the prisoners.

Source 18b

Juries

Twelve men from each district must come before the judges. They must say whether any man in their area is a robber, or murderer, or thief. If a man is accused, and says he is not guilty, there must be a trial by ordeal.

A law passed by King Henry II in 1166.

B Trial by Ordeal and Trial by Combat

Trial by ordeal was the way of judging an accused person. The idea was that God would decide who was guilty and who was innocent. So the man or woman had to take a test. The result would show God's verdict. If God, through the ordeal, said 'guilty', the accused was punished.

In **ordeal by fire**, the accused had to walk a few paces, carrying a piece of red-hot iron in the palm of his or her hand. The hand was burned, so it was

Trial by ordeal.

Trial by combat

94

bandaged. After three days, the judges took off the bandage and looked at the burned hand. If it was starting to heal, the person was innocent. If it was not healing, he was guilty.

Ordeal by water was simpler. The accused was thrown into a pond. If he sank, he was innocent. (If he was lucky he was fished out before he drowned.) If he floated, he was guilty.

In **trial by combat**, the man who brought the charge had to fight the person he accused. The first one to be knocked down had to admit he was in the wrong. Women and children could hire 'champions' to fight for them.

By the year 1300, trial by ordeal had been given up. Instead, a jury decided whether the accused was guilty or not. Trial by combat lasted a little longer. But it too has been abolished. A thief cannot now offer to fight his accuser!

Now try Exercises 18.2 and 18.3.

C Punishments

You could be hanged for all sorts of crimes in the Middle Ages. But not all criminals were put to death. Many had to pay fines. A law passed by King Henry II in 1176 said that thieves had to have a hand and a foot cut off. Then they had to go into exile (leave England for ever). The king got all their money and goods.

Sheriffs' prisons were mainly for persons waiting to be tried. There were **dungeons** in lords' castles, of course. Powerful lords kept their enemies locked up for years. The stocks, pillory, and ducking-stool were for small-scale crime. Traders who cheated in the market would get a spell in the pillory. It taught them a lesson and warned other traders. And it was cheap entertainment for the public.

Exercise 18.2

Read **Section B. Written sources** tell us what happened in trial by ordeal and trial by combat. But there are very few **pictures** from the Middle Ages.
　How might pictures have helped us?
　Write down some questions which you could have answered if there had been pictures. (The cartoon might give you some ideas.)

Exercise 18.3

a Before Henry II's time, each **lord** had his own court. The lord acted as judge. He could hang the peasants, or make them pay fines. Henry II changed this. He said the courts were under the king's control. He sent his judges round England to hear cases.
　Suggest a reason why this change was popular with the common people.
b In the thirteenth century, trial by ordeal was stopped. Instead, **juries** decided whether accused persons were guilty.
　Suggest a reason why this was a change for the better.
c Which people might have been sorry to see the end of trial by combat, and why?

A ducking stool, which was often used for punishing women who had done wrong.

The Legend of Robin Hood

Men who had done wrong, but did not turn up in court, were condemned as **outlaws**. For the rest of their lives, they had no rights. It was not a crime to kill them, or steal from them. Many outlaws fled to the **forests**. These were partly wooded places where only the king could hunt. It was a crime for anyone else to kill deer there. Outlaws in the forests robbed travellers and killed the deer.

The most famous outlaws are **Robin Hood** and his 'merry men'. The story is a legend, but some things in it are true. There was a forest called Sherwood. There was a sheriff of Nottingham. In about 1230, in Yorkshire, there was even an outlaw called **Robert Hood**.

Now try Exercises 18.4 and 18.5

This picture was painted in about 1840. It shows Robin Hood and his men dining with the king in Sherwood Forest. The ballads say that this happened, but they do not say which king it was. King Edward II did pass through **Sherwood Forest in** 1323. Perhaps he met Robin Hood then.

Source 18c

The story told in the ballads written in the fifteenth century

Robin Hood was an outlaw. Little John and Will Scarlett were members of his band. Robin and the 'merry men' lived in Sherwood Forest and Barnsdale in Yorkshire. They dressed in Lincoln green. They were good archers, and their main food was the king's deer. Their enemies were the sheriff of Nottingham and the Abbot of St Mary's in York. They robbed rich travellers, but took nothing from the poor.

Robin Hood – drawn in 1795.

An archer – drawn in the Middle Ages.

Source 18d

The story as it is told today

Robin Hood was the leader of a band of outlaws. Among his 'merry men' were Little John, Will Scarlett, and Friar Tuck. His girl-friend was called Maid Marion. Robin and the outlaws lived in Sherwood Forest. They dressed in Lincoln green. They were expert archers, and lived by killing the king's deer. Their great enemy was the sheriff of Nottingham. They robbed the rich, and gave money to the poor.

Exercise 18.4

Read **Section C** and **Sources 18c** and **18d**.
How has the legend of Robin Hood changed between the fifteenth century (Source 18c) and today (Source 18d)?
Write notes, answering the questions below.

a What changes have taken place in the **people** in the legend? Which persons have stayed the same? Which persons have been added? Which persons have dropped out?
b Do the events happen in the same **place**? Have there been any changes?
c Have there been changes in the outlaws' **dress** and **food**?
d Have there been any changes in the **events** – the things the outlaws did?

Exercise 18.5

Most legends have some truth in them. We can study legends, and find out which things **are** true, which things **may be** true, and which things **are probably not** true.

How much of the Robin Hood story is **true**, and how much is **fiction**?
Read **Section C** and **Sources 18c** and **18d** again.
Note down the answers to these questions, then discuss your answers in a group:

a Which things in the Robin Hood story are **true**? (Use these words as a guide: outlaws, forests, Sherwood, sheriff of Nottingham, deer, robbery.)
b Was there ever a real Robin (or Robert) Hood, and did he live in the right place? (Look at the map.)
c Which things in the story (**Source 18d**) do you think are **fiction**?

Your group should make a chart or wall display with drawings, a map, and written pieces. It should show which things in the story are true, which are fiction, and which you are not sure about.

19 The Village, 1500-1750

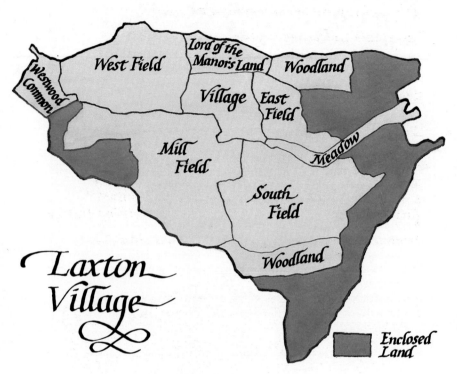

Laxton Village

Enclosed Land

All the villagers would grow the same crop (e.g. barley) in east field and west field. They would grow another crop (e.g. peas) in south field. Mill field would be left empty (or 'fallow') to let the land rest. Next year, east and west fields would grow peas, south field would be fallow and mill field would grow barley. This is called 'crop rotation'. In Laxton, the same crop was grown in east and west fields.

A farm labourer

A The manor

In the year 1500, nine out of ten English men, women, and children lived in the countryside. They worked on the land. Their homes were in villages or small hamlets. They ate mainly what they grew themselves.

In many places there were still villages with three (or four) **open fields**, divided into **strips**. Most of the villagers had one or two strips in each field, and paid rent for them to the **lord of the manor**. Each year, the peasants grew crops (such as wheat, barley, or beans) in two (or three) of the fields. (Look at **the plan** of **Laxton**.) All the peasants worked together to plough, sow the seed, and reap the harvest. Each man kept the crops which grew on his strips.

As well as the open fields, each manor had some **common** land. The villagers could keep animals there — sheep, cattle, or pigs. Even the poorest peasants could use the common. Most of the animals had to be killed in the autumn, because there was no food for them in the winter. The meat was salted to preserve it, and kept until it was eaten or sold.

You could find villages with open fields all over the Midlands of England. In much of the north and the southeast, the land was divided into smaller fields without strips, and there was no common. These were called **enclosed** villages.

Now try Exercises 19.1 and 19.2.

Exercise 19.1

Read **Section A** and study **the plan**.
Draw a plan of the village of Laxton in 1635. Shade, in different colours if possible:

a The lord of the manor's land,
b The open fields,
c The meadow land,
d The common land,
e Woodland,
f Enclosed land.

Sources

We find out about the past from **sources**. Some of them are **written sources**, such as books. John Leland's account of his travels through England in 1540 (see **Source 19a**) is a good example.

Old coins, maps, and pictures are also sources. We can learn a lot about the past by visiting churches, old houses, and museums, and studying the sources which are kept there.

Source 19a

a *The south and east of Leicestershire is 'champain', and has little wood growing.*
b *From Wakefield to Pontefract (in Yorkshire) is six miles, partly through enclosed land, and partly through 'champain'.*
c *From Wikham to Bishop Waltham (in Hampshire) it is three miles. The land is all enclosed, with good pasture, wood, and corn.*

Three passages from John Leland's account of his journey through England in about 1540. By 'champain' Leland meant open fields.

Source 19b

In villages which have not been enclosed, the poor keep cattle on the common. From the milk, they make cheese and butter, which they sell – the money helps them keep their families. If the common were enclosed, these people would not be able to keep cattle, and would be ruined.

Letter to a Lancashire newspaper, written in 1725.

Source 19c

In the places where the sheep produce the best wool, landlords are not content with rents from their land. They enclose the fields and make pastures. They have houses and whole villages pulled down. The poor farm workers and their families wander about until they have nothing left.

From a book written by Sir Thomas More in 1516.

Harvest time: the Lord of the Manor's reeve keeping an eye on the peasants

Source 19d

My father was a yeoman. He paid three or four pounds a year rent to his landlord. He kept a hundred sheep and thirty cows. He was able to afford to send me to school. And when my sisters were married, he gave each of their husbands five pounds. He would always welcome his poor neighbours into his house, feed them, and give them money.

From a sermon preached by Bishop Latimer in 1547.

Exercise 19.2

Examine **Sources 19a, 19b, 19c,** and **19d**.
For each of the sources, find out the answers to these questions:

a What is it?
b Who wrote it or made it? (Write 'Not known' if you do not know.)
c When was it written or made?

Write out your answers in the form of a chart or table.

B Gentry, yeomen, and labourers

The lords of the manor (often called the **gentry**) were the leading men of each district. Everyone looked up to them. All men with money (and their wives) wanted to belong to the gentry. Many a rich merchant from the towns bought land and turned himself into a lord of the manor.

Kings and queens relied on the gentry to keep order and enforce the law. As **Justices of the Peace** (J.P.s), they sat as judges in the local courts, fixed food prices, and collected the taxes that were used to help the poor.

J.P.s got no pay for their work, but they did not complain – they liked being in charge.

The better-off villagers were called **yeomen**. They owned part of their land, and rented the rest from the gentry. Yeomen worked on their own farms, but also employed labourers, and paid them wages. Yeomen made money by selling the corn they grew and the wool from their sheep. Some of them grew rich in the sixteenth century. A few rose to join the ranks of the gentry. (Read **Source 19d**.)

Villagers' wives kept hens and geese. They sold the eggs (and sometimes the birds themselves) at market to make a little extra money.

Below the yeomen were the **tenants** and **labourers**, who owned no land. Tenants rented some land (strips in the open fields) from the lords of the manor, but also earned wages, working for the lords or the yeomen. Labourers had no strips, and worked full-time for wages. Both they and the tenants grew poorer in the sixteenth century.

Now try Exercises 19.3 and 19.4.

Centuries

A **century** is a period of a hundred years.
The **first century** was the hundred years from AD 1 to AD 100.
The **fourth century** was the hundred years from AD 301 to AD 400.
The **tenth century** was the hundred years from AD 901 to AD 1000.
The **fifteenth century** was the hundred years from 1401 to 1500.

Exercise 19.3

Read **Section B** and look again at **Source 19a**. Copy the sentences and write 'True' or 'False' after each one.

a The gentry were the most important people in each district. _____

b All rich people wanted to belong to the gentry. _____

c J.P. stands for Justice of the Peace. _____

d The king paid the J.P.s wages. _____

e No-one liked being a J.P. _____

f Yeomen owned some land, and rented some. _____

g Yeomen did not have to work in the fields. _____

h At least one bishop was a yeoman's son. _____ (see **Source 19d**.)

i Tenants rented land from the gentry. _____

j Labourers got richer in the sixteenth century. _____

Exercise 19.4

Read the note on 'Centuries.' Now copy the sentences below and fill in the spaces.

a The third century was the _____ years from AD 201 to AD 300.

b The twelfth century was the hundred years from 1101 to _____

c The sixteenth century was the hundred years from _____ to _____

d The _____ century was the hundred years from 1701 to 1800.

e The year 673 was in the _____ century.

f The year 1381 was in the _____ century.

g The year 1620 was in the _____ century.

Draw a time-line, starting at the year 1500 and ending at 1800. Mark the sixteenth, seventeenth and eighteenth centuries.

A J.P. sorts out squabbles with patience and fairness.
Well, you'll just just have to cut it in half, then, won't you?!

C Enclosures

In the sixteenth century, men could become very rich by keeping sheep and selling the wool. Some landowners turned their open fields and commons into pasture for sheep. (Read **Source 19c**.) They put hedges round the new grass fields, so they were called **enclosures**. (The plan of Laxton village shows that in some villages only part of the land was enclosed.)

Enclosures were good for the landowners. But they were not good for the tenants and labourers. They were forced to leave their villages, for they now had no jobs, no land, and no common for their cattle and sheep. Many of them ended up in the towns, as beggars.

Before 1600, men enclosed land to make pasture for sheep. After 1650 there was a change. The population was growing, and the people needed food. So farmers ploughed up the enclosed fields. Some grew wheat, barley, and rye for bread. Others grew clover and turnips, to feed the cattle during the winter. The result was more meat, milk, and butter.

Enclosures cost money. Landowners had to pay for ditches, hedges, and new stock. Very rich **nobles**, who owned big **estates** (more than one manor) could afford the expense. So they enclosed land, and became richer still. But not all gentry could afford to enclose. A lot of them sold their land to the nobles after 1660. And many yeomen sank to the level of labourers.

Now try Exercise 19.5.

Above: Hunting was the favourite sport of the gentry. This picture shows them fox hunting in the eighteenth century.

Above right: Peasant's sport – a village festival with feasting, dancing, and a friendly game of skittles in the sixteenth century

Exercise 19.5

Read **Section C** and **Sources 19a** and **19b** again.
Answer the questions in short paragraphs.

a Which people were in favour of enclosures? Why?
b Which people were against enclosures? Why?
c Had all the villages in England been enclosed,

(i) in 1540? (See **Source 19a**.)
(ii) in 1725? (See **Source 19b**.)

20 Towns and Industry, 1500-1750

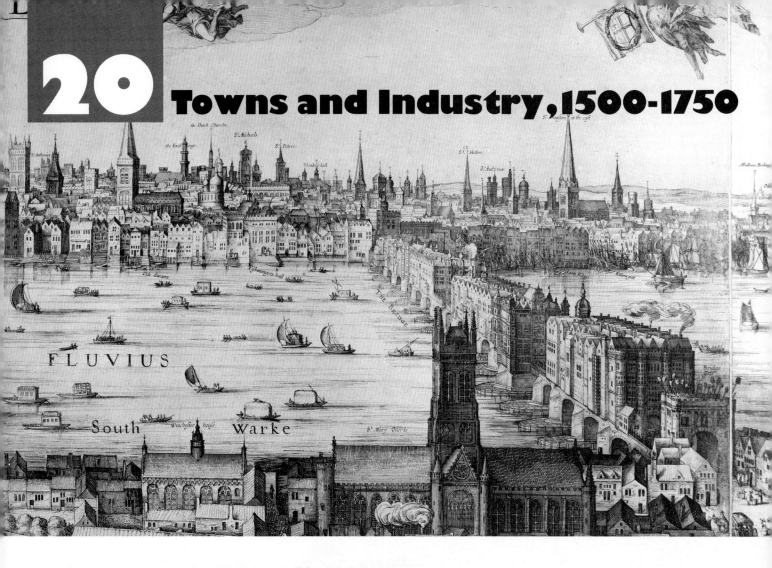

FLUVIUS

South Warke

London in 1616, seen from the south end of London Bridge

A Expanding towns

Only one person in ten lived in a town in England in 1500. The towns were all small. Even London's population was only 50,000. And no other town had more than 20,000 people. Many of England's 700 'market towns' were just big villages.

Things changed between 1500 and 1750. Many thousands of men and women moved from the country to the towns. By 1750, more than 500,000 people lived in London. After 1700, ports such as Bristol and Liverpool, and industrial towns like Birmingham and Leeds grew fast. Even so, no town apart from London had more than 50,000 inhabitants in 1750. The great mass of people still lived in villages or on farms.

All towns were dirty and unhealthy. Houses were packed together in narrow lanes, and families were packed into the houses. (Ten to a room was common.) There were no proper sewers or water supplies. Refuse was thrown into the streets and left to rot. Disease ran riot.

Towns were violent places. The hungry poor easily turned to crime. And since there was no proper police, they often got away with it. Mobs sometimes ran through the streets, looting and burning. Gentlemen in London complained that they were beaten and robbed by drunken roughs outside their own homes.

Now try Exercises 20.1 and 20.2.

TOWNS IN ENGLAND IN 1525

SCOTLAND

WALES

- Newcastle
- York
- Hull
- Lincoln
- Boston
- Norwich
- King's Lynn
- Shrewsbury
- Yarmouth
- Coventry
- Bury St. Edmunds
- Worcester
- Lavenham
- Ipswich
- Hereford
- Hadleigh
- Gloucester
- Colchester
- Reading
- LONDON
- Bristol
- Canterbury
- Salisbury
- Southampton
- Exeter
- Totnes

0 50 100 150 200
Kilometres

KEY:
- ▣ Population over 50,000
- ■ Population between 10,000 and 20,000
- ◉ Population between 5,000 and 10,000
- • Population between 3,000 and 5,000

Exercise 20.1

Read **Section A** and study the map. Copy the questions and fill in the blanks.

a After London, which were the three largest towns in England in 1525? _____, _____, and _____

b How many people lived in London, (i) in 1500? _____ and (ii) in 1750? _____

c Which was the largest of these towns in 1525: Hull, Exeter, Hereford? _____

d In which part of England were there most towns in 1525 (north-east, south-east, north-west, south-west)? _____

e In which part of England were there fewest towns in 1525? _____

f Which two ports were growing quickly in the eighteenth century? _____ and _____

g Apart from ports, what other kinds of towns were growing fast in 1750? _____

Source 20a

London is a mighty city of business. It is a very busy place, and you can hardly walk along the streets for the crowds. The men and women are well dressed and very proud. They don't like foreigners. They scoff and laugh at them. The boys gather in crowds in the streets and beat them up.

Written by a German visitor to London in 1600.

Source 20b

In every street in London, carts and coaches go thundering past. At every corner, men, women, and children meet in crowds. Hammers are beating in one place, pots clinking in another. There are porters carrying loads, and merchants' men with bags of money. The tradesmen never stand still.

Written by Thomas Dekker, a playwright who lived in London, in 1606.

Exercise 20.2

Read **Sources 20a** and **20b**. Then answer the questions – write one or two sentences about each.

a When were **Sources 20a** and **20b** written?
b Which source was written by an Englishman, and which by a foreigner?
c Both sources say what about London?
d Which things about London are mentioned in **Source 20a**, but not in **Source 20b** – write about two of them.
e Which things are mentioned in **Source 20b**, but not in **Source 20a** – write about two.

B The craftsmen

All towns had weekly **markets**, and villagers would come in on foot to sell butter, cheese, and eggs. They bought what they could not make for themselves, such as cloth, boots, pots and pans. Towns were where these things were made. Skilled **craftsmen** made shoes, hats, barrels, and horses' harness. Dozens of trades were carried on in every town. There were 60 different kinds of tradesmen in Leicester in 1500, and 90 in York.

In the Middle Ages, each trade was organised in a **guild**. The shoemakers' guild said how shoes should be made. They fixed the prices. They made rules about what apprentices had to learn. Craftsmen who did not belong to the guild could not make and sell shoes. And the guild looked after its members – it paid them money when they were ill, and it paid pensions to widows when members died.

Between 1500 and 1750, most of the guilds disappeared. In 1700, fifty towns still had some guilds, but new, go-ahead places like Birmingham had none. Without guilds, tradesmen could make their goods in new ways and use different tools, or even machines.

Now try Exercise 20.3.

A carpenter at work in the Middle Ages

Exercise 20.3

Read **Section B**. Write down this list of tradesmen in a column on the left-hand side of your page:

Baker   Butcher   Hatter   Cooper
Tanner   Saddler   Goldsmith   Lorimer.

Opposite each tradesman, write down what he did, or made. Here are the right answers (but they are in the wrong order!):

made hats   made jewellery and ornaments   made bread
prepared leather   sold meat   made horses' bits
made barrels   made saddles and harness.

A royal charter (agreement) between Richard III and the wax chandlers guild in 1484

C Industry

A weaver

A sixteenth-century mine

The making of **woollen cloth** was the main industry in England in 1500. (English wool was the best in Europe.) Nearly everyone in England dressed in woollen clothes. England's most important export was cloth. It was sold for high prices in Flanders (modern Belgium).

By 1500 most cloth was no longer made in towns. Country people, working for low wages in their own homes, spun yarn and wove cloth. Rich **clothiers** from the towns sent them the raw wool, collected the woven cloth, and paid their wages.

Between 1550 and 1600 the weavers learned to make a new, lighter kind of cloth, called **worsted**. (They were taught by men from Flanders who settled in eastern England – see **Source 20d**.) The lighter cloth was popular in warm countries, such as Spain and Italy.

Another growing industry was **coal-mining**. In the Middle Ages, wood fires kept houses warm in the winter. But by the sixteenth century there was not enough wood for all the houses in London. Instead, they burned coal, most of which was brought by ship from north-east England.

Experts think that the mines of the north-east produced about 65,000 tons of coal in 1550. By 1690, this had grown to well over a million tons. Londoners wanted more coal, so the mines had to be bigger and deeper on Tyneside. (Most of the coal near the surface had been mined.) Deeper mines meant more danger for the miners – a greater risk of flooding, roof-falls and explosions. (See **Source 20c**.)

Now try Exercises 20.4 and 20.5.

Source 20c

A sad accident happened at a pit at Lumley Park (in Durham), not long before we passed through. As the miners were digging out the coal, they came to a hollow place, which may have been part of an old mine. As soon as they broke through into it, there was a great explosion. The force was so great that the earth trembled for miles around. Nearly sixty men lost their lives.

From a book written by Daniel Defoe in 1724.

Causes (or reasons) and Results

A **cause** is a **reason** for something. It is the answer to the question '**Why** did it happen?' or '**Why** was it like that?' e.g. **Why** did so many people move from the countryside to the towns?

Often, there is more than one answer to the question 'Why?' – There are a number of **causes** or **reasons** for most things. Causes come **before** events.

Results come **after** events. For example, one **result** of so many people moving to the towns was overcrowded housing in the towns.

Source 20d

The Flemish workers make kinds of cloth that were never made here before.
Our people copy the foreigners, and make cloth like theirs. The result is more jobs for young people.
The Flemish merchants give jobs to local men and women as well as their own people.
These foreigners live in houses that were empty before, and pay good rents.
The Flemish merchants do a great deal of buying and selling. The extra trade is good for our shopkeepers.
They pay their fair share of taxes and rates.
They work hard, obey the law, live in peace, and in all ways make our city a better place.

Written in Norwich in 1575, after Flemish workers had been there for about ten years.

Exercise 20.4

Read **Source 20d**.
What were the **results** of the Flemish merchants and cloth-workers coming to Norwich?
Write notes for an essay, using this plan:

a What were the results for the English cloth-workers in Norwich?
b What were the results for the landlords and shopkeepers in Norwich?
c What were the results for all the people of Norwich?

Exercise 20.5

Read **Section C** and the note on 'Causes (or reasons) and Results'.

Answer these questions by choosing sentences from the list marked 'Answers' and writing them down.

a What was the **reason** why English woollen cloth was so good?
b What were two **reasons** why English clothiers were so rich?
c For what **reason** were merchants able to sell English cloth in warmer countries after 1600?
d What was the **reason** why people in London wanted to buy coal?
e What was the **reason** why coal-mines became bigger and deeper?

Answers:
i The coal that lay near the surface had already been mined.
ii English workers learned to make a new, thinner kind of cloth.
iii They paid low wages to the workers and got high prices for the cloth.
iv There was not enough wood for everyone to burn.
v English wool was the best in Europe.

English merchants make a charter with the Flemish

21 Henry VIII

A King and Parliament

In 1509 England's new king was the eighteen-year-old Henry VIII. He was the ruler of Wales as well, and his family, the Tudors, were partly Welsh. But he was not king of Scotland. (Scotland had its own king.)

The king was the real ruler, too. He was the head of the Government. He chose his ministers and advisers, and if he did not like their advice he could ignore it. If they displeased him he could sack them. Unlucky or careless ministers sometimes lost their heads.

The king could declare war and make peace as he liked. Most kings were soldiers, and led their men into battle. But to pay for wars, the king needed taxes. And to charge taxes, or make new laws, the king needed the help of **Parliament**. (Look at the cartoon.)

There were (and still are) two **houses** of Parliament – the **House of Lords** and the **House of Commons**. All nobles (dukes, earls, and barons) and bishops sat in the House of Lords.

Source 21a

A portrait of Henry VIII, painted when he was 45 years old

The KING

The House of Lords

(Lords, landowners and all bishops)

The House of Commons

(Mainly gentry and some rich merchants)

When a bill (a plan for a new Law) is passed by both Houses (the Lords and the Commons) it is sent to the King. If the King gives the Royal Assent (he agrees with it) it will become an Act – a new Law.

The House of Commons contained some of the **gentry** (see Chapter 19), and some rich merchants from the towns.

Parliament did not sit all the time. There was a meeting when the king decided to have one. Usually, this was when he needed money, and wanted new taxes. Between 1509 and 1529, Parliament met only four times, each time for just a few weeks. (After 1529 it met much more often.)

Now try Exercises 21.1 and 21.2.

Exercise 21.1

Read **Section A**, and study the diagram on page 108.
Copy the diagram (with or without the cartoon drawings).
Then add notes answering these questions:

a Parliament had the power to do which two things?
b Who decided when there should be a meeting of Parliament?
c How often did Parliament meet?
d Who were the members of the House of Lords?
e Who were the members of the House of Commons?
f What is a bill?
g What is the 'Royal Assent'?
h What is an Act of Parliament?

Source 21b

I am accused of breaking the law made by Parliament. But I say that this law goes against God's law and the law of the Church. Therefore, I must not obey it. No-one can change God's law, and only the Pope can change the Church's law.

Words spoken in 1534 by Sir Thomas More, who had been Henry VIII's chief minister.

Thomas More

Source 21c

Parliament can abolish old laws and make new ones. It can change the Church. It can make new taxes. It can change men's rights. It can pardon some men, and it can condemn others. Whatever Parliament passes, all must obey.

Written by Sir Thomas Smith in 1565.

Exercise 21.2

Sometimes the sources do not agree with each other. Men and women in the past, just like people today, did not always have the same ideas. It helps us understand the events, and the people who made them, if we look at what they disagreed about.
Read **Sources 21b** and **21c**, then answer the questions.

a Who wrote **Source 21b**, and when did he write it?
b Who wrote **Source 21c**, and when did he write it?
c **Source 21b** says that there are two other kinds of law, apart from the laws made by Parliament. What are they?
d According to **Source 21b**, who is the only person who can change the Church's law?
e **Source 21c** says that Parliament can do what?
f Does the author of **Source 21c** agree or disagree with the author of **Source 21b**? (Write two or three sentences explaining your answer.)

B A son and heir

Henry VIII was clever, handsome, strong, and good at all sports. But he was also selfish, and he could be cruel. He showed his cruelty, above all, in the way he treated his wives.

Like most men in his days, Henry VIII thought that ruling England was a man's job. So he wanted a son to take over when he died. By 1527, though, his only child was a daughter (Mary). (Look at the cartoon opposite.) He, therefore, decided to divorce Catherine, his first wife, and marry again. He hoped that a new wife would give him a son.

As England was still a **Catholic** country, Henry needed the **Pope's** permission for a divorce. The Pope said 'No'. Henry then said that he, not the Pope, was head of the Church in England. He got **Thomas Cranmer**, the Archbishop of Canterbury, to say that he was free to marry again.

Henry did marry again, but his second queen, **Anne Boleyn**, also gave birth to a daughter. A third marriage, to **Jane Seymour**, led at last to the birth of a son, but Queen Jane died in childbirth. Three more wives followed, but no more children.

Now try Exercise 21.3.

Catherine of Aragon was a Spanish princess. She married Henry VIII in 1509. They had six children, but only one of them survived – a daughter called Mary. Mary was born in 1516. Henry divorced Catherine of Aragon in 1533.

Henry VIII married **Anne Boleyn** in 1533. She gave birth to a daughter (Elizabeth) later in the same year. Anne had a son also, but he died at birth. Henry accused Anne of being unfaithful, and had her beheaded in 1536.

Jane Seymour married Henry in 1536. A son (Edward) was born in the next year. Jane died a few days after her son was born.

Henry married **Anne of Cleves**, a German princess, in 1540. Thomas Cromwell, Henry's chief minister, arranged the marriage. Henry had not seen Anne until she arrived in England. When he did see her, he thought she was too plain, and divorced her straight away. Cromwell got the blame, and lost his head.

Catherine Howard was a girl of 19 when Henry married her in 1540. By then he was middle-aged, fat and ugly (see **Source 21a**). Catherine was unfaithful, and Henry had her beheaded in 1542.

Catherine Parr was a widow of 31 when she married Henry in 1543. She looked after him and his younger children in the last years of his life. Henry died in 1547, and Catherine died in 1548.

Exercise 21.3

Read **Section B** and study the cartoon above.

Write out these events in the right order (earliest first).
Put the correct date next to each event.

Henry married Anne of Cleves.
Henry's daughter Elizabeth was born.
Henry VIII died.
Prince Edward was born.
Henry married Catherine of Aragon.

Catherine Parr died.
Anne Boleyn was executed.
Henry's daughter Mary was born.
Catherine Howard was executed.

C The English Reformation

A lot of men and women thought there were things wrong in the Catholic Church. Some of them became **Protestants**, or reformers. Protestants were against the Pope. They were against rich bishops living in grand palaces. They thought that priests should pray in their own language, not Latin. They said that priests should be allowed to marry.

The Protestants were pleased when Henry VIII got Parliament to pass laws ending the power of the Pope. The laws said that the king was the head of the Church in England. Bishops had to swear to be loyal to him, not to the Pope. These changes were the start of the English **Reformation**.

Henry VIII was not a Protestant. (He did not want to change the Church service, and he did not want priests to marry.) But he allowed Thomas Cranmer to translate some prayers into English. And he agreed that there should be a copy of the Bible in English in every church.

The idea of closing the monasteries came from Thomas Cromwell, Henry's chief minister. His reason was that the monasteries had masses of silver and jewels, and great estates of land. If the king closed them down, he could take all that they owned. Like all kings, Henry was always short of money.

By 1539 the monasteries and nunneries were closed. The monks and nuns had to leave. The buildings either became parish churches or private houses, or they were left to fall down. The king sold most of the land, silver, and jewels. Then he wasted the money on a useless war.

Now try Exercises 21.4 and 21.5.

Thomas Cromwell

A cartoon from a Protestant book published in 1563. It shows Henry VIII trampling on the Pope.

Exercise 21.4

Read **Section C**. Copy the sentences below and use the answers to complete them.

a Protestants did not think that _____

b Parliament passed an act that said that _____

c Henry VIII did not think that _____

d Thomas Cranmer was the _____

e Henry VIII said that every church _____

f Thomas Cromwell suggested that _____

g Henry agreed with Cromwell's idea _____

Answers:
- priests should be allowed to marry.
- should contain a Bible in English.
- because he wanted the monasteries' land and wealth for himself.
- Archbishop of Canterbury.
- the king was head of the Church of England.
- Henry should close down the monasteries.
- the Pope should be head of the Church.

Source 21d

The king is the most handsome prince I ever saw. He is above average height. His complexion is fair and bright. He has short auburn hair, combed straight. He has a round face, so beautiful that it would suit a pretty woman. He speaks French and Latin, and some Italian. He plays the lute and harpsichord well. He draws the bow with greater strength than any man in England, and is marvellous at jousting.

Written by an Italian visitor to England in 1515.

Source 21e

A portrait of Henry VIII painted when he was 29 years old

Fact and Opinion

A **fact** is something which is, or was, true. It is a fact that Anne Boleyn was beheaded.
An **opinion** is what someone thinks, or thought. Henry VIII's opinion was that Anne of Cleves was very plain.

Exercise 21.5

Read **Source 21d** and look at **Source 21e**. Read the note 'Fact and Opinion'.

a Write down two **facts** about Henry's appearance that are mentioned in **Source 21d**.

b What was the Italian visitor's **opinion** of the king's appearance?

c Was the king good at languages? Write down a **fact**.

d Was the king good at music? Write down the Italian visitor's **opinion**.

e Write down a **fact** which shows that Henry was strong.

f Look at **Source 21e**. Do you agree with the Italian visitor's description of Henry VIII? Do you agree with his opinion? (Write a paragraph.)

22 Queen Elizabeth I

A Henry VIII's children

When Henry VIII died in 1547, his only son became **King Edward VI**. But Edward was too young to rule. So England was governed by **Protectors** – first Edward's uncle, the Duke of Somerset, then the Duke of Northumberland.

Both dukes were Protestants, and keen on Church reform. They said that priests could marry. They made people use a new English prayer book. And they got rid of some of the statues and pictures from the churches.

Edward was always a sickly boy, and he died at the age of fifteen. His half-sister **Mary Tudor** then became queen. Mary was a keen Catholic. She brought back the Catholic mass, and said the Pope was in charge of the Church in England again. Many Pro-testants fled abroad. About 300 who stayed were burned to death by Mary. One of them was Thomas Cranmer.

Burning the Protestants was unpopular. Mary's marriage to King Philip II of Spain was worse. Philip and his Spanish courtiers, who looked down on the English, were hated.

Mary died in 1558, and Henry VIII's other daughter, **Elizabeth**, came to the throne. She was twenty-five years old, unmarried, and alone. Most men (and women) said that she needed a husband to guide her. But who would the husband be? No-one wanted Philip of Spain, or any foreign king. And if the queen married an English lord, all the others would be jealous. Elizabeth's answer was not to marry at all.

Now try Exercise 22.1

Below right: Edward VI and his Protectors continue Protestant reform

Below left: The Catholic Mary Tudor as a young woman

KING HENRY VIII AND HIS CHILDREN

HENRY VIII King 1509-1547

1st marriage to **Catherine of Aragon**

2nd marriage to **Anne Boleyn**

3rd marriage to **Jane Seymour**

MARY
born 1516
died 1558
Queen 1553-1558

married Philip II of Spain (no children)

ELIZABETH
born 1533
died 1603
Queen 1558-1603

EDWARD
born 1537
died 1553
King 1547-1553

Exercise 22.1

Read **Section A** and study the family tree, then answer the questions.

a For how long was Henry VIII king?
b How old was Mary Tudor when she became queen?
c For how long was Elizabeth queen?
d How old was Elizabeth when her father died?
e For how long was Edward VI king?

Draw a time-line from 1509 to 1603, showing England's kings and queens.

B Catholics and Puritans

The first of Elizabeth's problems was religion. The Protestants who had fled from Mary streamed back, hoping for support from the new queen. By and large, they were satisfied. Elizabeth said that she, not the Pope, was head of the Church of England. The service would be read from an English prayer book, not sung in Latin. Priests were to be free to marry.

Some English people stayed Catholic, and worshipped in secret. Priests moved by night from house to house, hiding in lofts or in holes between walls. A few Catholics plotted to kill Elizabeth and put her cousin, **Mary Queen of Scots**, on the throne. (See Chapter 23.) They got support from the Pope, who said that Elizabeth had no right to be queen. Priests and plotters who were caught were killed.

Europe's leading Catholic king was Philip of Spain. When Elizabeth had Mary Queen of Scots put to death in 1587, he went to war. He tried, with his **Armada**, to invade England in 1588, but failed. England and Spain were at war for the next sixteen years.

Puritans were also against the Church of England. They said it was just like the Catholic Church, with priests dressed in special robes. They did not like having the service read from a prayer book. Puritans wanted plain churches and services in plain English. They thought the minister should preach a sermon, not read prayers from a book. Elizabeth disliked the Puritans. In the last years of her reign, many of them were thrown into prison, and some were put to death.

Now try Exercises 22.2 and 22.3.

Exercise 22.2

Read **Section B**, then copy the chart and fill in the blank spaces.

	Catholic Church	Church of England	Puritans
Who was head of the Church?			Queen
Did they use a prayer book?	Yes		
The Church service was in which language?			
Could priests (or ministers) marry?			Yes
Did the priests wear special robes?	Yes		

An English galleon from the time of the Spanish Armada

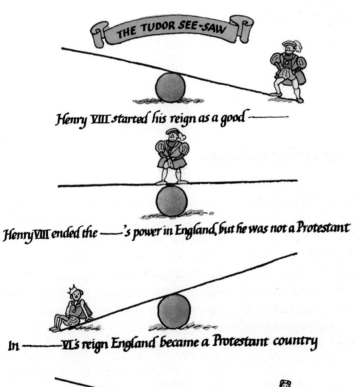

THE TUDOR SEE-SAW

Henry VIII started his reign as a good ————

Henry VIII ended the ————'s power in England, but he was not a Protestant

In ————— VI's reign England became a Protestant country

————— Tudor was a keen Catholic

Elizabeth made England ————— again

Exercise 22.3

Copy the five drawings of the Tudors on the see-saw. (Draw pin-men and pin-women if you wish.) Copy the captions, and fill in the blank spaces, using words from this list:

Edward   Protestant   Mary
Pope   Catholic

C A woman fit to rule

Henry VIII thought that a woman would not be able to rule England. Elizabeth proved him wrong. There was no doubt that she was in charge of the Government. She chose her ministers, and they obeyed her orders. She listened to her council of advisers, then made up her own mind.

The **court** was where the queen was at any time. It might be in one of her palaces, or it might be in the house of a great lord, when the queen was on tour. She, and all around her, put on a great show. They dressed in fine clothes and jewels, and took part in grand pageants and banquets. All this display was meant to let men know that the ruler of England was a rich and mighty queen, so they should treat her with respect.

Parliament met every three or four years, mainly when the queen needed taxes. And when it met, the Commons were always anxious for the queen's safety. They asked her to marry. They urged her to make stricter laws against the Catholics. They begged her to get rid of Mary Queen of Scots.

Elizabeth had more than one quarrel with the Puritan gentry in the Commons. The Puritans dared to attack the Church of England. She told them that the Church was her affair, not theirs. They replied that the Commons had a right to free speech – they could talk about the Church if they wished. But in the end, the Puritans gave in. Like other Englishmen, they were devoted to their queen.

Now try Exercise 22.4 and 22.5.

Source 22a

We are supposed to have freedom to say what we wish in this House. We need that freedom so that we can advise and warn the queen. But sometimes she does not like what we say. Once she sent us a message saying that we must not talk about religion. Later, she refused to agree to the laws we passed. This pleased the Catholics and traitors, and made them laugh at us.

From a speech made by Peter Wentworth in the House of Commons in 1576.

Source 22b

The queen told me to remind you that she is head of the Church of England. She has the power to put right anything that is wrong in the Church. And she will correct its faults, if it has any. She has told you not to meddle with matters of religion, but you have not obeyed her. She is sorry to have to say these things, for she knows that you are her loyal subjects. But she must warn you not to discuss religion again.

Report by the Speaker to the House of Commons in 1585. He had just had a meeting with the queen.

Source 22c

(The House of Commons) wanted to give the queen advice on the problem of whether she should marry or not, on who should take the throne when she died, and on what to do with Mary Queen of Scots. Most of all, they wanted the 'freedom of speech' to discuss these matters openly.

From a book written by Haydn Middleton in 1987.

Source **22d**

A drawing of Queen Elizabeth I made by Frederico Zuccaro in 1575, when the Queen was 42 years old

Source **22e**

A portrait of Queen Elizabeth I, painted in 1590, when she was 57 years old. Artist unknown.

Primary and Secondary Sources

Letters, diaries, and books written by people who were present, and saw the things they wrote about, are called **primary sources**.

Papers and books written by people who were **not** present are called **secondary sources**. The authors of **secondary sources** must have heard about the events from someone else, or read about them in books. Books that were written hundreds of years after the events they describe, therefore, are **secondary sources**.

Exercise 22.4

Read **Section C** and **Sources 22a**, **22b**, and **22c**. Then read the note on 'Primary and Secondary Sources'.
Write out the sentences, filling in the missing words.

a **Source 22a** is part of a speech made by _____ _____ in 1576.

b The speech in **Source 22a** was made in the _____ of _____ during Queen Elizabeth I's reign.

c **Source 22a** is a _____ source.

d The words in **Source 22b** were spoken by the _____ to the House of Commons in 1585.

e The Speaker (**Source 22b**) had just had a meeting with the _____

f **Source 22b** is a _____ source.

g **Source 22c** was written by _____ _____ in _____

h **Source 22c** was written _____ years after Queen Elizabeth I died. (She died in 1603.)

i **Source 22c** is a _____ source.

Exercise 22.5

Look at **Sources 22d** and **22e**. Discuss the questions in a group, then either write out your answers in paragraphs, or make a tape giving the group's answers.

a Who were the artists, and when did they make their pictures?

b In what ways are the two pictures **i** similar, **ii** different?

c Can you think of any reasons for differences between the pictures?

d Did the artists actually see Queen Elizabeth I?

e Should we believe what the pictures tell us about the queen's appearance?

23 Scotland in the Sixteenth Century

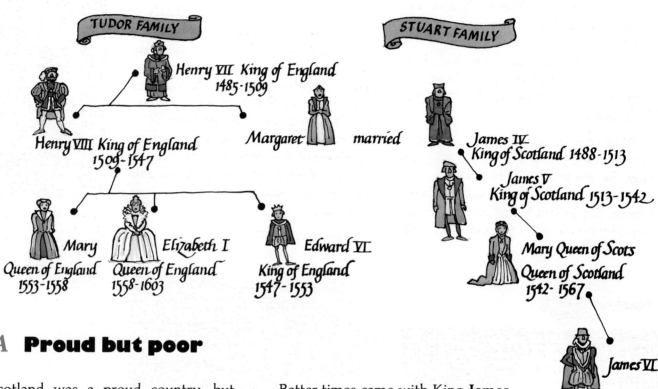

TUDOR FAMILY

Henry VII King of England 1485-1509

Henry VIII King of England 1509-1547

Margaret married

Mary Queen of England 1553-1558

Elizabeth I Queen of England 1558-1603

Edward VI King of England 1547-1553

STUART FAMILY

James IV King of Scotland 1488-1513

James V King of Scotland 1513-1542

Mary Queen of Scots Queen of Scotland 1542-1567

James VI

King of Scotland 1567-1625 (King James I of England 1603-1625)

A Proud but poor

Scotland was a proud country, but poor. Its soldiers had fought for, and won, their freedom from England. Scotland had its own king, laws, and army. But the people were mainly peasants. Their food was porridge and oatcakes – from the barley and oats that they grew. They sold the hides of their cattle and the wool from their sheep to pay the rent. Their homes were rough shacks, with earth or stone walls and turf roofs.

Scotland's kings spent a lot of their time at war, either with the English or with their own subjects. The wildest of these were the clan chiefs of the **Highlands** in the north. They stole each other's cattle, fought local wars, and cared nothing for the king. But the earls and lords of the **Lowlands** were not much better, with their plots and civil wars.

Better times came with King **James IV**. James was only fifteen when he became king in 1488. He was a bright young man, quick to learn, full of energy, and well liked. Within a year, he beat the rebel lords in battle, and brought order to the Lowlands. Trade increased, and the towns began to grow. Peace with England was settled when James married an English princess (Henry VIII's sister Margaret).

Then in 1513 James IV foolishly joined the side of France (Scotland's old ally) in a war with England. The Scots were crushed at the Battle of **Flodden**, where James and thousands of his men were killed. His son, King James V, was less than two years old. Scotland sank back into quarrels and civil war between groups of lords, all wanting power for themselves.

B Queen of Scotland and France

In December 1542, James V died, aged 30. The crown of Scotland passed to his daughter, Mary, less than a week old. (We call her **Mary Queen of Scots**.) While Mary was a child, her mother, who was French, governed in her place. When Mary was five, her mother sent her to France, to learn to speak French and behave like a lady of the French court.

At the age of fifteen, Mary married a French prince called **Francis**. A year later, he became king of France – so Mary was now queen of Scotland and France. But in less than two years, she was a widow. And in August 1561, still not nineteen years old, Mary sailed home to Scotland. It was a cold, foreign land that she hardly knew.

When Mary left for France, Scotland was a Catholic country. When she returned, it was Protestant. A preacher called John Knox was now the leading man in Edinburgh. He stirred up the mobs to break the statues in Catholic churches, and burn the pictures. The Scots Parliament passed acts ending the power of the Pope, and banning the Catholic mass. Mary was a Catholic all her life, but could do nothing to save her Church.

Now try Exercise 23.1.

George Wishart, one of Scotland's first Protestants, who was burned to death in 1546. He became a Protestant martyr.

Source 23a

Mary Queen of Scots, aged 16 – A painting made by François Clouet, who lived from about 1520 to 1572. He worked at the French court in the 1550s.

John Knox

Exercise 23.1

Read **Section B**. Draw a time-chart of the early life of Mary Queen of Scots (from 1542 to 1562). Mark the following on the chart:

a Mary was born and became queen of Scotland.
b Mary was sent to France.
c Mary married her first husband.
d Mary's first husband became king of France.
e Mary's first husband died.
f Mary returned to Scotland.

Shade in two different colours the time Mary spent in Scotland, and the time she spent in France.

C Mary's adventures

In July 1565, Mary married **Lord Darnley**, her handsome but foolish cousin. Mary soon found out that he could be jealous and cruel. Darnley hated **David Rizzio**, Mary's secretary, and one night in March 1566, he killed him. Darnley led a gang of thugs into the room where Mary, her ladies-in-waiting, and Rizzio were sitting. The thugs dragged Rizzio out, and stabbed him to death, just outside the door. Mary never forgave Darnley.

A year later, Darnley himself was murdered. The house where he was staying in Edinburgh was blown up in the middle of the night. His body was found outside – he had been strangled. It was said that the **Earl of Bothwell** had killed Darnley. Some people thought that Mary was involved.

Three months after the murder, Mary married the chief suspect, the Earl of Bothwell. This made the Scots think that she was guilty. They rose in revolt, seized her, and put her in prison. But she soon escaped. She fled to England, and begged her cousin **Queen Elizabeth** to protect her.

If Elizabeth had sent Mary back to Scotland, the Scots would have killed her. Instead, she kept her in prison for nineteen years. During that time, some English Catholics plotted to murder Elizabeth, and put Mary on the throne. In the end, Mary was charged with taking part in one of the plots. She was found guilty, and beheaded.

When the Scots rebelled against Mary, they made her year-old son king as **James VI**. The new king was brought up by strict Protestants, who had no time for fun. Meanwhile, the lords and clan chiefs ignored the law and fought their private wars.

Now try Exercises 23.2, 23.3, and 23.4.

The murder of David Rizzio. This picture was painted by Sir William Allan in 1833.

Source 23b

Mary Queen of Scots, aged about 35, when she was a prisoner in England. This miniature (small portrait) was painted by Nicholas Hilliard, who lived from 1547 to 1619. It was probably painted from life.

Exercise 23.2

Read **Section C**, and study **Sources 23a** and **23b**.
Answer questions **a** to **f** in sentences, and question **g** in a paragraph.

a Who painted **Source 23a**, and when did he live?
b When was **Source 23a** painted? Where was Mary when it was painted?
c Could the artist have painted **Source 23a** from life? Is it a primary or a secondary source?
d Who painted **Source 23b**, and when did he live?
e When was **Source 23b** painted? Where was Mary when it was painted?
f Did the artist paint **Source 23b** from life? Is it a primary or a secondary source?
g What differences between the two portraits can you see? Can you think of any reasons for the differences?

Source 23c

I know for certain that the Queen regrets her marriage. She hates the King (Darnley) and all his family. David Rizzio, with the consent of the King, will get his throat cut within the next ten days.

From a letter written by the English ambassador in Scotland, three weeks before Rizzio's murder.

Source 23d

No more tears now. I will think about revenge.

Words spoken by Mary Queen of Scots soon after the murder of Rizzio.

Source 23e

It breaks her heart to think that he (Darnley) is her husband. She cannot think how to be rid of him.

From a letter written by William Maitland, one of Mary's ministers.

Source 23f

The King's (Darnley's) death is planned. If I do not kill him, I cannot live in Scotland. He will destroy me.

John Hay's account of what the Earl of Bothwell said to him in 1566.

Source 23g

You and I are the most faithful couple that were ever united. Cursed be this fellow (Darnley) that troubles me so much.

From a letter which Mary was supposed to have written in 1567 to the Earl of Bothwell. Some historians think that it is a forgery.

Evidence

The student of history is like a judge in court. He looks carefully at the pieces of evidence (or sources) left by the people of the past. He asks questions about each source, including: Who wrote or said it and when? Can I believe what this source says? What does it prove?

Exercise 23.3

Read **Section C** again, and read **Sources 23c, 23d, 23e, 23f,** and **23g.** Now it is your turn to be the judge in 'The case of the Darnley murder'. There are five pairs of sentences below. From each pair, choose the one you think is true, and write it out.

a i **Source 23c** proves that Mary was happy before the murder of Rizzio.
   ii **Source 23c** proves that Mary hated Darnley before Rizzio's murder.
b i **Sources 23d** and **23e** prove that Mary planned to kill Darnley.
   ii **Sources 23d** and **23e** prove that Mary wanted to be rid of Darnley. She was probably thinking of divorce.
c i **Source 23f** proves that Bothwell planned to kill Darnley.
   ii **Source 23f** proves that Bothwell knew about the plan to kill Darnley.
d i **Source 23g** proves that Mary knew about the plot to kill Darnley.
   ii **Source 23g** may be a forgery, so it proves nothing.
e i By marrying Bothwell, Mary proved that she had been involved in the murder plot.
   ii Her marriage to Bothwell only proves that Mary was foolish.

The execution of Mary Queen of Scots

Exercise 23.4

Elizabeth was very unhappy about sending Mary to her death. There were reasons for and against it. Here are some of them:

Reasons for having Mary executed:
a Mary was guilty of taking part in plots to kill Elizabeth.
b The Catholics would stop plotting against Elizabeth if Mary was dead.
c Most of Elizabeth's Council and Parliament wanted Mary killed.

Reasons against having Mary executed:
a Mary was Elizabeth's cousin.
b Mary was a queen, and killing a king or queen is a terrible crime.
c Killing Mary might make the Catholics hate Elizabeth even more.
d The kings of France and Spain might go to war to punish Elizabeth.

What would **you** have done if you had been in Elizabeth's position? Discuss what you think with others in a group. One member of the group could tell the class what you think, or you could make a group tape.

24 Ireland in the Sixteenth Century

A Irish and English

England's kings said that Ireland belonged to them. But Ireland's real rulers were its earls and lords. They owned the land, and kept some kind of order among the peasants. Each lord had his castle and his own army. The English ruled only **the Pale**, a small district around Dublin. (Look at the map.)

The lords and peasants were Irish, not English. They had their own language and laws, their own poetry and music. The English, to them, were foreigners. The lords were **vassals** (subjects) of the English king, but that did not mean much to them.

Some English kings tried to take control of Ireland. **Henry VII** knew that rebels might land there, and use Ireland as a base to attack England. So he got **Sir Edward Poynings**, his governor of Ireland, to put Englishmen in charge of all the main castles. And Poynings said that the Irish Parliament could debate no bill that the king of England had not approved.

But to control Ireland, the English had to keep an army there. And that cost money, which few kings could afford. **Henry VIII**, in the first part of his reign, used the old, cheaper ways. He made the Irish lords swear to be loyal, then left them alone. The Irish paid some taxes to Henry, but he did not try to make them obey English laws.

Now try Exercise 24.1.

Exercise 24.1

Read **Section A**, and study the map. Write down the answers to the questions. Choose your answers from the list below.

Waterford Connaught the king of England's judges Munster Limerick the Pale foreigners Drogheda Leinster the governor of Ireland's soldiers Ulster Dublin vassals

a Which was the only part of Ireland that the English really ruled?
b Irish lords and peasants thought of the English as what?
c Poynings said that the Irish Parliament needed whose permission before it debated a bill?
d The English could control Ireland only if they kept what there?
e The north of Ireland is in which province?
f Which two towns were inside the Pale?
g Which town is at the mouth of the River Shannon?
h The south-west of Ireland is in which province?

B King of Ireland

Peace in Ireland never lasted long. In 1534 the Earl of Kildare, the leading Irish lord, was in London as a guest of Henry VIII. Soon a rumour spread in Ireland that Kildare had been killed. The Irish rose in revolt. They were led by **'Silken Thomas'** Fitzgerald, Kildare's son. Henry sent troops, crushed the revolt, and had Silken Thomas put to death.

Henry thought that Ireland needed a firm hand. He made the Irish Parliament pass an act saying that he was **King of Ireland**. (Before then, English kings had been 'Lords of Ireland'.) Another act said that all the land in Ireland belonged to him. The Irish earls and lords had to give him their land. Then he gave it back **on condition that they obeyed him**.

Henry also said that he was head of the Church in Ireland, as he was in England (see Chapter 21). And he closed down the monasteries in the Pale. When he did these things in England, the Protestants were pleased. But there were hardly any Protestants in Ireland – the lords and peasants remained Catholic. To them, the Pope was still the head of the Church.

From this point on, there were **two** main reasons why the Irish did not like the English. The first was the same as before – the English were foreigners. (They did not understand Irish law or history, or the Irish language.) The second was new – the English were Protestants, and the Irish were Catholics.

Now try Exercise 24.2.

Source 24a

Mellifont Abbey, one of the Irish monasteries closed down by Henry VIII

Source 24b

This shows both sides of an Irish coin issued by Henry VIII. One side (left) shows Henry's name and coat of arms. The other side (right) has the Irish harp stamped in the centre, with the letters 'H.R.' on either side. This stands for 'Henricus Rex' – i.e. King Henry of Ireland.

Source 24c

Irish brigands burning villagers' homes and stealing their cattle. (From a book printed in 1581.)

Source 24d

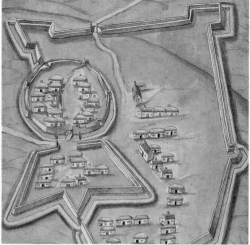

Mount Norris in Armagh – one of the forts the English built to help keep law and order in Ireland

Exercise 24.2

Read **Section B**, and look at **Sources 24a, 24b, 24c,** and **24d**.
On the left side of the page below, you will see the **first halves** of seven sentences about Ireland. On the right side are the **second halves**, but in a different order. Put the correct halves together, and write out the complete sentences.

First half
a **Source 24a** shows an Irish monastery that was . . .
b One one side (above) of the coin in **Source 24b** . . .
c The other side (below) of the coin in **Source 24b** proves that . . .
d **Source 24c** shows that Irish brigands . . .
e **Source 24c** shows that Irish villagers were . . .
f **Source 24c** shows why . . .
g The fort in **Source 24d** had . . .

Second half
• the fort in **Source 24d** was needed.
• Henry VIII claimed to be King of Ireland.
• a ditch and a stockade, but not high stone walls.
• closed down by Henry VIII.
• Henry VIII's name and coat of arms can be seen.
• came out of the woods to destroy and steal.
• not able to defend themselves against the brigands.

An Irish chief surrenders to the English governor in the time of Queen Elizabeth

C Elizabeth and Ireland

Soon after Henry VIII's death, the Irish found a **third** reason to hate the English. Queen Mary Tudor began the **plantations**. English troops pressed west from the Pale, drove out the Irish lords and peasants, and gave their land to English settlers – English farmers were 'planted' on Irish land.

Queen Elizabeth I tried more plantations, further to the west and north. But plantations led to revolt – angry Irishmen attacked the settlers. Lords (such as the **Earl of Desmond** in Munster) and their peasants were ready to fight for their laws, their Church, and their land. English troops crushed the revolts. They killed the rebels, and burned their crops and homes.

The most serious Irish revolt began in Ulster in the 1590s. It was led by **Hugh O'Neill**, Earl of Tyrone. He called on all Irishmen to fight for the Catholic Church and an Ireland free from English rule. The lords and peasants of Ulster and Munster answered his call. His armies won battles, and the English seemed to be on the run.

In the end, though, the English were too strong. O'Neill got some help from abroad – a Spanish army landed in Ireland in 1601, but it was soon rounded up by the English. In 1603, O'Neill gave up the fight. Four years later, he left Ireland for good. By then, there were English governors and forts in all parts of Ireland – the conquest seemed complete.

Now try Exercises 24.3, 24.4, and 24.5.

A Dutch sixteenth-century drawing, showing an Irish peasant and a lady from the Pale

---

Exercise 24.3

Read **Sections B** and **C**.
What were the **causes** of the Irish revolts against the English? Copy the sentences and write TRUE or FALSE after each one.

a The Irish thought that the English were foreigners.

_____

b Irish law and English law were the same. _____

c The English did not understand the Irish language.

_____

d The Irish peasants soon became Protestants. _____

e 'Plantations' means growing trees in Ireland. _____

f Irish lords and peasants were angry about losing their land. _____

g Hugh O'Neill asked all Catholic Irishmen to join his revolt. _____

h The three main causes of the revolts were that the Irish did not want to be ruled by Englishmen, they wanted to remain Catholic, and they did not want to lose their land.

_____

Source **24e**

The conquest was a good thing for Ireland. It gave her law and order. It ended the wars between the Irish tribes, the raids, and the killing. England's victory let the Irish grow into a nation.

Adapted from a book written by G. R. Elton in 1955.

Source **24f**

At the end of the revolt, Ireland was in a dreadful state. The English had won, but the Irish were reduced to hunger and misery. Wolves roamed the countryside. Children crawled on all fours, eating grass. Some men and women were so hungry that they became cannibals.

Adapted from a book written by Sir Keith Feiling in 1927.

Source **24g**

The Irish live like beasts in the mountains. Their homes are huts made of straw. The men are tall and broad, and can run like deer. They eat only once a day, at night. What they eat is usually butter with oatmeal bread. They drink sour milk, not water. There is no justice or law and order in the land – everyone does as he likes.

Written by a Spanish noble who was shipwrecked on the Irish coast in 1588.

Exercise 24.4

Read **Sources 24e** and **24f**.
Discuss these questions in a group, then write four paragraphs – one answering each of the questions.

a Which source says that conquest by the English was a good thing for Ireland? In what ways was it good?
b Which source says that conquest by the English was a bad thing for Ireland? In what ways was it bad?
c Which author was thinking of the short-term results of the conquest (i.e. what Ireland was like just after the English conquest)? Which author was thinking of the long-term results of the conquest (i.e. what happened in Ireland in the next hundred or two hundred years)?
d Is it possible that both authors were right?

Source **24h**

The Irish peasants live in fear of attacks by robbers and rebels. So they make no attempt to grow crops. They roam about with their cows like nomads. They have no fixed homes, but sleep in the open, or in clay huts, or wooden cabins covered with turf. They light a fire in the middle of the hut, and sleep on the ground, with no bedding under them.

Written by Fynes Moryson, who was in Ireland in 1600.

Exercise 24.5

Read **Sources 24g** and **24h**.
Which of these things do **Sources 24g** and **24h** tell us about?

a The homes the Irish lived in.
b The language the Irish spoke.
c The clothes the Irish wore.
d The food the Irish ate.
e Irish schools.
f Law and order in Ireland.

Choose three topics from the list, and write brief notes (which you could later use as an essay plan) about each of them.

Henry VII, the first of England's Tudor Kings, had a Welsh grandfather. Henry was born at Pembroke Castle.

A The Acts of Union

The Norman **marcher lords** conquered east and south Wales after 1066. **King Edward I** conquered the rest of Wales between 1272 and 1300. But English rule did not bring peace and justice to Wales. Great lords, with their bands of armed men, bullied the peasants and stole their cattle. The courts were no help, for the lords and their men controlled them too.

In 1493, **King Henry VII** set up a **Council for Wales** to try to bring law and order where there was none. The Council did some good work, but only made a start. Then, in 1534, **Henry VIII** chose **Rowland Lee** to be the Council's head. He gave Lee the job of stamping out crime. And for the next nine years, Lee toured eastern Wales, torturing, hanging, and flogging. His victims were more often rich than poor, but he was hated by all.

Henry VIII's main plan for Wales, though, was **Union with England**. Two acts, passed by Parliament in 1536 and 1543, said that Wales and England were one. English law, they said, applied to Wales, so Welshmen had the same rights as Englishmen (which they had not had before). And Welsh members would sit in Parliament in London.

The Union was good for the poor of Wales. The courts became fair, the armed bands were crushed, and peace was restored. The Welsh gentry took the chance to move up in the world. The acts said that Welshmen could be magistrates (J.P.s), so long as they spoke English. So the gentry sent their sons to English schools, and became English in their ways.

Now try Exercises 25.1 and 25.2.

Exercise 25.1

Read **Section A** and the sentences below.
Ask the questions 'Who did it?' and 'When was it done?' about each of the sentences. Write your answers in a chart or table.

a They conquered south Wales.
b He conquered the rest of Wales.
c He set up a Council of Wales.
d He stamped out crime in eastern Wales.
e He got Parliament to pass the Acts of Union.
f They took the chance to become J.P.s.

A miniature portrait of Henry VIII from one of the first legal documents produced in the Welsh county of Brecon after the first Act of Union

Aims

Students of history try to find out the **aims** of the people in the past. This means asking, 'What were they **trying** to do?' or 'What were their **reasons** for acting as they did?'

For example, 'What were Henry VIII's aims when he got Parliament to pass the Acts of Union with Wales?'

Sometimes the people in the past have told us what their aims were. More often, we have to guess at their aims by looking at what they did. Not all authors agree about people's aims – see **Sources 25a** and **25b**.

Source 25a

The Acts of Union put Wales completely under English rule. Their aim was to crush the Welsh language and nation. Only those who knew English could take part in the government of Wales. (And only one Welshman in twenty could speak English.) The Welsh could enjoy the same rights as the English, but only if they stopped being Welsh.

Adapted from a book written by Gwynfor Evans in 1974.

Source 25b

Welshmen at the time did not object to the Acts of Union. For them, the really important thing was that Englishmen and Welshmen were now equal in law. Also, Welshmen no longer needed special permits to live in towns. The Acts did not try to crush the Welsh language. Their aim was to unite England and Wales. No-one was punished for speaking Welsh. Judges did not object when Welsh was used in their courts.

Adapted from a book written by W. Vaughan-Thomas in 1985.

Exercise 25.2

Read **Sources 25a** and **25b**, and the note on 'Aims'. Then answer the questions in sentences.

a Write down any facts that you can find in **Source 25a**.
b What was the aim of the Acts of Union, according to **Source 25a**?
c What does the author of **Source 25a** think about the Acts of Union?
d Write down any facts that you can find in **Source 25b**.
e What was the aim of the Acts of Union, according to **Source 25b**?
f What does the author of **Source 25b** think about the Acts of Union?

Source 25c

Tintern Abbey in Monmouth

B From Reformation to Methodism

The Welsh did not complain when Henry VIII took the Pope's place as head of the Church in 1534. They did not object when he closed the monasteries. But they were not pleased when pilgrimages to saint's shrines were banned. For the Welsh were proud of their ancient saints.

The main event of the Reformation in Wales, though, was the translation of the Bible into Welsh. (Look at **Source 25e**.) Most of the people of Wales spoke only Welsh, and understood neither Latin nor English. Now they could understand when the Bible was read to them in church. (Very few could read it for themselves.) The translation gave a boost to the Church, and a boost to Welsh.

Source 25d

Ewenny Priory in Glamorgan

Henry VIII closed down the monasteries in Wales, as well as in England.
Tintern Abbey (**Source 25c**) fell into ruins. Ewenny Priory (**Source 25d**) became a country house.

Source 25e

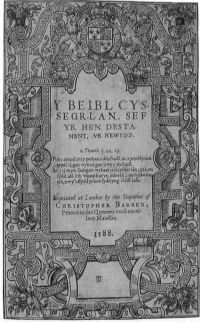

The title page of the first Bible in Welsh, published in 1588

By the time of Queen Anne (1702–1714), though, the Church in Wales had become poor and backward. All the bishops were English, and some of them did not even visit Wales. The priests were badly paid, and ignorant – many of them knew no Welsh. Even the buildings were falling down.

Methodist preachers like **Howell Harris** tried to put life back into the Church. In the 1730s and 1740s, they travelled through Wales, preaching outdoors, in Welsh, often two or three times a day. Excited crowds listened, and sang, shouted, and clapped. The English called them 'Welsh Jumpers', and said that they were mad. But the movement grew into a Church that gripped the whole of Wales.

Now try Exercise 25.3.

'Welsh Jumpers' – early Methodists

Exercise 25.3

Read **Section B** and look at **Sources 25c, 25d,** and **25e.**
Write notes (in your own words), describing:

a **Three** important things that happened to the Church in Wales in the **sixteenth century.**
b The state of the Church in Wales in the **eighteenth century,** and how some people tried to improve it.

C Farmers and miners

Until long after 1750, Wales was a country of farmers. Some of them grew crops, such as wheat and barley, for bread and beer. Most of them grew leeks, cabbages, peas and beans for themselves and their families. But to all Welsh farmers, their animals mattered most.

Peace and order followed the Acts of Union. This was good for Welsh farmers, for the cattle-thieves had been stamped out. **Drovers** could now walk herds of cattle slowly along the tracks and roads from north Wales to London. As London grew, so the demand for Welsh beef grew too. By 1750 as many as 30,000 cattle a year went over the border to England.

Welsh drovers with a herd of cattle on the way to England

On the hills, the Welsh kept sheep, chiefly for the wool. In the Middle Ages, the farmers sold the wool in English markets. After about 1500, though, the Welsh did more spinning, weaving and knitting themselves. In 1750, Welsh knitted woollen stockings were fashionable in England.

Some peasants mined coal as well as working on the land. (Men had dug for coal in south Wales since the Middle Ages.) As demand grew, more and more Welsh coal was sent by ship to Bristol or France or Ireland. Iron ore was also mined in south Wales. And after 1600, foundries in Cardiff were making cast-iron guns.

Apart from some fighting in the Civil War (see Chapter 26), Wales enjoyed peace between 1500 and 1750. Peace was good for everyone, and the population grew steadily, from 225,000 in 1550 to 480,000 in 1750. In that time, the gentry grew richer, and more English. The peasants remained poor, and stayed Welsh.

Now try Exercises 25.4 and 25.5.

Source 25f

Our subjects in south Wales are so poor that they do not send their sons to school. In any case, there are no schools in those parts. The result is that Welshmen of all ages and every class do not know God's laws. They do not know the law of the land either. And they do not know any English, so they do not understand the laws which they are supposed to obey.

Henry VIII's order to open a school at Brecon in 1541.

Exercise 25.4

Read **Section C**, and ask yourself the question, 'Which things changed, and which things stayed the same?' Copy the sentences and write **TRUE** or **FALSE** after each one.

a Most Welsh people made their living from farming between 1500 and 1750. _____

b The Acts of Union made things worse for the farmers. _____

c The number of Welsh cattle sold in England increased between 1500 and 1750. _____

d The Welsh farmers stopped keeping sheep after 1500. _____

e Coal-mining in Wales did not begin until after 1600. _____

f Iron guns were made in Cardiff in the seventeenth and eighteenth centuries. _____

g The population of Wales more than doubled between 1500 and 1750. _____

h The peasants continued to speak Welsh between 1500 and 1750. _____

Exercise 25.5

Read **Source 25f**. What were Henry VIII's aims when he set up the school at Brecon? Look at the list below, then write out the aims which you think are the same as Henry VIII's.

a To teach the children the Welsh language.
b To set up schools where there were none.
c To provide free schooling for the sons of Welshmen.
d To teach Welsh people God's commandments.
e To teach Welsh boys to speak English.
f To teach Welsh boys to read and write in English.
g To teach mathematics and science.
h To make sure that the people of Wales understood and obeyed the laws.

26 The Civil War

A Puritans and the Church of England

The **Puritans** (see page 114) were unhappy with the Church of England. They thought that there was no need for bishops as well as priests. They did not want priests to wear special robes. They did not like having to use a Prayer Book. In all these ways, they said, the Church of England was too close to the Catholic Church.

In 1603, King James VI of Scotland became **James I** of England. (Look at the family tree on page 118.) The English Puritans were pleased, for James had been brought up in Scotland by strict Protestants, men like themselves. So the Puritans hoped that he would alter the Church of England to suit them. But they were disappointed. James I made no changes.

In 1625, James died and **Charles I**

became king. The Puritans did not trust him, for his queen was a Catholic, and they thought he had plans to make the Church of England Catholic too. Priests made the sign of the cross as they prayed, and used altars instead of simple tables. William Laud, whom Charles chose to be Archbishop of Canterbury, sent inspectors round the churches to make sure that the Prayer Book was used. Puritans who broke the rules were put in prison.

When Charles tried to make the Scots use the Prayer Book in 1637, they rebelled. (See Chapter 30.) A Scots army invaded England, and took Newcastle. Charles had to pay them £850 a day to advance no further.

Now try Exercise 26.1.

Source 26a

Of God,   Of Man,   Of the Divell.

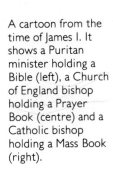

A cartoon from the time of James I. It shows a Puritan minister holding a Bible (left), a Church of England bishop holding a Prayer Book (centre) and a Catholic bishop holding a Mass Book (right).

Thomas Percy   Guido Fawkes   Robert Catesby

In 1605 there was a Catholic plot to blow up Parliament while King James I was present. The plot was discovered and the plotters were executed. The most famous plotter was Guy Fawkes.

Exercise 26.1

Read **Section A**, and study **Source 26a**.
Copy the sentences filling in the blank spaces as you go.

a The artist says that the Puritan minister stands for
_____'s religion.

b He says that the Church of England bishop stands for
_____'s religion.

c He says that the _____ bishop stands for the devil's religion.

d The Puritan minister is holding a _____

e The Church of England bishop is holding a
_____ Book, and the Catholic bishop is holding a _____ Book.

f Apart from the books they are holding, there is no difference between the _____ of
_____ and the _____ bishops.

g The artist is saying that there is not much difference between the _____ Church and the Church of
_____

h The artist must have been a _____

B Parliament and Taxes

James I and Charles I were always short of money. Most of what they spent came from the people, as taxes passed by **Parliament**. The gentry and merchants who sat in the House of Commons did not much like their Stuart kings. They said that they both wasted money, and would not agree to all they wanted.

The quarrel between Charles I and the Commons was so bad that after 1629 the king tried to rule without Parliament. He collected some taxes without Parliament's permission. Men who refused to pay were fined or put in prison.

Some gentry thought that Charles

King Charles I

was becoming a **despot** – a ruler who ignored the law. His governor of Ireland, the tough **Earl of Strafford**, did ignore the law. (See Chapter 31). In 1639, Charles ordered Strafford to return to England and take command. The gentry grew even more alarmed.

King Charles, on the other hand, thought that ruling the country was **his** job, not the people's. Most other countries had kings who were above parliaments and the law. Why should England be different?

Parliament met in 1640 because King Charles needed money to pay the Scots. (See Section A.) The House of Commons was full of men who objected to what Charles had done. They said that in future the king must not rule without Parliament. They condemned Strafford to death. Then they began to attack the Church of England as well. Charles could stand no more. In 1642 civil war broke out between him and Parliament.

Now try Exercises 26.2 and 26.3.

Exercise 26.2

Read **Section B**.
On the left side of the page below, you will see the **first halves** of seven sentences on the causes of the Civil War. On the right side are the **second halves**, but in a different order. Put the correct halves together, and write out the complete sentences.

First halves
a The members of the House of Commons thought that...
b After 1629, Charles I made people...
c Some gentry accused Charles I...
d A lot of people said that the Earl of Strafford had...
e Charles I thought that it was the king's duty...
f Charles I had to call Parliament in 1640...
g Civil war broke out in 1642 because Charles I...

Second halves
● objected to the changes Parliament was making.
● of trying to make himself a despot.
● because he needed money for the war with Scotland.
● to rule the country as he thought fit.
● James I and Charles I did not spend their money wisely.
● behaved like a despot in Ireland.
● pay taxes without asking for Parliament's consent.

Source 26b

Strafford was a would-be tyrant. He said that Parliament had gone too far, and he wanted to set King Charles free from its controls. He thought that the king had a right to absolute power. And he saw that the only way of giving him that power was by force, and fear.

Adapted from a book written by John Richard Green in 1874.

The House of Commons in the seventeenth century

Source 26c

Strafford said that the king was the 'father' of the country. It was his job to look after the people in it. To do his job properly, he had to be strong. He must not let the gentry and lawyers in Parliament take his powers away. His servants must work hard to keep justice and order. 'Less than Thorough (see page 159) will not do', as he said.

Adapted from a book written by Sir Keith Feiling in 1927.

Exercise 26.3

Read **Sources 26b** and **26c**.
Discuss these questions in a group:

a Who wrote the two sources, and when were they written? Are they primary or secondary sources?
b Both sources tell us how Strafford wanted England to be governed. What sort of government did he want? Do the two sources give us the same answer to this question?
c What did Strafford think about the Members of Parliament? Do the two sources give us the same answer to this question?
d Is **Source 26b** on Strafford's side, against him, or neutral? (Give some reasons for your opinions.)
e Is **Source 26c** on Strafford's side, against him or neutral? (Give some reasons for your opinions.)

After discussing the questions, either **i** Write your answers in a short essay in your own words, or **ii** Make a group tape.

ENGLAND AT THE TIME OF THE CIVIL WAR

Roundhead Cavalry officer and trooper

Royalist Cavalry officer and trooper

SCOTLAND

Newcastle

Marston Moor × York

Hull

Nottingham

Naseby

Worcester × Edgehill

Oxford

Bristol

London

WALES

Plymouth

☐ Areas held by the King in 1642

☐ Areas held by Parliament in 1642

0   50   100   150   200
Kilometres

C Cavaliers and Roundheads

Charles left London and in August 1642, he raised his standard above Nottingham Castle. This was a signal that all men who were loyal to the king should prepare to fight for him. The Civil War was about to begin. (The king's army were called the **Cavaliers**.)

Parliament's leaders did not want to get rid of the king, but they could not trust Charles I. He had to be made less powerful. So they too raised an army. It was called the **Roundhead** army, because many of the men were Puritans, and Puritans cut their hair short.

The two armies were about equal at first. The Cavaliers had better cavalry, commanded by the king's nephew from Germany, Prince Rupert. They tried to advance on London, but failed. Then the Roundheads, with help from the Scots, started to win.

In 1644 and 1645 the Roundheads formed the **New Model Army**, a force of well drilled and well armed troops.

They were properly paid, and their officers were men who knew their job. The New Model Army won the Battle of Naseby for Parliament in June 1645, and the war ended in 1646. Charles gave himself up to the Scots, and they handed him over to Parliament.

Charles I could have remained king if he had agreed to share his power with Parliament. But he tried to be clever. He escaped and made a deal with the Scots, who promised to put him back in control. A Scots army invaded England in 1648, but it was beaten by **Oliver Cromwell** and the New Model Army. Cromwell and the other generals were now in charge.

Now try Exercises 26.4 and 26.5

A pikeman

Exercise 26.4

Read **Section C**.
Write sentences to show that you know what these words mean:

Standard Civil War Cavaliers Roundheads Cavalry Infantry Officers Generals

Source 26d

My own regiment of foot (infantry), at push of pike, forced back the enemy's strongest regiment. In the meantime, the cavalry beat back all the other side. They charged through the enemy's cavalry and their foot.

From Oliver Cromwell's account of a battle fought in 1650.

Exercise 26.5

Study the pictures on page 136 and **Source 26e**, and read **Source 26d**.

a Write notes about the following:
  i How Civil War soldiers were dressed.
  ii How pikemen marched, and how they fought in battle.
  iii How the cavalry fought in battle.
b Draw pictures (pin-men if you wish) showing pikemen
  i marching, and ii in battle.

Source 26e

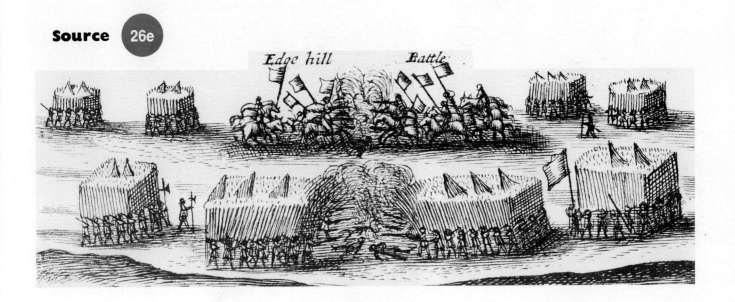

27 The Commonwealth

A The English Republic

At the end of the Civil War, power was in the hands of the House of Commons. (Most of the House of Lords had sided with the king.) The Commons decided to make England a **Commonwealth**, or republic. It announced that in future there would be no king, and no House of Lords.

It was the Commons that put King Charles on trial. They charged him with making war on his people. Charles refused to answer the charge. He said that he was king, and only God could judge him. The court did not agree. It found him guilty and sentenced him to death. He was beheaded in front of a big crowd outside Whitehall Palace on 30th January 1649.

The army took its orders from the House of Commons. But the army's generals had got used to **giving** orders, not **taking** them. Before long, it was clear that the **army** was really in charge. The most powerful man in England was the leading general, **Oliver Cromwell**.

In 1653, Cromwell quarrelled with the members of the Commons, and threw them out. Later that year, he agreed to become **Lord Protector**, or

Oliver Cromwell

The execution of Charles I in 1649

138

head of the State. Some men even wanted to make him 'King Oliver'. He might have agreed, but the other generals would not stand for it.

At one stage, Cromwell split England and Wales into eleven districts, and put a major-general in charge of each of them. They kept good order, but the people did not like being ruled by soldiers. Not even Charles I had done that.

Now try Exercise 27.1.

Exercise 27.I

Read **Section A**, then answer the questions.

a Who was in charge of England at the end of the Civil War?
b What did 'Commonwealth' mean?
c When Charles I was put on trial, he was accused of doing what?
d Charles I said that the court had no right to try him. Why?
e What happened to the House of Commons in 1653?
f In which year did Cromwell take the title 'Lord Protector'?
g Why did Oliver Cromwell not become king?
h Why was government by the major-generals unpopular?

B The Commonwealth and its enemies

The family of Charles I fled abroad after the Civil War. But his eldest son, Prince Charles, hoped that he would return to England one day. Cromwell's army and navy kept watch to see that he did not.

Cromwell's first task was to deal with rebels in Ireland who took the side of Prince Charles. Cromwell and the army crossed to Ireland and crushed the revolt. The Irish people have hated the name Cromwell ever since. (See Chapter 31)

The prince also got help from the Scots. They crowned him King Charles II in 1650. A Scots army invaded England, but Cromwell beat it at the Battle of Worcester. Roundhead troops searched for the prince after the battle, but he managed to escape to France. (See **Source 27a**.)

Cromwell had spies all over England, and secret agents abroad. Men who had fought for the king had to pay a special tax, and many lost their land. The major-generals had to watch **Royalists** (men known to be on the prince's side). Some of them banned horse-racing, so that there would be less chance for crowds to gather, and for the prince's friends to meet.

Now try Exercise 27.2.

Below: Commonwealth soldiers taking pictures out of a church, and breaking down altar rails

Below left: Prince Charles, later King Charles II

The Souldiers in their passage to York, turn unto reformers pull down Popish pictures, break down rayles, turn altars into Tables.

Source 27a

Between the Battle of Worcester on 3rd September and going on board the ship at Brighton on 15th October, he travelled nearly 300 miles. He went sometimes on foot, and sometimes on a horse. Often he was disguised in coarse linen and a leather jacket. He had to spend one day in a barn, and another in a tree. He was glad to stay one night in a secret place at Boscobel which was never meant to be a king's bedroom. When he thought he was almost safe, he ran right into some of the rebels who were so greedy for his blood. Yet, thanks be to God, they did not recognize him.

From Thomas Blount's account of Prince Charles's escape.

Source 27b

A Parliamentary cartoon showing a Royalist with a wolf's head and eagle's claws.

Exercise 27.2

Read **Section B** and **Source 27a**. Write notes in answer to the questions.

a Which do you think are the five most important **facts** in **Source 27a**?

b Write down any **opinions** that you can find in **Source 27a**.

c Whose side was Thomas Blount on – the Commonwealth's or the prince's? Give reasons for your answer.

C Puritan England

Before the Civil War, the Puritans complained about the Church of England. Now the Puritans were on top. The Commons said that there would be no bishops, and the Prayer Book was banned. Statues and pictures were removed from churches. There were no more 'holy days'.

The law was strict about what was allowed on Sundays. No-one could travel on a Sunday, except to and from church. Shops and public houses were closed. Dancing and singing were banned. Sundays would have been very dull if all the rules had been kept, but they were not.

The major-generals had to make sure that there was no drunkenness or swearing, and that everyone went to church. They could close down theatres and public houses if they wished. Some of them used these powers, but others were not so hard.

Oliver Cromwell died in 1658. His son Richard took his place, but Richard was weak. He was not a soldier or a statesman. He soon gave up, and the army took control. It called a new Parliament, and the members invited Prince Charles to return to England to become King Charles II.

Now try Exercises 27.3, 27.4, 27.5, and 27.6.

Exercise 27.3

Read **Section C**, and look at **Sources 27b** and **27c**.
Now think about this question:

'Were the artists who drew these cartoons on the side of the Commonwealth or against it?'

Do not write out a full answer to the question. Just write an essay plan – notes for four or five paragraphs, saying what you can see in the cartoons, and what the cartoons tell you about the artists who drew them.

Source 27c

A Royalist cartoon, showing Oliver Cromwell and other leading men of the Commonwealth sitting in the 'Cabinet Council'. The Chairman of the Council is the devil!

Source 27d

People who go to the theatre know that we have put right a lot of things that were wrong. Bad language and rude jokes have been cut out of our plays now. We no longer make fun of famous men. Off the stage, actors have stopped borrowing money and cadging drinks from rich young men. These days, you never find an unruly mob or pick-pockets at a theatre.

A protest made in 1643 by some London actors who did not want Parliament to close the theatres.

Exercise 27.4.

Parliament closed the London theatres during the Civil War. Why did it do so? What were the **motives** of the members of Parliament?
Read **Source 27d**, then copy the sentences below and fill in the blank spaces. The Members of Parliament objected to:

a Plays that contained _____ language and rude _____

b Plays that contained jokes about _____ _____

c Actors borrowing _____ from rich young men.

d Actors who _____ too much, and did not pay for their _____

e Disorderly crowds at _____

f _____ operating among the theatre crowds.

Source 27e

The soldiers and the Puritans thought he was wonderful. The Cavaliers hated him. I think he was modest most of the time, until success spoiled him. Then he gave in to temptation. He thought that God had made him great, and given him victory against the king. He thought that if God was with him, he must be always right. Pride made him selfish and greedy.

Written by Richard Baxter, a Puritan minister who knew Oliver Cromwell.

The sources do not all say the same

As you have seen, writers do not always say the same thing about the people of the past. There are many reasons why this may be so. Here are a few of them:

a Writers who met and talked to the people of the past knew more than writers who got what they knew from books.

b Authors of some **primary sources** had strong **opinions** – they took one side or the other.

c Authors of some **primary sources** took part in the events themselves. They tried to show that they had always been right.

d As time has passed, many sources have been lost or destroyed.

e Modern writers can read **all** the sources that remain. Some of these sources were kept secret in the past.

f Authors take the side of their own country. For example, English writers take the English point of view, and Irish writers take the Irish point of view.

Source 27f

He was a modest man, keen to do his duty. His enemies said he was ambitious, of course. But he was not out for himself. He wanted, above all, to serve his country, understand his friends, and forgive his enemies. He did not often boast, though he got excited in battle. When victory was won, he gave thanks to the Lord and his men.

Adapted from a book written by Dr. Maurice Ashley in 1957.

Exercise 27.5

Read **Sources 27e** and **27f**, then read the sentences below. Write out the sentences which you think are true.

a Richard Baxter knew Cromwell, but Dr. Ashley is a twentieth-century writer.
b Both authors thought that Cromwell was a modest man.
c Richard Baxter thought that Cromwell was spoiled by his own success.
d Dr. Ashley thought that Cromwell was more concerned for his country than himself.
e Richard Baxter said that Cromwell thought God was always on his side.
f Both sources said that Cromwell believed that he was always right.
g Only Dr. Ashley said that Cromwell gave credit to God and his men.
g Both sources said that Cromwell became selfish and greedy.
i Richard Baxter said that success made Cromwell proud, and that pride made him selfish and greedy.

Exercise 27.6

Look again at **Sources 27e** and **27f**, read your answer to Exercise 27.5, and read the note 'The sources do not all say the same.'
Discuss this question in a group: 'Why do you think that Richard Baxter and Dr. Ashley had different opinions of Oliver Cromwell?'

After the discussion, either a Make a group tape (or a member of the group could give a talk); or b Write out your answer in a paragraph.

28 Restoration and Revolution

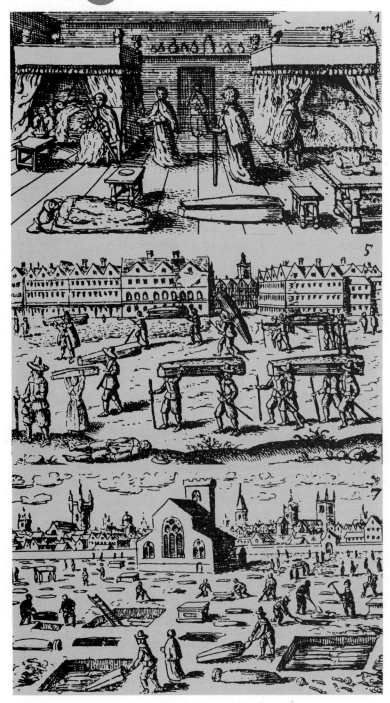

Pictures from a book published at the time of the Great Plague

A Plague and fire

Charles II was restored (allowed to return to England as king) in 1660. Most people were glad to have him back after the bleak years of the Commonwealth. The laws that made Sundays so dull were cancelled. In London, the theatres were open again.

For some people, London was a cheerful place in Charles II's reign. But it was also deadly dangerous. Disease was everywhere, and the smell must have been awful. The heaps of rubbish in the streets were perfect breeding-places for black rats. And the fleas that lived on the rats carried **bubonic plague**.

The plague had never gone away since the **Black Death** of 1348–9. Every few years there was an outbreak. In 1665, after a pause of 30 years, it swept London again, and nearly 70,000 people died. Those who could afford to do so fled, taking the disease with them.

Plague was highly infectious, and killed its victims within hours. Houses where it struck were locked and barred, and those inside could come out only at night. That was when the carts rumbled through the streets, and you could hear the mournful cry, 'Bring out your dead!'

By the end of 1665 the worst was over, and the plague did not come back. The reason was not that doctors found a cure. It was that **brown** rats drove out the black rats. Brown rats had different fleas, ones that did not carry plague.

A second disaster hit London in 1666. In five days in September, fire wiped out the city's heart. Wooden buildings burned easily, and there was no proper fire brigade. Men pulled down houses, or blew them up, to stop the fire spreading. For a second time, the rich and famous fled.

After the fire, a great chance was missed. London could have become a new, planned city with wide streets and proper sewers. But the houses were put up just as before, with no thought for health or hygiene. On the other hand, fine new churches were built, to **Sir Christopher Wren's** designs. His greatest work was the new **St. Paul's Cathedral**.

Now try Exercises 28.1 and 28.2

Source 28b

7th June. I saw two or three houses in Drury Lane marked with a red cross on the doors, and 'Lord have mercy upon us' written there. It was the first time I had seen that.
12th July. So many are dying that they have to bury some in daylight. (There is not time to bury them all at night.)
15th September. What a sad time it is! So many people have left London that there are no boats on the river, and grass is growing in Whitehall court.
26th October. The town is beginning to be lively again, though the streets are still empty, and most of the shops are shut.

From the diary of Samuel Pepys.

Source 28c

Number of deaths from plague in London in 1665.

May	43	September	26,219
June	590	October	14,373
July	4,127	November	3,451
August	19,046	December	940

Exercise 28.1

Read **Section A** and **Sources 28b** and **28c**, and study **Source 28a**.

a Put the halves of the sentences together, then write out the complete sentences.

First half of sentence.

i Pepys (**Source 28b**) first saw signs of plague in June, but **Source 28c** shows . . .

ii **Sources 28b** and **28c** agree that the greatest number of deaths occurred . . .

iii **Sources 28a** and **28b** both tell us that . . .

iv Only **Source 28a** shows . . .

v **Source 28c** tells us that the number of deaths fell in October, and **Source 28b** says . . .

vi We can see what it was like inside a house hit by plague by . . .

Second half of sentence.

• in the summer and autumn of 1665.
• some bodies were buried in daylight.
• looking at **Source 28a**.
• that there were some plague deaths in May.
• how and where the victims were buried.
• that London was getting back to normal then.

b Draw a bar-graph of plague deaths in London, May to December 1665.

These Engins,(which are the best)to quench great Fires; are

A fire engine from the time of the Fire of London

Sir Christopher Wren, who designed the new St. Paul's Cathedral (in the background) and many other churches

Exercise 28.2

Study the fire-engine.
Write notes, saying

a How you think the fire-engine worked;
b What you think was wrong with the fire-engine – why it would not work very well.

B Whigs and Tories

Charles II had spent twelve years abroad, while England was a republic. For the rest of his life, his main aim was to remain king of England. He said, 'I do not want to go on my travels again.'

To be secure, he had to stay on good terms with the most important of his subjects, the **nobles** and **gentry**. They forced Charles to share his power with **Parliament**. They had good reason, for the nobles controlled the House of Lords, and the gentry controlled the House of Commons.

Charles II was an **Anglican** – a member of the Church of England. (Secretly, he may have been a Catholic.) Most of the nobles and gentry were Anglicans. They disliked both Catholics and **Dissenters** – Protestants who did not belong to the Church of England. They got Parliament to pass acts which kept Catholics and Dissenters out of all the top jobs.

Charles II had no children. His heir was his brother **James**, who was a Catholic. None of the nobles and gentry liked the idea that the next king would be a Catholic. One group (called the **Whigs**) wanted to pass a bill saying that James could not be king. But the others (called the **Tories**) said that James was the heir, and had a right to be king.

Charles took his brother's side. With the help of the Tories, he made the Whigs give in. And when Charles died in 1685, his brother took the throne as James II.

Now try Exercise 28.3.

King James II

Exercise 28.3

Read **Section B**. Find words from this list that fit the descriptions below. Copy the descriptions and write one of the words from the list after each one.

Nobles Tories Heir Bill Anglicans Dissenters Whigs Gentry

a The man who was to be the next king. _____

b Members of the Church of England.

   _____

c Dukes, earls, and lords. _____

d Landowners who were not nobles. _____

e The party who did not want a Catholic king.

   _____

f The party who took the side of King Charles and his

   brother James. _____

g A plan for a new law. _____

h Protestants who were not Anglicans.

   _____

C The Revolution of 1688

The Whigs were always against James II, because he was a Catholic. The Tories, at first, were on his side. They began to change their minds when James said that he wanted a full-time army. Both Whigs and Tories were afraid that a king with a **standing army** would have too much power.

When James put Catholics in command of the army, the Whigs and Tories grew more alarmed. He chose Catholics as his ministers, too. The Whigs and Tories, who were all Anglicans, were angry at being pushed out of these top jobs.

Parliament had passed laws against Catholics and Dissenters in high office. But James said that the laws did not apply. The Whig and Tory lords were furious – **Parliament** made the law, and **they** controlled Parliament. The king was taking their powers away.

James II, whose first wife was dead, had no sons. His two daughters were both Protestants. In time, he would die, and England would have a Protestant queen again. But James took a second wife, a Catholic. In June 1688 she gave birth to a **prince**. The prince would be a Catholic, and he was James's heir. (Look at the cartoon.)

The Whigs turned to **William of Orange** for help. William was the husband of James's elder daughter, and a Protestant. In November 1688, William and his army sailed from Holland to Devon. As he marched on London the nobles and gentry, Whig and Tory, took his side. James, finding himself with no friends, fled. Parliament said that he had resigned the crown, and offered it jointly to William and his wife Mary.

Now try Exercises 28.4 and 28.5.

THE KING

James II, who was a Catholic, became king in 1685.

He gave the top jobs in the government, army and navy to Catholics.

He built up a standing army for service in peacetime, as well as war.

Cancelled
James II cancelled the laws against Catholics and Dissenters.

WHIGS

A group of lords, gentry and rich merchants.

I don't want a Catholic king.

I think that Whigs should have the top jobs.

Queen Mary, James II's second wife, gave birth to a son in 1688.

TORIES

Another group of lords and gentry.

He has a right to be King. Give him a chance.

I think that Tories should have the top jobs.

We both think that the standing army might be used to crush Parliament, and force the people to obey the king.

King James thinks that he can change the law as he likes. Only Parliament can make and change laws.

The prince will be brought up as a Catholic. He will be the next King. His sons will be Catholics. England's Kings will always be Catholics.

THE COMMON PEOPLE

The common people (farmers, craftsmen, labourers, and their wives and children) were neither Whigs nor Tories. They owned no land and not much money. Most of them had no votes. No-one asked them what they thought.

Exercise 28.4

Read **Section C** and study the cartoon. Answer the questions in sentences.

a Which people supported **i** the Whigs, and **ii** the Tories?
b Which party was always against James II, and why?
c What turned the Tories against James II? (Mention two facts.)
d Why did the Whigs and Tories think that the birth of a prince in 1688 was so important?
e How was William of Orange related to James II?
f Who asked William of Orange to help them?
g Why did James II leave England?
h What part did the common people play in the Revolution of 1688?

Exercise 28.5

Plan an essay on the causes of the Revolution of 1688.

a Write out these paragraph-headings in the correct order:
  i James made himself powerful and gave some top jobs to Catholics. This made the Tories and Whigs angry.
  ii James found that he had no supporters left, so he fled to France.
  iii At first, the Whigs were against James II, and the Tories were on James's side.
  iv The Whigs invited William of Orange to come over from Holland.
  v The queen gave birth to a son in June 1688.
b Write out any one paragraph in full. (Use your own words.)

From Stuart to Hanover

A The end of the Stuarts

James II was **deposed** (thrown out) mainly because he was a Catholic. The Protestant William and Mary took his place, but James always hoped to return. At first, there seemed a good chance that he would succeed, for he got help from King Louis XIV of France. So Parliament agreed to taxes to pay for a war with France. And it passed a law which said that no Catholic could be king or queen of England.

William and Mary had no children. When William died in 1702, the last

Protestant Stuart, Mary's sister **Anne**, became queen. Anne had eleven children, but they all died young. So there was no Protestant Stuart heir when Anne died in 1714.

In the time of Queen Anne, the Whigs and Tories were at odds again. Both sides wanted power for themselves, as the queen's ministers. They quarrelled about the war with France, which was still going on. And they fought about the **succession** – who

THE STUART FAMILY

JAMES I b.1566 d.1625
King of England
1603-1625

Names underlined in red – Catholics

CHARLES I b.1600 executed 1649
King 1625-1649

Elizabeth
married Elector Frederick (a German prince)

The Hanover Family

Mary
married
William II
of Orange

CHARLES II
b.1630 d.1685
King 1660-1685
married
Katherine of
Portugal (no children)

JAMES II
b.1633 d.1701
King 1685-1688
married

1st   2nd

Sophia married Ernest, Elector of Hanover

Anne Hyde

Mary of Modena

GEORGE I
b.1660 d.1727
King of England
1714-1727

James Edward
b.1688 d.1766

WILLIAM III married MARY
of Orange   Queen
King 1689-1702   1689-1695
(no children)

ANNE
Queen
1702-1714
(11 children, all die young)

Charles Edward
b.1720 d.1788

GEORGE II
b.1683 d.1760
King of England
1727-1760

should be king when Queen Anne died?

Some Tories would have liked **James Edward Stuart** (James II's son) on the throne. But the law said the king must be a Protestant, and James Edward was a Catholic. The Whigs wanted the Protestant **George**, elector (ruler) of **Hanover** in Germany, and got their way. When Anne died, 'German George' became king. (Look at the family tree.)

A few Tories would have liked the Stuarts to return. (People on the side of the Stuarts were called **Jacobites** at that time.) There were Jacobite risings in 1715 and 1745, and they had some success in Scotland. (See Chapter 30.) But in England, the Protestant Hanovers, with their Whig ministers, were firmly in control.

Now try Exercise 29.1.

William of Orange, later King William III of England and his wife, Mary (James II's daughter)

Exercise 29.1

Read **Section A**, and look at the family tree. Then write sentences to show that you know what these words and phrases mean:

a To depose the king.
b Catholic.
c Protestant.
d The Stuart family.
e The king's (or queen's) ministers.
f The succession.
g The elector of Hanover.
h The Jacobites.

B The victory of the Lords

In 1689, Parliament passed acts which took power from the king (or queen). They said that only Parliament could change the law – the king could not do it alone. Taxes were legal only if Parliament agreed to them. There could be a **standing army**, but it too needed parliament's consent. And that consent had to be given **each year**. This meant that Parliament had to meet at least once a year. Therefore, the king or queen could not rule without it.

Parliament said that it had a right to these powers because it spoke for the people. In fact, it spoke for a few of the people – the rich ones, those who owned the land. These were the nobles who sat in the House of Lords, and the gentry who sat in the Commons.

The House of Commons was **elected**. But not many men (and no women) had the right to vote. Men who could vote had to do so in public, so their landlords and employers could see how they voted, and **force** them to vote the right way. Those who could not be forced might be **bribed**.

The forcing and bribing were done by men with land and money – the gentry and the nobles. The most powerful men were the richest, and they were the nobles, with their huge estates. That is why the House of Lords was more important than the Commons at this time. Many of the gentry in the Commons followed the orders of nobles in the Lords.

Now try Exercise 29.2.

An election to choose the Member of Parliament for Oxford, held in Oxford Town Hall in 1687. Only a small number of people had the right to vote, and they did not vote in secret.

Exercise 29.2

Read **Section B**, then copy the sentences and write TRUE or FALSE after each one.

a Acts passed in 1689 made the king (or queen) stronger. _____

b The king had to call a meeting of Parliament each year, so that he could ask for permission to keep a standing army. _____

c Kings could no longer rule without Parliament. _____

d Most men, and some women, had the right to vote. _____

e People could not vote in secret.

_____

f Some employers sacked their workers if they voted for the wrong man. _____

g The House of Commons was more important than the House of Lords in the eighteenth century.

_____

h The gentry were the owners of the biggest estates. _____

C Cabinet and Prime Minister

King George I

In the time of William and Mary, the king was still the head of the Government. William had ministers to help him, of course. But he chose them, and he could sack them. The king made the big decisions, such as when to go to war.

Queen Anne, George I and George II still had a lot of power. They picked their own ministers, and discussed Government business with them. But they learned that they could not do just as they pleased.

After 1688, the ministers had to ask Parliament **each year** to agree to taxes and the army bill. And if Parliament did not like the king's ministers or what they did, it might not pass these bills. So the king or queen had to pay attention to Parliament, and to the great lords who controlled it. (See Section B.)

The king or queen and the chief ministers met once a week in the **Cabinet**. William attended the Cabinet when he was in England (he was often away at war). Queen Anne was always there. So was George I, for the first three years of his reign.

150

After 1717, the Cabinet usually met without the king. When it did so, one of the ministers was chairman. After the meeting, he went to the king and told him what the Cabinet advised. **Sir Robert Walpole** did this job from 1722 to 1742. He was the head of the king's government – Britain's first **Prime Minister**.

Now try Exercises 29.3, 29.4, and 29.5.

Exercise 29.3

Read **Section C**, and look at the cartoons.
Make your own notes answering the questions below.

a Compare the '1620' cartoon with the '1705' cartoon:
  i What had changed?
  ii What had not changed?
b Compare the '1705' cartoon with the '1750' cartoons:
  i What had changed?
  ii What had not changed?

1620 King James I asked his Council for advice.

The king made the decisions.

1705 Queen Anne attended meetings of her Cabinet.

The Queen and the Cabinet made decisions together. No Prime Minister.

1750 The Cabinet made the decisions. The Prime Minister was the chairman.

The Prime Minister told King George II what the Cabinet had decided.

The Duke of Marlborough (seated), who led the British armies to victory in the wars against the French in Queen Anne's reign, and his chief engineer

Source 29a

For a long time, the Duchess of Marlborough was Queen Anne's closest friend. But the duchess got ruder and ruder, and in the end the queen could stand her no more. The queen found a new friend, Mrs Masham, a cousin of the Tory leader Harley. The queen told the duchess to leave the court, and there was a great row. Before she left, the duchess wrecked her rooms in St. James's Palace. The Whig ministers were dismissed soon after. Harley and the Tories took their place.

Adapted from a book written by Sir Charles Oman in 1895.

Source 29b

Princess (later Queen) Anne with one of her children. The princess posed for this portrait in 1694. It was painted by Sir Godfrey Kneller.

Source 29c

Sarah, Duchess of Marlborough. This portrait was painted from life in about 1700. The name of the artist is not known.

Source 29d

The cunning Harley found a way to turn the queen against the Duke of Marlborough. He introduced the queen to Mrs Masham, who became her close friend, and a rival to the duchess. In 1710, Mrs. Masham got the queen to break with the duchess. Soon after, she dismissed the Whigs and brought in Harley and the Tories.

Adapted from a book written by G. M. Trevelyan in 1904.

The Duke of Marlborough was a supporter of the Whigs and an opponent of the Tories led by Harley. As a result of the argument between Queen Anne and the Duchess of Marlborough, the Whigs lost power at court.

Exercise 29.4

Look at **Sources 29b** and **29c**, and read **Sources 29a** and **29d**.

a Answer these questions in sentences or write 'not known':
  i Who painted **Source 29b**, and when?
  ii Did the artist who painted **Source 29b** see Princess (later Queen) Anne?
  iii Who painted **Source 29c**, and when?
  iv Did the artist who painted **Source 29c** see the Duchess of Marlborough?
  v Who wrote **Source 29a**, and when?
  vi Who wrote **Source 29d**, and when?
  vii Which **sources** (**29a, 29b, 29c, 29d**) are primary, and which are secondary?
b Draw a cartoon to show any event described in **Source 29a** or **29d**.

Exercise 29.5

Read carefully through **Sources 29a** and **29d** again. Then write two paragraphs about these two sources, answering these questions:

a In which ways do the two accounts say the same things?
b In which ways are the two accounts different?

30 Scotland in the Seventeenth and Eighteenth Centuries

A The National Covenant

King James VI of Scotland moved south to England as soon as he heard that Queen Elizabeth was dead. From 1603 until his death in 1625 he was king of England **and** king of Scotland. But in those twenty-two years he came back north only once.

James preferred England. The English lords obeyed the king, and were not always at war with each other. England was a richer land, so the king was better off. (He soon had a crowd of courtiers, English and Scots, keen to flatter him in return for gifts and favours.) Also, James thought Scotland's **Presbyterian** church was dull and boring. He much preferred the Church of England, with its bishops, Prayer Book, and priests in robes.

James brought back bishops in Scotland. In 1637, his son, Charles I, went further, and ordered that the Scots had to use a Prayer Book. This caused a huge storm – nobles, gentry, and townspeople joined in the protest. In 1638, they drew up the **National Covenant**, which said that they would not stand for changes in Scotland's Church. Charles tried to use force, but his army was beaten. In 1640 the Scots invaded the north of England.

The crisis that began with the Scottish Prayer Book led to the first Civil War. (See Chapter 26.) The Scots took the side of Parliament, and helped defeat the king. But in 1648 King Charles got the Scots to change sides. By then, though, the New Model Army was too strong. The Scots were beaten in the second Civil War, and King Charles went to his death.

Now try Exercises 30.1 and 30.2.

In 1637, Charles I ordered that a Prayer Book had to be used in churches in Scotland. This order caused riots, and was the main reason why the National Covenant was drawn up in 1638.

The Arch-Prelate of St Andrewes in Scotland reading the new Service-booke in his pontificalibus assaulted by men & women, with Cricketts stooles Stickes and Stones.

Craigievar Castle in Scotland

Exercise 30.1

Read **Section A**, then answer the questions in sentences.

a When did James VI of Scotland become king of England?
b Why did James prefer England to Scotland?
c What did James like about the Church of England?
d What change did James make in the Church of Scotland?
e What change did Charles I try to make in the Church of Scotland?
f What did the National Covenant say?
g Why did the row over the Prayer Book lead to the English Civil War? (Look back at Chapter 26, then write two or three sentences.)
h Which side did the Scots take in i the first Civil War, and ii the second Civil War?

Source 30a

The lords think that they are above the law. They mistreat the common people, and force the men to join their private armies. Then if they fall out with their neighbours, they start a war. It's one family against another, with not a thought for the king or the law.

From a book which King James VI wrote in 1597.

Exercise 30.2

Read **Source 30a**.

a Write down three **facts** from **Source 30a**.
b What do you think were King James's **opinions** about the Scottish lords? (Write one or two sentences.)

B Union with England

The Scots were angry about the execution of Charles I. In 1650, they crowned his son (Prince Charles) king of Scotland. But Cromwell would not permit that. He invaded Scotland, and beat the Scots army at Dunbar. When the Scots invaded England in the next year, Cromwell beat them again at Worcester. Charles II fled, and Scotland was occupied by English troops.

When Charles II was restored in England in 1660, he was restored in Scotland as well. When James II was deposed in England in 1688, he was deposed in Scotland also. England and Scotland had the same king, but that was all. They were not yet one country. Scotland had its own Parliament, laws, and Church.

In the time of Queen Anne, England's trade with its colonies was making it rich. (See Chapter 32.) Scotsmen had tried to found their own colony, but it failed. So Scottish merchants wanted the right to trade with England's colonies. The English were willing to agree to free trade, but at a price.

The price was accepting the English law on the **succession** (who should be the next king). The English were afraid that when Queen Anne died, England and Scotland would have different kings again. In England, **George of Hanover** was Queen Anne's heir, but the Scots had not made up their minds.

The Scots were not against George, but thought they had a right to choose their own king.

In 1707, agreement was reached on an **Act of Union**. It said that England and Scotland were to be one country – **Great Britain**. There would be one king or queen. (George of Hanover would be Queen Anne's heir). And there would be one Parliament. Trade between Scotland and England was to be free, and Scottish merchants could trade with English colonies. But Scotland kept its own Church, and its own laws and courts.

Now try Exercises 30.3 and 30.4.

Exercise 30.3

Read **Section B**. You will see that the English and Scots had different opinions and points of view. Make notes on

a Scottish opinions and points of view on
   i trade, and **ii** the succession.
b English opinions and points of view on
   i trade, and **ii** the succession.
c What the Act of Union said about
   i trade, **ii** the succession, **iii** Parliament, and **iv** the Scottish Church and laws.

The development of the first Union flag in 1707 from the Scottish and English flags. The English flag is on the left and the Scottish flag is in the middle.

Source 30b

For the English, the Union will make no change. They will keep the same Parliament, the same taxes, the same laws, and the same courts. But the Scots will have to pay the English debts, now and in the future. Scotland will lose the right to manage its own affairs. For the Scots, the Union will be a complete surrender.

From a speech made by Lord Belhaven to the Scots Parliament in 1706.

Source 30c

For Scotland, the Union brought nothing but good. The farmers of the Lowlands learned new skills. Glasgow, which had been just a fishing port, grew into a rich and mighty city. Peace changed the wild men of the Highlands into peaceful herdsmen. The only thing the Scots lost was their old hatred of England.

Adapted from a book written by the English historian J. R. Green in 1874.

Exercise 30.4

Read **Sources 30b** and **30c**, and discuss these questions in a group:

a What did Lord Belhaven think about the idea of an Act of Union? What results did he expect it to have, **i** for England, and **ii** for Scotland?
b What did J. R. Green (**Source 30c**) think about the results of the Act of Union? J. R. Green wrote his book how many years after the Act of Union was passed?
c Can you think of any **reasons** why there was such a difference between what Lord Belhaven expected and what later writers said about the Act of Union?

Then do one of the following:

i Make a group tape, giving your answers to the questions.
ii Make a wall-display, with pieces of written work and cartoons.

The JACOBITE REBELLION of 1745

Prince Charles Edward

The Duke of Cumberland who defeated the Jacobites at Culloden

→-→ Prince Charles carried on French ship
- - → His advance from Eriskay to Derby
←- - His retreat
⚔ Battle won by Jacobites
⚔ Battle lost by Jacobites

C The Jacobites

Many Scotsmen were against the Act of Union. Lowlanders said that Scotland would lose its freedom – Parliament in **London** would make laws and fix taxes for Scotland. A lot of Highlanders were against it as well. Their reason was that the Campbells, whom they hated, were for it.

In 1715, some of the clan chiefs rose in revolt against George I. Their aim was to make James VII's son **James Edward (the Pretender)** king instead. (They were called **Jacobites**.) Where the chiefs led, the clansmen followed, with sword in hand. But they did not get much support from the Lowlands or England, and the revolt fizzled out.

The second Jacobite revolt was more serious. Prince **Charles Edward**, the Pretender's son, raised his standard at Glenfinnan in August 1745. The chiefs obeyed the call, and a Highland army was formed. They took Edinburgh, beat King George's army at

Above: The Duke of Cumberland, the general who defeated the Jacobites at Culloden

Opposite page: The Battle of Culloden

Prestonpans, then marched into England. (Look at the map.)

There was panic in London. King George II prepared to leave for Germany. But not many Englishmen joined the prince. When he reached **Derby**, he could see that he had too few men to take London. In great sadness, he decided to turn back.

Charles retreated to Scotland with his tired and hungry Highlanders. The king's army advanced north to meet him. They met at **Culloden**, near Inverness. It was a slaughter, not a battle. The badly armed, exhausted Highlanders were cut down on the field, or in the flight that followed.

The prince escaped to the west, and by ship to France. His followers were hunted down. Some were hanged, others transported to the colonies for life. New laws said that Highlanders were not allowed to carry arms, wear the tartan, or play the bagpipes.

Now try Exercise 30.5.

Exercise 30.5

Read **Section C**, and look at the map.
Copy the passage below and fill in the blank spaces, using words from this list:

Dumfries York Glenfinnan Culloden Carlisle Orkney Eriskay Edinburgh French Glasgow Irish Derby Prestonpans Newcastle Skye Manchester

Prince Charles landed from a _____ ship on the island of _____ in the Outer Hebrides in August 1745. He crossed to the mainland, and raised his standard at _____, where a lot of Highlanders joined him. His army marched south, entered _____, and beat the king's army in battle at _____.

In November, they entered England and marched through _____ and _____. In December, they reached _____.

On their retreat, they went through Carlisle, _____, and _____ on the way to Inverness. At _____, in April 1746, the Jacobites were crushed by the king's army. Prince Charles fled to the west, and the island of _____. He set sail on a _____ ship in September 1746.

31 Ireland in the Seventeenth and Eighteenth Centuries

A Plantations and 'Thorough'

In the year that James I became king of England, revolt in Ireland ended. (See Chapter 24.) But James could not feel secure in Ireland. Most of the Irish were Catholics, and hated the Protestant English (and Scots). Revolt could break out again at any time. And England's enemies (such as Spain) might use Ireland as a base.

James I tried more **plantations**. He got about 20,000 Protestant settlers from England and Scotland to move to Ulster. Most of them were farmers, but some built new villages and towns, such as **Belfast**. And the London guilds that took over Derry changed its name to **Londonderry**.

A lot of Catholic Irish were driven out, and many lost their land. To them, the settlers were thieves. To the settlers, the Irish were wild beasts, or traitors, or both. The plantations were supposed to prevent revolt, but in fact they made it more likely.

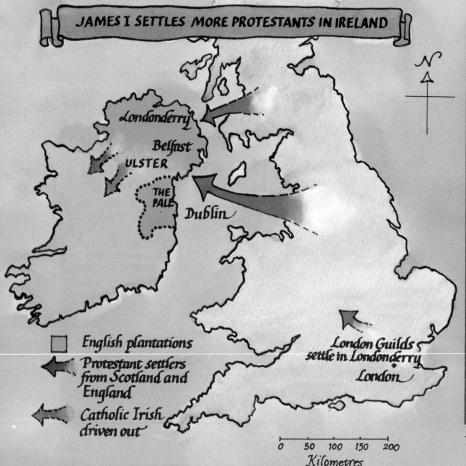

JAMES I SETTLES MORE PROTESTANTS IN IRELAND

Londonderry
Belfast
ULSTER
THE PALE
Dublin

☐ English plantations

◄ Protestant settlers from Scotland and England

◄ Catholic Irish driven out

London Guilds settle in Londonderry
London

N

0 50 100 150 200
Kilometres

The Earl of Strafford

Charles I's governor in Ireland was **Thomas Wentworth** (later **Earl of Strafford**). His aim was to keep Ireland quiet by making the king strong. This meant forcing the people to pay taxes and fines, and using the money to pay for an army.

Strafford called his policy '**Thorough**' – he meant **tough**. He forced the Irish Parliament to pass extra taxes. He made landlords (Catholic and Protestant) pay fines, or face losing their land. He allowed Catholics to worship in their own way, in return for money. When Strafford returned to England, the Irish were glad to see him go. But the English thought that it was their turn to next. (See Chapter 26.)

Now try Exercise 31.1.

Exercise 31.1

Read **Section A**, then look at the list of motives below. Decide **i** What were the motives of James I in Ireland?
ii What were the motives of Strafford in Ireland?

a He wanted to get more money out of the Irish.
b He wanted to make work for the unemployed from England.
c He did not want England's enemies to use Ireland as a base.
d He wanted to prevent another revolt in Ireland.
e He wanted to crush the Catholic Church.
f He wanted to be able to afford to keep an army in Ireland.
g He wanted the land to be properly farmed.
h He wanted to make the king strong.
i He wanted more Protestants in Ireland.

Write out James's motives and Strafford's motives in two columns.

B Rebellion and Civil War

The Ulster plantations did lead to more trouble. The Catholic landlords and peasants rose in revolt in 1641, and attacked the settlers who had taken their land. Protestants claimed that thousands of settlers were killed. But we now know that, at the same time, Protestant settlers were murdering Catholics.

The revolt spread to the whole of Ireland. In the 1640s, while King Charles I was at war with Parliament in England, there was civil war in Ireland too. But there it was Catholics against Protestants, and in most parts the Catholics came out on top.

As soon as Charles I was dead, the Commons turned to the problem of Ireland. They were worried that the Catholics there might do a deal with the late king's son. And with a base in Ireland, Prince Charles would be more of a threat to England.

They sent Oliver Cromwell and the army to Ireland. Cromwell crushed the rebels, but it was **how** he did so that made him hated. At **Drogheda**, 3,000 men, women, and children were killed by the soldiers. At **Wexford**, the same thing happened. Cromwell said that his actions saved lives – the other towns gave in without a fight. But the Irish never forgot.

Like James I, Cromwell tried to keep the peace in Ireland by means of **plantations**. But he went much further than King James. Cromwell said that Catholics could own land only in **Connaught** in the west. (Look at the map on page 123.) All the other land was given to former soldiers or sold to Protestants from England. The Catholics either moved to the west or became hired workers on what had been their own land.

Now try Exercise 31.2.

Source 31a

I think this is God's judgement on those barbarians who spilt so much innocent blood. Also, it will save lives in the future. These are good reasons for what was done. Otherwise, there would have been cause for sorrow and regret.

From a letter written by Oliver Cromwell after the massacre at Drogheda.

Source 31b

For the Irish, the way the revolt was crushed was the most important thing. Cromwell said that the massacre would save lives in the future. But in the long run it helped to make bitterness. And that caused far more blood to be spilt. Cromwell's name was branded on the memory of the Irish. To this day, it comes first to mind when Irishmen speak of the wrongs done to them.

Adapted from a book written in 1956 by Brian Inglis. The author grew up in Ireland, and used many Irish sources in his work.

A cartoon of an English soldier raised for service in Ireland in the 1640s

Exercise 31.2

Read **Section B**, and **Sources 31a** and **31b**. Then answer the questions **a** to **f** in sentences, and question **g** in a paragraph.

a Who wrote **Source 31a**, and what was he doing in Ireland?

b Who did the author of **Source 31a** mean by 'barbarians who spilt so much innocent blood'? (Look at the first paragraph of **Section B**.)

c What did he mean by 'it will save lives in the future'? (Look at the fourth paragraph of **Section B**.)

d Who wrote **Source 31b**, and when? What was the author's connection with Ireland?

e On what important point do **Sources 31a** and **31b** disagree?

f What do you think the words 'Cromwell's name was branded on the memory of the Irish' (**Source 31b**) mean?

g Why do you think that **Sources 31a** and **31b** say different things about Cromwell in Ireland? (Look back to the note 'The sources do not all say the same' in Chapter 27.)

C **Wild geese and penal laws**

A few Irish Catholics got their land back when Charles II was restored in 1660. But the main hope of the Irish was the Catholic **James II**, who became king in 1685. Catholics got jobs as mayors, judges, and officers in the army. James' governor of Ireland was a Catholic. There was even talk of giving Catholics back their land.

Then came the revolution of 1688. (See Chapter 28.) James II fled from England, but he tried to make a comeback through Ireland. He got help from the French, landed at Kinsale in 1689, and soon nearly all of Ireland was in his hands.

Protestant **Londonderry** held out

against him, though. Then, in 1690, **William of Orange** himself came to Ireland, and beat James in the **Battle of the Boyne**. James fled again, and the 'wild geese' followed. These were Catholics who had fought for James, and now left Ireland for good. Many of them later served in the armies of the king of France.

After 1690 came the Protestant '**Ascendancy**'. This was the time when the Protestants were in control, and showed that they meant to stay there. They passed a string of acts (called the '**penal laws**') which kept Catholics out of all the top jobs. They said that Catholics could not buy land, or keep weapons, or vote in elections. Catholic priests were allowed, but not bishops, and there were to be no Catholic schools.

Now try Exercises 31.3, 31.4, and 31.5.

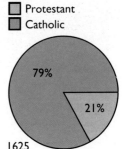

Who owned the land in Ireland, 1625–1750?

◻ Protestant
◻ Catholic

79%
21%
1625

59%
41%
1641

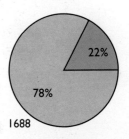

22%
78%
1688

A modern Protestant wall painting of William of Orange

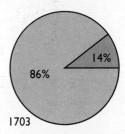

14%
86%
1703

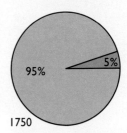

95%
5%
1750

In 1600, more than 90% of the population of Ireland was Catholic

In 1750, about 75% of the population of Ireland was Catholic

James II appointed the Catholic Earl of Tyrconnell as his governor of Ireland. The Protestant playing-card calls him a 'knave'.

Exercise 31.3

Read **Section C**.

a Make rough notes of your own, listing all the Catholics' grievances (things they would have grumbled about) in Ireland in 1750.
b Discuss your list with other pupils in a group. See if you have missed any grievances that they have noticed.
c Make a group wall-display, with pieces of written work, drawings, and cartoons.

Exercise 31.4

Look at the charts which show who owned the land in Ireland between 1625 and 1750.

a Draw a graph, showing how much of the land in Ireland was owned by Catholics between 1625 and 1750.
b Write at least one sentence saying what the charts and your graph tell you.
c Try to find at least three facts in Chapter 31 explaining why the amount of land owned by Catholics changed. (Write three sentences.)

Source 31c

A stranger would not think that Ireland had fertile soil and a mild climate. He would see families living in filth on butter-milk and potatoes. He would see people without shoes or stockings on their feet, living in houses that are worse than English pig-styes. But this would not trouble him. He only comes for a short time, then goes back to England. And it is to England that all of Ireland's wealth is sent.

(This was written in 1727 by Jonathan Swift, who lived for many years in Ireland.)

Source 31d

An Irish peasant's cabin in the eighteenth century

Source 31e

Bantry House, County Cork – an eighteenth-century country house in Ireland

Exercise 31.5

Read **Source 31c**, and study **Sources 31d**, and **31e**.
Copy the sentences below and write TRUE or FALSE after each of them.

a The author of **Source 31c** lived in Ireland. _____

b The author of **Source 31c** knew how Irish peasants lived.

   _____

c Everyone in Ireland probably lived in the way described in **Source 31c**. _____

d **Source 31c** does not say why Irish peasants were poor.

   _____

e **Source 31d** is a photograph of Irish peasants.

   _____

f **Sources 31c** and **31d** tell us the same kind of thing about Irish peasants. _____

g We should believe what **Sources 31c** and **31d** tell us.

   _____

h **Source 31e** shows a rich man's house, built in Ireland in the eighteenth century. _____

i **Source 31e** proves that some people in Ireland had a lot of money. _____

j **Source 31e** proves that **Sources 31c** and **31d** are wrong.

   _____

32 Trade and Colonies, 1500-1750

Merchant ships trading in the East in the seventeenth century

A The East India Company

In 1500, **England** was a small country that did not count for much. By 1750, **Britain** (made up of England, Scotland, Wales, and Ireland) was a **great power** – one of Europe's leading states. This change took place because Britain grew rich from **trade**.

In the time of the Tudors, England's main trade was selling woollen cloth to Antwerp in the Low Countries (now Belgium). But the Low Countries belonged to the king of Spain. And when Queen Elizabeth I fell out with King Philip of Spain, he banned the English from Antwerp.

The merchants searched for new markets. Some sailed to Russia, and others to Turkey. In 1600, trade began with India. A group of London mer-chants started the **East India Company**. Their money paid for the ships and the crews. It was their gold and silver which the ships carried on the outward journey. They paid for the trading stations which Indian rulers allowed them to set up in certain ports. (Look at the Map on pages 164–165.)

The risks were great – many a ship was lost in a storm or taken by pirates. Sometimes there was a fight at sea with the French or Dutch. But when a ship did come home, laden with Indian silks and cottons (and later China tea), the merchants got the profits. A successful voyage would pay their costs five times over.

Now try Exercise 32.1.

Exercise 32.1

Read **Section A** and study the Map.
Then copy the questions and write your answers in the spaces.

a What did English merchants sell in Antwerp?

_____

b Who banned English merchants from Antwerp?

_____

c When was the East India Company set up?

_____

d What did English ships carry to India?

_____

e What did English ships bring back from India?

_____

f How much profit might a successful merchant make?

_____

g Ships going to India had to sail in which two oceans?

_____

h Name two places where the East India Company had trading stations.

_____

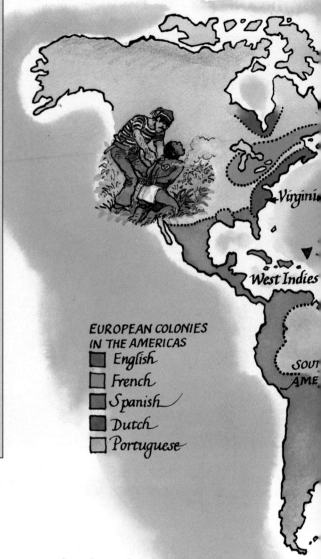

EUROPEAN COLONIES
IN THE AMERICAS
■ English
□ French
■ Spanish
■ Dutch
□ Portuguese

Virginia

West Indies

SOUT
AME

B Colonies in America

The Spanish were the first to explore America. It was not long, though, before the English followed. Some went as pirates, and some as traders. But some set out to found **colonies**. (A colony is a group of people who make new lives in a far-off part of the world.)

Rich men **invested** in colonies. They put up money for the ships and supplies. They hoped to make profits from the clothes, nails, guns, etc. which they would ship to America for the settlers to buy. And more profits would come from the goods the settlers sent home for sale.

The settlers risked shipwreck, disease, famine, and attacks by the native

A Puritan settler in America

people whose land they were taking. But land was cheap in the colonies, or even free, so most settlers soon had farms of their own. Some people hoped to find gold or adventure. Many Puritans went to America for freedom to worship as they wished. But some settlers had no choice – seven years' hard labour in the colonies was the punishment for quite small crimes.

The first English colony was founded in **Virginia** in 1607. (Look at the Map.) The first Puritans came to **New England**, further north, soon after. As more settlers arrived the colonies spread and new ones were started. In 1664 the English took over a

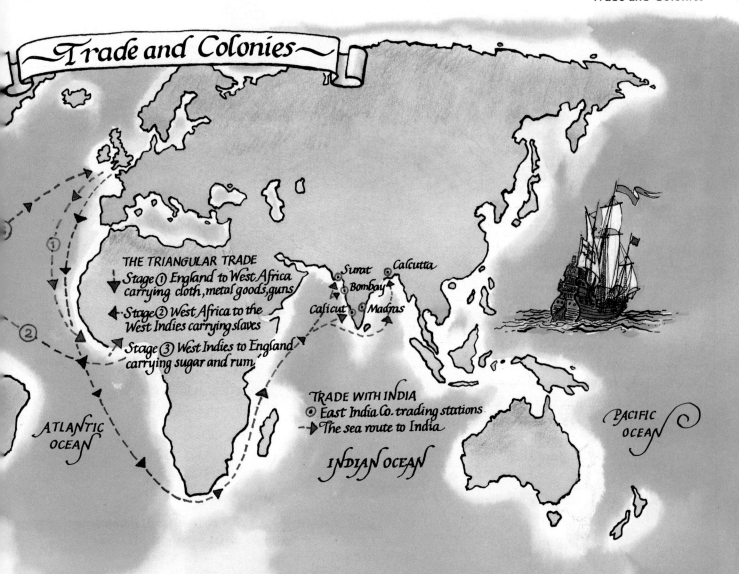

Trade and Colonies

THE TRIANGULAR TRADE
➤ Stage ① England to West Africa
  carrying cloth, metal goods, guns
➤ Stage ② West Africa to the
  West Indies carrying slaves
➤ Stage ③ West Indies to England
  carrying sugar and rum.

TRADE WITH INDIA
⊙ East India Co. trading stations
➤ The sea route to India

ATLANTIC OCEAN

PACIFIC OCEAN

INDIAN OCEAN

Surat   Calcutta
Bombay
Calicut   Madras

Dutch colony and named it **New York**. By 1750, the British controlled most of North America's east coast.

In New England and New York, the settlers were farmers and fishermen. In Virginia, they learned to grow **tobacco**. (Smoking was a new habit in Europe, and tobacco was much in demand.) Rich 'planters' came over from England and bought up big estates. Convicts and, after 1700, black slaves, worked the land for them. The planters made fortunes. So did the merchants of Bristol and Glasgow who shipped and cured the tobacco.

Now try Exercise 32.2.

Exercise 32.2

Read **Section B**.
What were the **motives** of **i** the men who invested in colonies, and **ii** the settlers who went to live in the colonies? Read the list of suggestions below, then make two lists of motives – investors and settlers.

a To help poor people find a better life.
b To find gold and make their fortunes.
c To make money by selling things to the settlers.
d To find a place where they did not have to work hard for a living.
e To set up their own farms.
f To make money by selling what the settlers produced (e.g. tobacco).
g To find a more healthy place to live.
h To be able to worship in their own way.
i To do something different and exciting.

C Sugar and slaves

Silk, cotton, and tobacco were important for the growth of English trade, but not as important as **sugar**. Between 1600 and 1750 people began to eat much more sugar with their food. The sugar came from the West Indies, where the cane grew in 'plantations'. (Look at the Map on pages 164–165.)

Ships laden with sugar (and rum) sailed from Barbados to Bristol and Liverpool. Factories there refined it (made it pure). Then it was sold to merchants in English towns and cities, or abroad.

The owners of the plantations were rich English landlords. Many of them stayed at home, and lived on their profits. They had agents in the islands to manage their estates. The hard work of cutting and carting the cane and milling the sugar was done by black slaves.

The slaves came from West Africa. A lot of them were prisoners, captured in wars between tribes. Their captors sold them to white slave-traders, or exchanged them for cloth, metal goods, or guns from Europe. The traders branded them with their marks, and packed them into ships. The voyage to the West Indies took about eight weeks. A quarter of the slaves died at sea.

The slaves were sold in the West Indies to the planters' agents. There was always a brisk trade, for slaves lasted only a few years in the cane fields. Meanwhile, the ships were loaded with sugar and rum, and set sail for home. (Look at the Map again.) The trade made the merchants and planters rich. Most of them never saw the inside of a slave ship.

Now try Exercise 32.3.

Source 32a

A slave being branded

Source 32b

We brand the slaves on the chest with a hot iron. We do it so that we will know which ones are ours. It may seem cruel, but we try not to burn them too hard. We pack them on board – often six or seven hundred on a ship. The captains do it very cleverly, and much better than the French and English. Their slave ships are foul and stinking, but ours are clean and neat.

Written by a Dutch slave trader in West Africa in 1705.

Exercise 32.3

Look at **Source 32a** and read **Source 32b**.
Write notes on the sources:

a Who can you see in **Source 32a**?
b What examples of cruelty to slaves are mentioned in **Source 32b**?
c What excuses does the author of **Source 32b** give for the slave-traders' cruelty?

33 Daily Life, 1500-1750

How a family lived depended on **who** they were. The courtiers set the fashions in clothes, food, and homes. The gentry and rich merchants copied what they could afford. The farmers and craftsmen came next, and last came the labouring poor. Fashion, of course, meant nothing to the poor – their concern was just to stay alive. (See Chapter 34.)

Source 33a

First course: A boiled pike or a stewed carp. A boiled pudding. A chine of veal and a chine of mutton. A calf's head pie. A roasted leg of mutton. A couple of large chickens, or a pig, or a piece of roast beef. A salad.

Second course: A dish of fat roasted chickens. A cold venison pasty. A dish of fried pasties. A fresh salmon. A couple of lobsters. A dish of tarts. A gammon of bacon. After this, serve cheese and fruit.

From a book of recipes written by Hannah Woolley in 1684.

A Food

In the time of the Tudors, most English people ate only two meals a day. They had dinner between eleven in the morning and twelve noon, and supper between five and eight o'clock in the evening. By 1750, nobles and gentry were dining at between two and three in the afternoon. To keep them going until then, they ate **breakfast** (tea and bread and butter) in the morning.

The nobles ate a great deal of meat. As well as beef, mutton, and pork, they were fond of rabbits, deer, and swans. And those who could afford it had sauces made from spices and herbs to go with the meat. They were fond of fish and shell-fish as well, and liked lots of tarts and puddings. But they were not so keen on vegetables.

In the sixteenth century, the law **forced** people to eat fish on two days each week. The reason was to strengthen the navy! By making people eat fish, the king made sure that there would be plenty of fishermen. And in time of war the fishermen were the crews of the ships in the navy.

A rich man's banquet consisted of three or more 'courses'. And a course meant a table filled with dishes. (See **Source 33a**.) At the end of the meal, what was left was taken out for the servants. What they did not eat was given to the poor.

Now try Exercise 33.1.

Source 33b

For broths of sundry tastes and sort,
For beef, veal, mutton, lamb, and pork,
Green sauce with calf's head and bacon,
Pig and goose, and crammed-up capon,

For pasties raised stiff with curious art,
Pie, custard, florentine, and tart ...
Thanks be given for flesh and fishes,
With this choice of tempting dishes.

From a made-up story told in a long poem written by Thomas Dekker in 1612.

Exercise 33.1

Read **Section A** and **Sources 33a** and **33b**.
Put the correct halves of the sentences together, and write out the complete sentences.

a **Source 33a** was written ...
b **Source 33b** was written ...
c **Source 33b** is part of a longer poem and is ...
d **Source 33a** is ...
e Both sources tell us that well-off people ate a lot of ...
f The sources show that people were not so keen on ...
g The fiction source tells us the same kind of thing ...

- vegetables and salads.
- a made-up story, or fiction.
- as the fact source about seventeenth-century food.
- by Thomas Dekker in 1612.
- from a real recipe book and is fact.
- by Hannah Woolley in 1684.
- meat, pies, pasties, and tarts.

B Clothes

Tudor courtiers were great show-offs, above all in their dress. Men and women liked fine materials and bright colours. They were fond of gold and silver thread stitched into fancy patterns. Both sexes wore garments edged with lace or fur. Everyone had lots of rings and bracelets.

Ladies' gowns had full skirts, slashed open at the front to reveal **farthingales** (hooped petticoats in fine lace). The men wore **doublets** (long tunics) and hose. Both men and women wore starched lace ruffs round their necks. (see **Source 33c**.)

After 1600, all men began wearing breeches instead of doublet and hose. At the time of the Civil War, how they dressed depended on which side they took. Roundheads wore plain, dark clothes. Cavaliers dressed brightly, with lots of lace and ribbon. Under the Commonwealth, England's rulers all dressed in Roundhead style. When Charles II was restored, the bright colours and ribbons made a come-back.

By the 1690s, ladies' gowns had full skirts, tight bodices, and low necklines. Ladies wore lots of make-up – paint, rouge, and beauty patches. Wigs, with long, curly ringlets (called 'periwigs') were the fashion for men. They were so heavy and hot that most men shaved their heads.

Now try Exercise 33.2.

Source 33c

Sir Thomas More and family in the sixteenth century

Source 33d

Lord Buckingham and family in the seventeenth century

Source 33e

The Shudi family in the eighteenth century

Ordinary people's clothing in the eighteenth century

C Education

Children were not forced by law to go to school in Tudor and Stuart times. If they did attend, in most cases, the parents had to pay fees. In spite of this, by 1700 most children in towns got some schooling.

The sons and daughters of great lords had private tutors. As part of their studies, the sons spent from three to five years with their tutors on a 'Grand Tour' abroad. They learned to speak French, looked at works of art and buildings, and studied the laws of the countries of Europe.

The gentry and merchants sent their sons to the **grammar schools**. This is where they learned to read, write, and speak **Latin**. Latin was still the language of scholars in the universities. And it was to Oxford or Cambridge that the young gentry went after grammar school. After that, they stud-

ied the law for a few years at the **Inns of Court** in London.

Girls were expected to marry at an early age. So the daughters of the gentry stayed at home. They were taught to read and write, and to sew and manage a home by their mothers. Neither their fathers nor their mothers wanted to waste money on education.

Parish schools and, by 1700, charity schools were for the sons and daughters of craftsmen and labourers. They were better than nothing, but only just. The children learned to read and write, and to do simple sums. A lot of time was spent on scripture. But the teachers were untrained and badly paid, and there were not many books or much equipment. As a rule, the pupils left school to start work when they were ten or eleven years old.

Now try Exercise 33.3.

Village schools in the sixteenth and eighteenth centuries

Source 33f

I could read when I was four years old. By the time I was seven, my father employed eight tutors – for languages, music, dancing, writing, and needlework. Father started me on Latin, and I made good progress. I was soon ahead of my brothers, even though my Latin tutor was a dull fellow.

I always liked my books best. My mother said that all the reading and study would harm my health. And she was not pleased when I would not practise my music and dancing. As for needlework, I hated it.

Written by Mrs. Lucy Hutchinson in about 1657.

Exercise 33.3

Read **Section C** and **Source 33f**. Answers the questions in sentences.

a Which facts can you find in **Source 33f**? (Write down four facts.)
b What was Lucy proud of?
c What did Lucy dislike?
d What did Lucy's father think about education for girls?
e What did Lucy's mother think about her daughter's education?
f What did Lucy think of her Latin tutor?

D Health

Between 1650 and 1750, more people moved to the towns, and the nation's health got worse. All towns were unhealthy – none of them had proper sewers or pure drinking water. Overcrowding helped disease to spread. And after 1700 cheap **gin** ruined the health of the poor.

Disease led quickly to death. A lot of children died young, and many women died in childbirth. People were saddened, but not surprised, by the sudden loss of a loved one. Most of them said that it was God's will that

the person should die – there was nothing that they could do about it.

Only those who could pay the fees could call in doctors. This was not such a bad thing for the poor, for doctors were not much use. They helped by giving good advice, such as not to eat or drink too much. But they also did harm – they still **bled** patients suffering from fever.

Each family had its recipes for cures, kept with the recipes for pickles and jam. Some contained good sense, but many were useless or worse. For example, 'to cure baldness, rub your head with garlic and wash it in vinegar.' In every market-place there was a man selling 'miracle' cures, and plenty of foolish buyers.

In one sense, though, the nation's health improved. The changes in farming (see Chapter 19) meant that there was more **fresh** meat – at least for those who could afford it.

Now try Exercises 33.4 and 33.5.

Source 33g

A brass memorial in Durnford Church, Wiltshire. The inscription says:
Here lyeth the body of Edward Young of Little Dorneford Esq:, sonne & heyre (son & heir) of John Young Esq: & of Mary his wife, one of ye fower (four) daughters & Coheyres (co-heirs) of Thom. Trapnell of Mounceton Farley, Esq:. Which Edw: (This man Edward Younge) married Joan, ye eldest daughter of Laurence Hide of West Hatche, Esq: & had by her 6 sones & 8 daughters, who dyed (i.e. Edward Younge died) Febr: 18, 1607.

Exercise 33.4

Read **Section D**.
Copy the sentences and write TRUE or FALSE after each one.

a Towns were healthier than the countryside. _____
b Gin was cheap between 1700 and 1750, so many poor people drank too much and ruined their health. _____
c Families were large, but many children died young. _____
d Sudden death was a common event and did not surprise people. _____
e Most doctors were glad to work among the poor without payment. _____
f Families kept their own lists of remedies and cures. _____
g No one was fooled by sellers of 'quack' medicines. _____

Exercise 33.5

Study **Source 33g**.

a Make your own notes, answering these questions:
  i What does **Source 33f** tell us about Edward Young and his family?
  ii What makes you think that Edward Young was a rich man?
  iii Did all families put up brass plates in churches? If not, why not?
  iv Are church brasses a useful type of source? What do they tell us? What do they not tell us?
b Discuss your answers to the questions with other pupils in a group.
c Make a group tape, or give brief talks to the rest of the class, giving your group's answers.

34 The Poor, 1500-1750

A Living conditions of the poor

About half the people in England were poor. They seldom had enough to eat, and sometimes starved. Their clothes were second-hand, and a lot of poor children had no shoes. In the villages, their homes were simple shacks, with clay or wooden walls, thatched roofs, and no glass in the windows. They had no chimneys, just a hole in the roof. A chest, a bench, and a trestle table would be their only furniture.

The poor in the countryside were farm labourers and their families. The men's wages were low, and their wives helped out by making cheese and spinning wool. As soon as they were able, children had to work. The girls helped their mothers at home, and the boys earned a few pence minding sheep or scaring birds from the fields.

Even so, farm workers were well off in some respects. They had gardens, where they grew cabbages, peas, and beans. And they could keep a cow and some sheep on the common. So they had butter, cheese and wool to sell. They needed the money to pay the rent and buy their bread.

But when common land was enclosed (see Chapter 19), the poor suffered. The land was carved up into fields, and there was nowhere for their animals to graze. As a result, they had nothing to sell, and became even poorer.

Labourers in towns had to buy all their food. Their wages were poor, if they could get jobs at all. They lived in crowded, dirty hovels. In parts of London the poor were crammed fifteen or twenty to a room. And there were some with no homes at all.

Now try Exercise 34.1.

A farm labourer's cottage

Source 34a

Only rich men can afford to eat a joint of fresh meat once a month. The poor have to sell their young pigs and chickens to pay the rent. They cannot afford to eat the eggs their hens lay, and they must sell the best of their butter and cheese. They make do with skimmed milk and curds.

Written by Richard Baxter in 1691.

Source 34b

Half the people in England eat meat every day. A quarter eat meat twice a week. The rest, who are the poor, have meat only once a week.

Written by Gregory King in 1696.

'Beer Street' in London – a drawing by the eighteenth-century artist, William Hogarth. He shows us what the London streets looked like, and warns us that he thought the problems of the poor were caused by too much drink.

Exercise 34.1

Read **Section A**, and **Sources 34a** and **34b**.

a Write out these sentences, and write TRUE or FALSE after each of them.

  i **Sources 34a** and **34b** were written in the same century.

  ii **Sources 34a** and **34b** were written by the same person.

  iii Both sources say that the rich ate a lot of meat.

  iv **Source 34b** says that even the poor ate meat once a week.

  v **Source 34a** says that the poor could not afford to eat fresh meat.

  vi **Source 34a** explains why poor people could not afford fresh meat.

b Can you think of any possible reasons why **Sources 34a** and **34b** say different things about poor people's food? (Write a short paragraph.)

BEER STREET.

Beer, happy Produce of our Isle / Can sinewy strength impart, / And wearied with Fatigue and Toil / Can chear each manly Heart. | *Labour and Art upheld by Thee / Successfully advance, / We quaff thy balmy Juice with Glee / And Water leave to France.* | *Genius of Health, thy grateful Taste / Rivals the Cup of Jove, / And warms each English generous Breast / With Liberty and Love.*

B Prices and wages

England's population increased from just over two million in 1500 to five million in 1650. (Look at Graph A.) The farmers grew more wheat, rye, and barley, but not as much as the people needed. So there was a shortage of bread, and the price rose. All the other prices followed.

Graph B shows how prices rose. It tells you that a 'basket' with so much bread, a piece of cloth, a pair of shoes, some candles, and a few other items would have cost £1 in 1505. It says that to buy exactly the same 'basket' of goods you would have had to pay £6.82 in 1645.

Wages also rose, but they did not go up as much as prices. Poor peasants, who could not afford to buy bread for their children, left their villages. They drifted to the towns, but soon found that life there was worse than in the villages they had left. In every town, gangs of men, women, and children begged in the streets.

Things got slightly better after 1650, when prices stopped rising. After 1700 they even fell a little. Wages did not fall, so men who were in work were better off. But the numbers of the poor did not fall much. And when there was a bad harvest, the price of bread shot up again.

Now try Exercise 34.2.

Exercise 34.2

Study **Graph A** and **Graph B**. Copy the questions and fill in the spaces as you go.

a What was England's population in 1500? _____

b What was the population in 1600?

_____

c By how much did the population increase between 1600 and 1700?

_____

d There were two periods when the population was not increasing. Which was the longer of these periods? From _____ to

_____

e What did the 'basket' of goods cost in 1505? _____

f When did the cost of the 'basket' reach £2. About _____

g What did the 'basket' cost in 1600?

_____

h By how much did the cost of the 'basket' fall between 1645 and 1685? About _____ pence.

i What did the 'basket' cost in 1745?

_____

j Why did prices rise when the population was rising? (See paragraph 1 of **Section B**.)

_____

Graph A: The population of England, 1500–1750

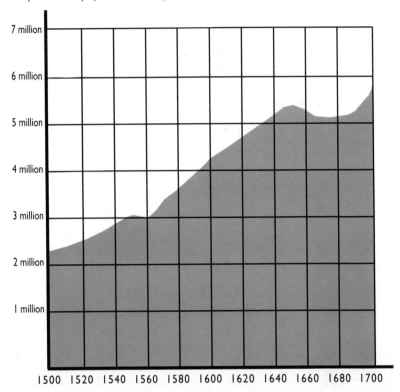

Graph B: Prices 1505–1745

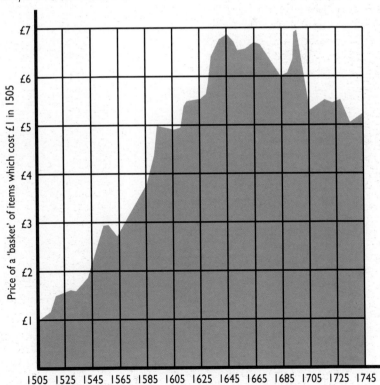

C The poor law

In the sixteenth century, there was no unemployment pay and no child benefit. There were no old age pensions and no National Health Service. Instead, each town had 'almshouses' and 'hospitals' to look after the old and sick. Rich merchants often left money to almshouses in their wills.

After 1550 there were so many poor that the almshouses could not cope. The bands of beggars worried the Government. It got Parliament to pass laws, partly to help the poor, and partly to force them to work.

The new laws said that those who could afford it should pay a tax to help the 'deserving poor'. This meant the old, the disabled, and the sick who could not work. But the Government said that healthy young men and women who had no jobs must be lazy. It called them 'vagabonds', and said that they had to be punished. Some were whipped, some were branded with red-hot irons, and some were put in the stocks.

People agreed that the poor could not be left to starve. But no-one liked paying taxes to help care for them. In the eighteenth century, some parishes built 'workhouses'. These were homes and work-places for the poor. To scare off the 'scroungers', they made the workhouses as unpleasant as they could.

Now try Exercises 34.3, 34.4, and 34.5.

Exercise 34.3

Read **Section C**.
Draw a time-line from 1450 to 1750. Mark the fifteenth, sixteenth, seventeenth, and eighteenth centuries. Write these sentences in the correct places on the time-line.

a In 1723 Parliament allowed parishes to combine to build workhouses.

b A law passed in 1572 said that all who could afford it had to pay a local tax to help the poor.

c In 1662 magistrates got the power to send strangers back to their own parishes if they looked as if they would need poor relief.

d An act passed in 1536 said that each parish had to have a fund of money to help to look after the poor.

e A law passed in 1597 ordered parishes to find work for the unemployed.

f In 1496 sheriffs and mayors were ordered to put vagabonds in the stocks for three days and nights.

Source 34c

A vagabond is whipped through the streets

Source 34d

A gentleman and a beggar

Exercise 34.4

Study **Sources 34c**, and **34d**.
Write a short essay, with the title 'How the artists saw the beggars'.
Use these notes as a guide:

a Describe what you can see in the pictures. – How are the beggars dressed? What are they doing, or what is happening to them?
b What do you think the artists thought about the beggars? Were they sorry for them? Did they think the beggars were layabouts? Did both the artists think the same?

Source 34f

The poor are lucky – they have a more godly life than the rich. They have no luxuries, and luxury just makes men proud. They have to work hard, so they are not tempted to be lazy. They can not afford to eat and drink too much, so they are healthy in body and mind. They know what it is like to go hungry, so they are kind to neighbours who fall on hard times. And they get very little happiness on earth, so they think a lot about Heaven.

Written by Robert Nelson in 1715.

Source 34g

There has to be poverty. If there were no poor, who would take orders from the rich? Who would do the humble and dirty jobs? Who would work the land? Who would do the tradesmen's labouring jobs? Without the poor, we should all go short, instead of just a few starving now and then.

Written by Soame Jenyns in 1761.

Source 34e

Labourers' children have to be kept by the parish. The more children a poor man has, the more money he gets from the parish. The allowance is paid to the father. He often spends it in the public house, and his children do not get enough to eat.

Written by John Locke in the 1690s.

Exercise 34.5

Read **Sources 34e, 34f**, and **34g**.
Then answer the questions in sentences.

a These sources tell us what some people thought about the poor in the seventeenth and eighteenth centuries. Are they primary or secondary sources?
b What does John Locke (**Source 34e**) say that makes you think that he had a low opinion of labouring men?
c Robert Nelson (**Source 34f**) thought that the poor were lucky. How many reasons did he give for this opinion?
d Do you think that Robert Nelson was a poor man? If he had been poor, would he have agreed that he was lucky?
e Soame Jenyns (**Source 34g**) thought that poverty was necessary. How many reasons did he give for his opinion?
f Do you think that Soame Jenyns was poor? (Give your reasons.)
g Why do you think that there are not many sources giving **poor people's** opinions?

35 Science and Superstition, 1500-1750

A Observation and experiment

The most important change that took place between 1600 and 1750 was the start of modern **science**. Before 1600, science was something you read in books. And the books had been written by **ancient Greeks**. After 1600, scientists began to believe what they saw with their own eyes.

In the Middle Ages, science and magic were not far apart. **Alchemists** tried to turn lead into gold. **Astrologers** told the future by looking at the stars. After the end of the Middle Ages (about the year 1500), there was still a lot of **superstition**. In 1700, educated

men still believed in lucky charms. And most common folk were still scared of witches.

Science began to change soon after 1600. **Sir Francis Bacon** said that a scientist's first task was **observation**. Bacon meant that he should look at things and describe what he saw (not what the books said he should see). In some cases, he had to do **experiments**, and write down the results.

To work this way, scientists needed new instruments. Between 1600 and 1750, they invented a lot of things that

Science in the sixteenth century – An alchemist's laboratory

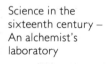

we now take for granted. First was the **telescope**, to look at the stars and the planets. Next came the **microscope**, to look at things too small for the human eye. Then, after long research, they made a **thermometer** that really worked.

All the leading men of the time became keen on science. In London, Thomas Gresham founded a college, which took his name. Its members met each week to listen to lectures and hear the latest news. In 1662, King Charles II gave the college his support, and it became the **Royal Society**. All the top scientists belonged to it, as they still do today.

Now try Exercises 35.1 and 35.2.

Source 35a

> *20th January 1665. Mr. Batten tells me that he has never had colic pain since he started to carry a hare's foot about with him. I bought a hare today and took it home. As soon as I touched its foot my pain went away.*
> *26th March 1665. I have never had the colic pain since I started wearing the hare's foot. On the other hand, it may be the turpentine pill I take each morning. Or it may be the two together.*

From Samuel Pepys's diary. Pepys went to Cambridge University, and became a Fellow of the Royal Society. He was one of the best-educated men of his day.

Exercise 35.1

Read **Section A**. Then write sentences to show that you know what these words mean.

scientists alchemist astrologer superstition observation experiment telescope microscope thermometer Royal Society

Exercise 35.2

Read **Source 35a**, and look again at what **Section A** says about superstition. Make your own notes to answer these questions:

a Is **Source 35a** a primary source?
b Who was the author of **Source 35a**? What do we know about him?
c What does **Source 35a** say to make us think that educated people in the 1660s were superstitious?
d Scientists are supposed to make up their minds after **observing** the facts. Which facts did Pepys observe? Did he make up his mind about the hare's foot?
e Most people were far less educated than Pepys. How superstitious do you think they were?

B Some great scientists

Robert Boyle was one man who took Bacon's advice to observe and record. In his laboratory in Oxford he did hundreds of experiments. He invented an air-pump, to pump air out of a vessel, and so make a **vacuum**. This made him think that air could be weighed. He went on to attack the Greek idea that there were just four **elements** – earth, water, air, and fire. In his day, men said he was wrong, but we know he was right.

Thanks to **William Harvey**, the science of **medicine** made a big leap forward. In a book which he wrote in 1628, Harvey said that blood moved round the body. He said that it flowed out from the heart through the arteries, and back through the veins. This was the idea of the **circulation of the blood**. Like Boyle, Harvey was not believed at first.

Sir Isaac Newton was the greatest scientist of his age. He was **not** the first man to say that the earth revolved round the sun. And he did **not** discover gravity. But he worked out laws to show how these things happened. And he showed that **mathematics** was at the heart of all **physics**. The men and women of his time did recognize Newton as a great man. His work made them think that science would soon solve all problems.

Now try Exercises 35.3 and 35.4.

Boyle's air pump, which he used to make a vacuum

William Harvey demonstrating his ideas to Charles I

Sir Isaac Newton as shown on a 1980s pound note

Exercise 35.3

Read **Section B**. Copy the questions and fill in the spaces using words from the list below.

telescope mathematics circulation veins Oxford sun space air-pump gravity Cambridge medicine chemistry fire moon arteries physics

a Where was Robert Boyle's laboratory?

_____

b What did Boyle invent to make a vacuum?

_____

c The ancient Greeks believed in four elements, which were water, earth, air, and what? _____

d Harvey did a great deal for which branch of science?

_____

e Which word used by Harvey means that the blood goes round and round the body? _____

f Harvey said that the blood flows out from the heart through what? _____

g Newton knew that the earth revolved around what?

_____

h Newton knew that what caused objects to fall?

_____

i Newton showed that you could use what to explain the laws of physics? _____

Source 35b

I began to think that the blood must go round in a circle. Later, I proved that it is true. I saw that the blood is driven out of the heart, through the arteries, into the lungs and other parts of the body. It returns through the veins to the heart. So it goes on in an endless motion, with the heart acting as a pump.

Written by William Harvey in 1628.

The Royal Observatory at Greenwich

Source 35c

I have heard Harvey say that when his book on the circulation of the blood came out he lost a lot of patients. The public thought that he was crack-brained. All the doctors were against him. Many of them wrote books attacking him. But 20 or 30 years later, all the world's universities thought that he was right. Soon, everyone else thought the same.

Written by John Aubrey, who lived from 1626 to 1697.

Exercise 35.4

Read **Sources 35b and 35c**. Then write two paragraphs in your own words:

a What were Harvey's ideas about these things?
  i How the blood moves round the body,
  ii What the arteries do,
  iii What the veins do,
  iv What the heart does.
b What did Harvey's patients, the public, and other doctors think about Harvey's theory,
  i at first, and
  ii twenty to thirty years later?

C Witches

Witches being hanged

Most men and women knew nothing of science. To them, the world was full of spirits and **witches**. Witches (nearly always women) were supposed to have sold their souls to the devil. In return, he had given them magic powers. They could cast spells and give people the 'evil eye'. If they did so, their victims would be taken ill, or die, or be hit by bad luck.

Witches, so they said, lived alone, apart from a spirit that helped them in their work. This often took the form of a pet, such as a cat. So village people kept clear of old women who lived alone with their cats. They hung horse-shoes and bunches of herbs over their own cottage doors to protect them from the witches' powers.

Not only the ignorant and poor believed in witches. In 1542, the gentry, merchants, and lords in Parliament made witchcraft a crime. The law stayed in force until 1736. In that time, a few hundred women, most of them old, were hanged. (Witches were not burned in England.)

A simple chain of events could bring a 'witch' to trial. An old woman would come begging at a farmhouse door. The busy farmer's wife would send her off with nothing. Shortly after, the farmer would fall ill and die. His wife would remember the old woman, and accuse her of being a witch. The old woman would be arrested and tortured. Under torture, she would 'confess' that she was a witch.

In the late seventeenth century, educated people stopped believing in witches. Poor old women were still brought to court, but judges refused to find them guilty. The last hanging for witchcraft in England took place at Exeter in 1685. The common folk, of course, went on believing in witches many years after witchcraft ceased to be a crime.

Now try Exercise 35.5.

Source 35d

David Seaton had a maid called Jill Duncan. This Jill often helped the sick, and many of her cures were so quick that they looked like miracles. Her master was surprised by her skill. Then he became suspicious. He began to think that Jill might be a witch.

When David asked Jill how she did these things, she made no answer. So he tried torture to make her talk. He crushed her fingers, then bound her head tightly with a rope. In the end, she confessed that she was a witch. She said that she worked with the devil, and that she was planning to make the king ill with her magic.

From a report of a witch trial in Scotland in 1591.

Exercise 35.5

Read **Section C** and **Source 35d**. Discuss the questions in a group. Then do one of these: **i** Write down your answers, **ii** Make a group tape.

a Which things in **Source 35d** are probably true?

b Which things in **Source 35d** could not be true?

c What makes you think that David Seaton believed in witchcraft?

d Do you think that Jill Duncan believed in witchcraft?

e Do you think that, in the end, Jill believed that she was a witch?

f Does the author of **Source 35d** say whether he believed in witches? Do you think that he believed in witches?

36 Architecture, Art and the Theatre, 1500-1750

Source 36a

Source 36b

Two views of Chipchase Castle in Northumberland, close to the Scottish border. **Source 36a** shows the part built in the fourteenth century, when there were regular border wars. **Source 36b** shows the part built in 1621, when there was peace on the border.

A Country houses

You can read the history of England in the buildings of the past. In the Middle Ages, a great deal of the nation's wealth was in the hands of the Church. The finest buildings at the time were the **cathedrals** and **abbeys**. Also, the kings and lords were often at war, so they built massive **castles**, with high, thick walls and small windows.

After the **Reformation**, in the time of the Tudors, the Church lost a lot of its wealth. Its land passed into the hands of the gentry and nobles. Now they were the ones who built in style. Also, apart from the 1640s, civil wars came to an end. Peace came even to the borders of Scotland and Wales. So the gentry and lords built **country houses**, not castles.

Houses varied in size, depending on how rich the owners were. But most of them had big windows, grand door-ways, and high, stylish chimneys. At first, the great hall was the main room in the house. Later, separate dining rooms and drawing rooms were built. Upstairs, most of them had a **long gallery**, where the lord and lady took exercise in bad weather.

The main rooms in the best houses had ornate plaster ceilings, and chimney pieces in carved wood or stone. Tapestries or oak panelling covered the walls. Later, the fashion changed to hanging paintings on the walls. Often,

Source 36c

Burghley House. A country house built in the reign of Queen Elizabeth I.

Source 36d

Belton House in Lincolnshire, built in the eighteenth century

these were portraits of the lord and his family.

Buildings tell the story of the growth of **trade** as well. (See Chapter 32.) Merchants, as they grew richer, built bigger, finer houses in the towns. Then many of them bought land, built country houses, and moved out to their new estates.

Now try Exercises 36.1 and 36.2.

Source 36e

A rich merchant's house in Coggeshall

Exercise 36.1

Read **Section A**, and look at **Sources 36a, 36b, 36c, 36d**, and **36e**.

a How did the nobles, gentry, and merchants become rich enough to build fine country houses? Why did they build houses, and not castles?
Copy the chart below and fill in the spaces.

Cause	Result
1. _____ _____ _____	Nobles and gentry got land that had belonged to the Church. They became richer, and built country houses.
2. No more civil wars (apart from the 1640s) in England. Peace also on the Scottish and Welsh borders.	_____ _____
3. Trade grew, so merchants became richer.	i _____ _____ ii _____ _____

b Draw a picture of a country house.

Source 36f

A sixteenth-century room with furniture at Moseley Old Hall, Staffordshire

Source 36g

An eighteenth-century room with furniture at Saltram in Devon

Source 36h

Anne of Cleves (Henry VIII's fourth wife) by Hans Holbein

B Painting and sculpture

Artists in the Middle Ages worked for the Church. They painted pictures of Jesus and the saints on canvas, or wood, or on church walls. Then, between 1400 and 1500, there came a change. Artists in Italy began painting **portraits** of the people of their time. Their subjects, of course, were the rich – lords and ladies, merchants and their wives.

The new fashion spread to the rest of Europe. Painters from Italy and Germany came to England to paint Henry VIII and his wives. Nobles and gentry copied the king. They too wanted to see themselves and their families on canvas.

All the best painters came from abroad, though. There were not many great English portrait painters before the year 1700. What the English were good at was **miniatures**. These were small portraits that men and women hung in lockets around their necks.

Sculptors, like painters, had worked mainly for the Church. But at the Reformation, stone carvings of saints were removed. In the 1640s and 1650s, the Puritans, who hated ornaments in churches, destroyed still more. But sculpture made a come-back. By 1750 the lords and gentry were filling their houses and gardens with sculptures, most of them from abroad.

Now try Exercise 36.3.

Source 36i

A miniature of Sir Walter Raleigh by Nicholas Hilliard

Source 36j

Source 36k

Above right: A formal garden, with its gravel paths, small flower beds, and clipped shrubs, all in regular patterns. Formal gardens were the fashion in the sixteenth and seventeenth centuries.

Above left: An eighteenth-century *landscaped garden* (at Stourhead in Wiltshire). Here, the trees and plants grew in a much more natural way.

Exercise 36.3

Read **Section B**, and look at **Sources 36h, 36i, 36j, and 36k**. Then write sentences to show that you know what each of these words and phrases mean:

portrait   miniature   sculpture   formal garden
landscaped garden

C The theatre

Source 36l

The Swan Theatre in London in 1596

People in Tudor times made their own amusements, such as music and dancing. But it was a special treat to see a **play**. This was very rare, for outside London there were no theatres. Once in a while, though, a band of **travelling players** arrived in a town and put on a show.

In the 1570s, the first theatres were opened in London. They looked just like inn yards. (Look at **Source 36l**.) Some of the spectators sat in the **galleries** round the sides, overlooking the stage. Rich lords sat on the edge of the stage, and sometimes joined in the play. The 'groundlings' – the poorer folk – stood in the **pit**.

In many ways, the theatres were different from those of today. There were no lights, so the plays were staged in daylight. There were no curtains, and there was very little scenery. The actors wore normal clothes, not special costumes, and **boys** took all the women's parts.

The greatest of the playwrights was **William Shakespeare**. As a young man, he came down to London from Stratford-upon-Avon. He joined a group of actors, started writing plays, and became famous. After his death his plays (more than thirty of them) were printed. They have been read ever since, and acted in theatres all over the world.

Puritans did not like the theatres. When they were in power, in the 1640s, they closed the theatres down. When Charles II was restored, though, they were opened up again. There were some changes – now the theatres had roofs, lights (candles), and curtains. Also, for the first time in England, women took part in the plays.

Now try Exercises 36.4 and 36.5.

Source 36m

Rich young men with nothing to do are always at the theatre. That's where they mix with the tramps, thieves, and tricksters who meet there to plot their crimes. And the plays they see are full of wickedness and cheating. Those who watch are soon persuaded to copy what they see.

Apprentices and servants waste their time at the theatre, neglecting their work. People who should know better go there instead of to church. On top of all that, theatres can make you ill – it's easy to catch an infection in the crowd.

Letter written by a Puritan Lord Mayor of London in 1597.

Source 36n

Going to the theatre does young people no harm. If they don't go they might get up to worse mischief elsewhere. Most of the plays set a good example – they tell about the brave actions of the men of the past. And if you do see cheats and liars on the stage, they always come to a bad end.

Written in 1592 by Thomas Nashe, a writer who hated Puritans.

Exercise 36.4

Look at **Source 36l**, read **Sources 36m** and **36n**, and read **Section C**. Plan and write an essay with the title: 'The theatre in the time of Elizabeth I'. Include paragraphs on:

i What the theatre looked like.
ii The sort of people who went to the theatre.
iii The sort of plays they saw there.
iv Different opinions about the theatre – who was against the theatre, who was in favour of it, and their reasons.

Exercise 36.5

Look at the cartoons and read the notes about Shakespeare's plays. Write out the sentences below. After each sentence, write either TRUE or FALSE.

a Everything in Shakespeare's history plays is true. _____
b Shakespeare sometimes borrowed stories from other authors. _____
c Henry V and Julius Caesar were real people. _____
d *Macbeth* was a tragedy. _____
e The story in *Romeo and Juliet* was true. _____
f *Romeo and Juliet* has a happy ending. _____
g The story in *A Midsummer Night's Dream* is fiction. _____
h Shakespeare made up the story of *The Comedy of Errors* himself. _____

William Shakespeare

William Shakespeare's Plays

Some of Shakespeare's plays were about real people who lived in the past. Shakespeare, of course, made up all of the speeches. But a lot of the facts in his <u>history</u> plays were true.

In other plays Shakespeare made up the whole story, or used a story which he knew was fiction. Some of the plays were <u>tragedies</u> (with sad endings). Others were <u>comedies</u> (with happy endings).

<u>Henry V</u> is about the great soldier-king and his wars in France. Most of the events really happened.

<u>Julius Caesar</u> tells the true story of murder and civil war in ancient Rome.

<u>Romeo and Juliet</u> were young lovers whose families were always at war. The made up story comes to a sad end.

The king of the fairies in <u>A Midsummer Night's Dream</u> quarrels with his wife. He makes her fall in love with a weaver called Bottom, and he gives Bottom an ass's head.

<u>Macbeth</u> is about a Scottish noble who killed the king and took his crown. Macbeth comes to a tragic end. Most of the story is fiction.

The story in <u>The Comedy of Errors</u> comes from an ancient Roman play. It is all about two sets of identical twins.

37 Agriculture, 1750-1870

A Squires and labourers

Britain was still a country of villages and farms in 1750. Far more people worked on the land than in any other trade. The landowners were the leading men. Some of them were great lords, with big estates and country houses. The **squires** (or **gentry**), owned less land than the lords. But the squires (see **Source 37a**) were still the top men in their villages.

Tenant farmers rented land from the lords or squires. Most of them employed **labourers** to work their fields. Some of these workers (the young, unmarried men and women) lived in the farmers' homes and worked full-time. The rest were employed by the farmers only at busy times of the year. They lived with their families in rough cottages, and had a hard life.

In 1750 many villages in England still had three or four **open fields**, divided into strips. Even more still had some **common land**. But open fields and common land were disappearing. **Enclosures** were eating them up, turning them into smaller fields, with hedges or fences round them. By 1830, there were hardly any open fields left.

Enclosures meant more money for landowners and tenant farmers. They were not so good for labourers, though. They lost the right to use the common land. That was where they had kept their cows and sheep. And money from selling butter, cheese, and wool had kept hunger from their doors. On the other hand, enclosures meant work and wages. Landlords and tenants needed labour to make fences, dig ditches, and till the fields.

Now try Exercises 37.1 and 37.2.

Source 37a

A poacher is brought before the squire. (The squire is both landlord and Justice of the Peace.) Poaching was a serious crime, and the punishment could be seven years' transportation. That is why the poacher's wife and child are on their knees.

Exercise 37.1

Read **Section A** and look at **Source 37a**. Copy the sentences and fill in the blanks.

a Great lords and squires owned _____ .

b Many squires were _____ of the Peace.

c Tenant farmers had to pay _____ to their landlords.

d Young, _____ farm workers often lived in the farmer's house.

e _____ meant turning open fields and common land into smaller, separate fields.

f By _____ hardly any villages still had open fields.

g Labourers lost the right to keep animals on the _____ land.

h Enclosures usually meant extra _____ and _____ for labourers.

Source 37b

A few days ago, a group of women were arrested for breaking down the fences that enclosed a common. The magistrates at Burton ordered them to be put in Stafford Jail. But the people heard what was going on, and gathered along the road. They attacked the guards with stones and lumps of soil, rescued the women, and led them off in triumph.

Adapted from the *Northampton Mercury* newspaper, 10 June 1771.

Source 37c

A million acres of land have been enclosed in the last 30 or 40 years. Most of it was open-fields before enclosure. The land used to grow crops worth 30 shillings [£1.50] an acre. Now it grows crops worth £3 an acre. So enclosing this land has brought in at least £1,500,000 more a year.

Adapted from an article written by Arthur Young in 1790.

Exercise 37.2

Read **Sources 37b** and **37c**, then answer the questions in sentences.

a Why was Arthur Young (**Source 37c**) in favour of enclosures?

b Who got the extra money that came from farming enclosed land?

c Which group of people did Arthur Young not think about?

d Why were the women in **Source 37b** sent to Stafford Jail?

e Why do you think the women broke down the fences?

f What does **Source 37b** tell us about the feelings of the common people?

B Improved farming methods

Enclosures made more money for land-lords and tenants. Landlords laid new drains, to make wet land drier, and put up new farm buildings. Then they urged their tenants to try new farming methods. The tenants made bigger profits, and the landlords put up the rents.

Enclosed fields. You can still see the Medieval strips in some of the fields.

On enclosed land, farmers made up their own minds which crops to grow, when to sow the seed, when to harvest the crop, etc. (They did not have to go along with the rest of the village.) This meant that they could try out new crops, such as turnips and clover. And farmers who grew clover found that they did not need to leave the land fallow every third year. (Look at the chart 'Crop Rotation'.)

Turnips and clover were winter food for cattle and sheep. Farmers who grew them did not need to kill off most of their animals in the autumn. And after enclosures, farmers kept their own cattle in their own fields – they did not have to mix with the others on the common. So careful farmers could be sure that their animals were kept free from disease.

For some, farming became a science. **Robert Bakewell** and the **Colling** brothers bred new kinds of sheep and cattle. They were bigger than other animals, gave more meat, and brought more profit to the farmer.

News of the farming changes was spread in books and papers. Great lords, and King George III himself, laid out 'model farms' to show what could be done. But not all landlords and farmers were quick to change. Most farmers did not start growing turnips and clover until after 1800.

Now try Exercises 37.3 and 37.4.

Selective breeding led to an increase in the size of cattle and sheep

Before

After

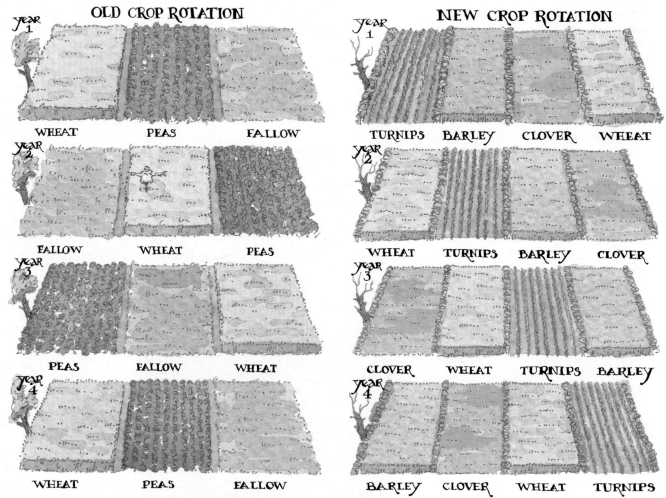

Farmers found that clover put nitrogen back into the soil, so there was no need to leave it to rest (lie fallow) every third or fourth year.

Source 37d

After the land had been enclosed, go-ahead farmers used machines like this seed drill on their land

This four Wheel Drill Plow, with a Seed and a Manure Hopper, was first Invented in the Year 1745. and is now in Use with Wm Ellis at Little Gaddesden near Kempstead in Hertfordshire, where any person may View the same. It is so light that a Man may Draw it, but Generally drawn by a pony or little Horse —

Source 37e

I have just seen one of the new seed-drills. It is strong, but not heavy, has two wheels, and is drawn by one or two horses. It makes three furrows at a time, sows seed into them, then covers the seed with soil. It does the work much more quickly and exactly than it can be done by hand.

Adapted from the *Leeds Intelligencer* newspaper, 5 June 1764.

Fact and opinion

Facts are things that are true, or were true in the past. An event that happened is a fact. Things that you can see, or touch, or hear are facts. These are facts: the women in **Source 37b** broke down some fences; the local people rescued the women.

An **opinion** is what someone thinks, believes, or feels. It tells us about a person's likes and dislikes, and whether he or she thinks things are good or bad. This is an opinion: the magistrates in **Source 37b** thought that the women were criminals.

Exercise 37.3

Read **Section B** and **Source 37e**, and study **Source 37d**.

a In what ways is the seed-drill described in **Source 37e** the same as the drill shown in **Source 37d**? In what ways are the two drills different? (Write a paragraph).
b Either copy **Source 37d** or draw a picture of the seed-drill described in **Source 37e**.

Source 37f

A hundred years ago, the potato was thought to be a food fit only for the poorest of the poor. Now it is eaten by rich and poor alike. But it is the poor who have gained most — it has given them a better standard of life and saved them from the famine. It can be roasted, boiled, fried, chopped up, or mixed with bacon, or onions, or flour.

Adapted from a book written by Sir Frederick Eden in 1797.

Exercise 37.4

Read the note on 'Fact and Opinion', and read **Source 37f**.

a Write down as many facts as you can find about potatoes in **Source 37f**.
b What were rich people's opinions about potatoes **i** in 1697, and **ii** in 1797?
c Why did the author of **Source 37f** have a good opinion of potatoes?

C Good times and bad

The years after 1750 were a time of high profits for farmers and good rents for landlords. The best years were from 1793 to 1815, when Britain was at war with France, and food prices were very high. It was a time of **boom** in farming.

When peace came in 1815, food prices, profits, and rents fell. The years 1815 to 1830 were a time of **slump** for farmers and their landlords. Some tenants gave up the struggle and became labourers. Others left the land, and looked for work in the growing towns. Labourers' wages were always low, but in times of slump they fell even lower. In the south of England in 1830 they sank to 10 shillings (50p) a week.

From about 1835, though, food prices rose again. And between 1850 and 1870 farmers and landowners enjoyed another boom. They spent money to improve the land, on drainage pipes and steam pumps, and on new fertilizers. They bought new machines such as binders and reapers, and steam-driven threshers. Even the labourers shared in the boom — in good times the farmers could afford to pay them a decent wage.

Now try Exercise 37.5.

Source 37g

A steam-driven threshing machine – to separate the ears of grain from the straw

Farm labourers at work without machinery

Exercise 37.5

Read **Section C**, and look at **Source 37g**.
Find words in **Section C** to fit the phrases below:

a Money to spare after the farmer had paid all his bills.
b A time of high prices and good profits.
c A time of low prices, low profits (or none at all), and low wages.
d Chemicals that farmers put on the land to make it more fertile.
e A horse-drawn machine to cut hay or corn.
f A steam-driven machine to separate the ears of grain from the straw.

38 Trade and Empire in the Eighteenth Century

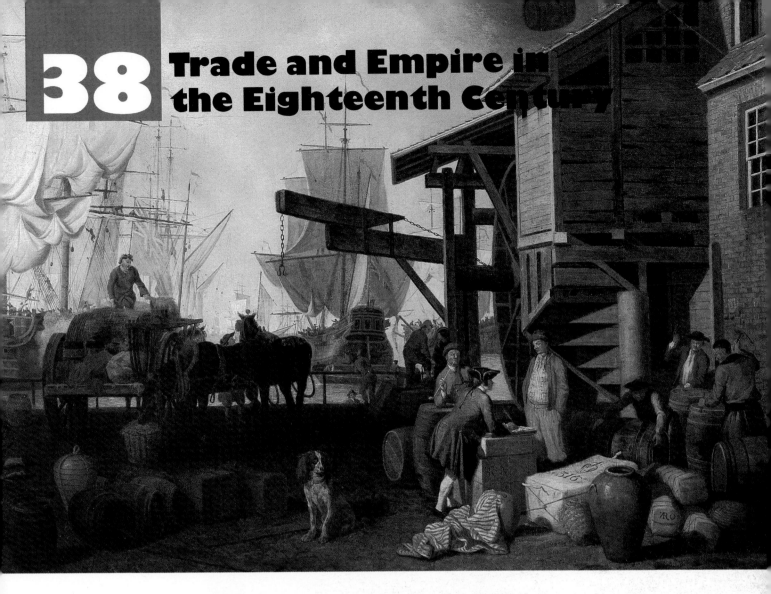

Goods being unloaded at the London customs house in the eighteenth century. A painting by Samuel Scott.

A Eighteenth-century trade

By 1750 Britain was the world's leading trading nation. Ships full of Swedish iron and China tea queued up to enter the ports. Cartloads of West Indian sugar and American tobacco rattled along the quays. Store-houses were packed with spices and rich cloths from India and the East.

Trade was growing all the time. In 1800, six times as much sugar reached Britain as in 1700. The ports were growing too — Bristol was twice as big in 1750 as in 1700. The merchants who owned the ships grew rich, bought land, and turned themselves into country squires.

Imports had to be paid for with **exports**. In 1750, Britain still sold her own woollen cloth to all parts of Europe. As well as cloth, though, she sold in Europe some of the spices and sugar that her merchants had brought from abroad. Each deal meant a handsome profit, of course.

Merchants also made big profits from the shameful trade in **slaves.** They bought slaves on the coast of West Africa, shipped them like cattle to the West Indies and America, and sold them to work cutting sugar-cane or picking tobacco and cotton. Then they brought home cargoes of sugar and tobacco to Britain.

Now try Exercise 38.1.

> **Exercise 38.1**
>
> Study **Section A**.
> British merchants in the eighteenth century bought and sold iron, spices, tea, sugar, tobacco, woollen cloth, and slaves.
> In which countries did they buy them, and where did they sell them?
> Make a chart with columns headed 'Goods' (iron, spices, etc.), 'Where Bought' and 'Where Sold'.

The Taj Mahal – built by the Mughal emperor Shah Jahan

B India

India's ruler was the **Mughal** emperor in Delhi. But the men with real power were the **princes** – the nawabs and rajahs who ruled the districts. They were just like kings, with their palaces, grand clothes, and hundreds of servants. Each prince had his army – men, horses, guns, and elephants.

India's wealth (in gems, perfumes, pepper, and fine cloth) attracted traders from Europe. And the Mughals allowed them to open 'factories', or trading posts, at places round the coast. (Look at the **Map**.)

By 1750, the British and French were the main westerners in India. They often quarrelled with each other, and took opposite sides in the wars among the nawabs and rajahs. In 1757 the British came out on top. They beat the French, and made themselves masters of Bengal. **Robert Clive** won his vital battle, at **Plassey**, by bribing an Indian prince not to fight.

The British in India were employed by the **East India Company**, a trading firm. Even the soldiers were paid by the company. After 1750, though, the

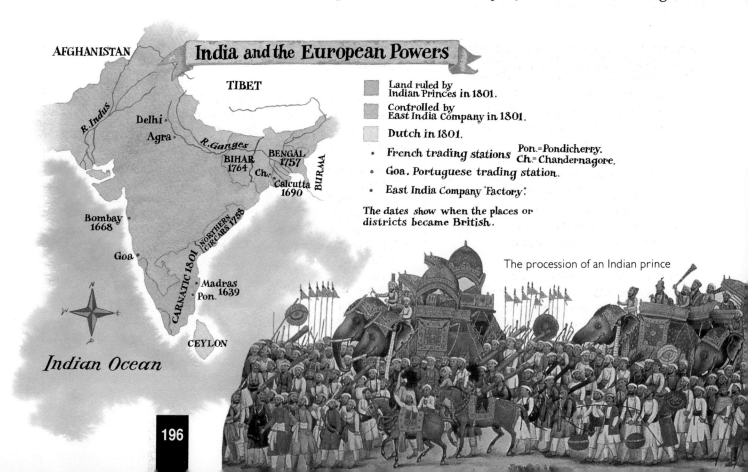

India and the European Powers

AFGHANISTAN

TIBET

R. Indus

Delhi
Agra

R. Ganges

BIHAR 1764
BENGAL 1757
Ch.
Calcutta 1690

BURMA

Bombay 1668

CARNATIC 1801

NORTHERN CIRCARS 1758

Goa

Madras 1639
Pon.

CEYLON

Indian Ocean

Land ruled by Indian Princes in 1801.

Controlled by East India Company in 1801.

Dutch in 1801.

• French trading stations — Pon.=Pondicherry. Ch.= Chandernagore.

• Goa. Portuguese trading station.

• East India Company "Factory".

The dates show when the places or districts became British.

The procession of an Indian prince

196

company dealt with more than just trade. It began to take control of India. One by one, the princes agreed to accept British 'protection'. (The **Map** shows the spread of British rule.)

In the parts which they ruled, the British collected taxes, ran law courts, and kept law and order. They said that their rule was honest and fair, and better than India had known before. In fact, most of the East India Company's men cheated and took bribes. Those who lived long enough to come home brought big fortunes with them.

Now try Exercises 38.2 and 38.3.

Exercise 38.2

Read **Section B**, and study the **Map**. Find out when the following places or districts became British:

Carnatic, Madras, Northern Circars, Bombay, Calcutta, Bengal, Bihar.

Write out the names and dates in the correct order (earliest first).

Source 38a

The nawab of Bengal was a cruel and wicked tyrant. In 1756 he picked a quarrel with the English, and captured their base at Calcutta. He told his guards to put all the English prisoners into a dungeon called the 'Black Hole'. No less than 146 persons were locked into this small, airless space for a night. Next morning, only 23 of them were left alive.

Adapted from a book written by an Englishman, Sir Charles Oman, in 1895.

Source 38b

The story of the Black Hole of Calcutta may not be true. Most historians now think that an Englishman called Holwell made it up. (He wanted to make the British hate the nawab of Bengal.) No-one else who lived at that time mentioned it. Clive says nothing about it in his letters. After the war, the British did not make the nawab pay money to the victims' families.

Adapted from a book written by D. P. Singhal, an Indian historian, in 1983.

Historians sometimes disagree

Writers do not always say the same things about the people or events of the past. Here are some reasons why this may happen.

  i Writers who were present when events happened might know more than writers who have only used other books.
  ii As time has passed, some sources have been lost or destroyed.
  iii As time has passed, new sources have been discovered.
  iv Some historians have not bothered to read or look at all the sources.
  v Some authors take the side of their own country.

Exercise 38.3

Read the note 'Historians Sometimes Disagree' and **Sources 38a** and **38b**. Write out the sentences, and write either TRUE or FALSE after each of them. 'Oman' was the author of **Source 38a**. 'Singhal' was the author of **Source 38b**.

a Oman thought that the story of the 'Black Hole of Calcutta' was true.
b Oman may have talked to people who survived the 'Black Hole of Calcutta'.
c Oman must have read all the sources.
d If events happened as Oman described, Englishmen living in India at that time would have talked and written about them.
e Singhal also believed the 'Black Hole' story.
f Singhal had probably read more sources than Oman.
g **Source 38a** was written by an Englishman, and **Source 38b** by an Indian.

C The loss of the American colonies

Most of the east coast of North America was British in 1750. From the farmers and fishermen in the north to the tobacco-growers in the south, they all flew the British flag and obeyed British laws. (Look at the **Map**.)

Canada was French, and the French were often at war with Britain. In some parts of the British colonies, the men always had to be ready to defend their homes. So they were glad to have British troops on their side. And they paid taxes to help pay for the troops.

In 1763, after victory in war, Britain took Canada from France. So the threat to the colonies was gone. But the taxes remained. And it was **Parliament** in London that fixed the taxes and made the laws.

The laws on trade said that Americans must buy imports (e.g. tea) from British merchants. And they said that

exports (e.g. tobacco) must be sold to British merchants. In the colonies, they said that this was unfair. They said that they should fix their own taxes, and make their own laws.

The quarrel turned to war in 1775. The American 'rebels' formed an army and chose **George Washington** as their leader. At first, the army was badly armed and clothed. It nearly lost the war. Then the French sent help, and the tide began to turn. In 1781, the British army at **Yorktown** had to surrender to the French and the 'rebels'.

Peace was made in 1783. The colonies got their freedom, and joined together to form the **United States of America**. Britain kept Canada, though, and some loyal subjects moved there from the new U.S.A.

Now try Exercise 38.4.

The Boston Tea Party

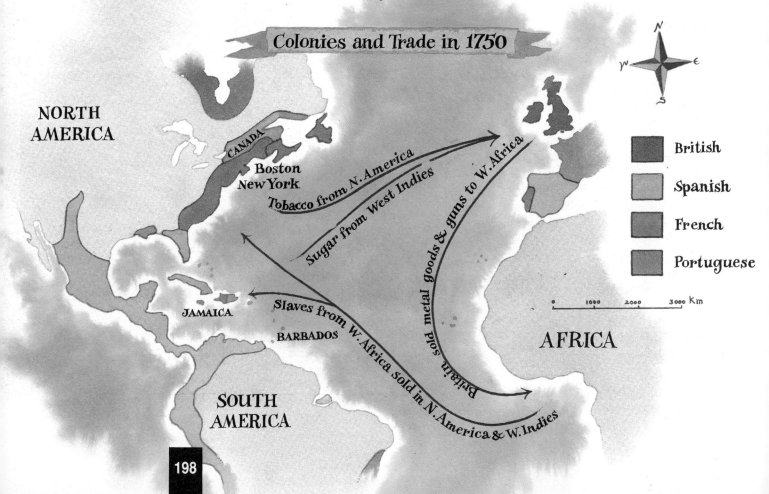

Colonies and Trade in 1750

NORTH AMERICA

CANADA

Boston
New York

Tobacco from N. America

Sugar from West Indies

Britain sold metal goods & guns to W. Africa

JAMAICA

BARBADOS

Slaves from W. Africa sold in N. America & W. Indies

SOUTH AMERICA

AFRICA

British
Spanish
French
Portuguese

1000   2000   3000 Km

Source 38e

A law passed in 1773 said that only the East India Company could sell tea in America. The Americans hated this law. They said that they should be free to buy tea from anyone. One night in December 1773, a band of men dressed as Mohawk Indians climbed aboard three ships in Boston harbour. They found the cargoes of tea, and tipped them into the sea. This was the famous 'Boston Tea Party'. Soon after, the British passed a law saying that the port of Boston was closed until the tea was paid for.

Adapted from a book published by the United States government in 1953.

George Washington

The Industrial Revolution — Iron, Steam and Coal

A The Industrial Revolution

Between 1750 and 1900 Britain went through a huge change in how and where men and women worked and lived. Students of history call it the **Industrial Revolution**.

In a few trades at first, people started to make things with **machines**, instead of by hand. The machines were in **mills** and **factories**, so men and women (and children) worked there, not in workshops or in their homes. Before long, **power** (first water, then steam) was used to drive the machines.

Farming ceased to be the main work of the people. Its place was taken by industry. And as the mills and factories were mainly in **towns**, that is where people had to live. And finally, the **population** rose — in 1900 it was six times as large as 150 years before.

Now try Exercise 39.1.

Exercise 39.1

Read Section A, then copy out the chart, filling in the blank spaces.

Before Industrial Revolution	During and after Industrial Revolution
a Craftsmen made articles by hand.	In many trades, goods were made by _____ .
b Craftsmen worked at home or _____ .	Men, women, and children worked in _____ or _____ .
c Craftsmen used their own skill and strength.	Machines were driven by power (_____ or _____).
d _____ was most people's occupation.	Industry employed more and more people.
e Most people lived in _____ districts.	Far more people lived in _____ .

B The iron industry

Iron ore has to be heated (or **smelted**) to extract the iron. Until after 1700, the fuel for smelting was **charcoal** (partly burnt wood). But the demand for charcoal was eating up England's forests. And the iron industry could not grow if there was not enough fuel. (The sulphur in coal had a bad effect on iron, so coal could not be used for smelting.)

In 1709, though, **Abraham Darby** of Coalbrookdale in Shropshire discovered that if you first made coal into **coke** it could be used for smelting. The invention was kept secret for 30 years. Even then, the news spread slowly. It was the 1760s before coke was widely used.

Darby's methods produced good **cast iron**, which was used for guns and pots and pans. But they were no use for **wrought iron**, to make plough shares, tools, and nails. It was **Henry Cort** in 1784, with his 'puddling process', who found a way of using coke to make wrought iron.

Source 39a

> *Mr. Crawshay's iron works (at Merthyr Tydfil) are now the largest in Britain. The biggest thing there is the great water wheel. It is fifty feet across, and it has the power of fifty horses. There are six smelting furnaces, and around them are the forges and rolling mills. Forty years ago, this place was just a village. Now it is the largest town in Wales.*

Adapted from a book written by Benjamin Malkin in 1804.

The first iron bridge, built at Coalbrookdale by Abraham Darby's firm in 1779

Source 39b

Iron works at Coalbrookdale in Shropshire in 1788

The work of Darby and Cort made iron cheap and plentiful. Big iron works were set up in South Wales, Scotland, the Midlands, and Yorkshire. By 1815 Britain turned out nearly ten times as much iron as in 1750.

The years 1750–1850 were the age of iron. It was used for beams in buildings, bridges, gas-pipes, and above all for machines. By the 1840s iron trains ran on iron tracks up and down the length of Britain. Iron was the key to the Industrial Revolution.

Now try Exercise 39.2.

Exercise 39.2

Read **Section B** and **Source 39a**, and look at **Source 39b**. Answer the questions.
a Who owned the iron works at Merthyr Tydfil?
b How do you know that the Merthyr Tydfil iron works used water power?
c What fuel do you think they used in the Merthyr Tydfil furnaces?
d About when did Merthyr Tydfil begin to grow into a town?
e How do you know that the Coalbrookdale iron works used water power?
f How do you know that the Coalbrookdale iron works used coke or coal?
g How many workers do you think that the Coalbrookdale iron works employed – under 20, between 20 and 100, over 100?

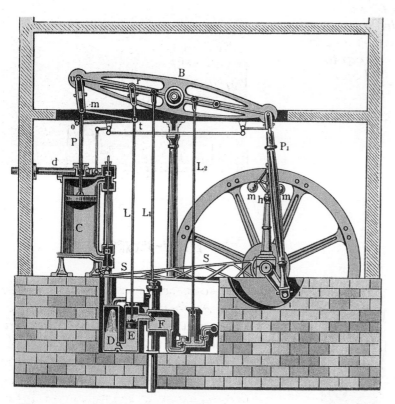

The steam engine designed by James Watt

C Steam engines

The most important of the iron machines was the steam engine. The looms and spindles of the mills were driven by steam. Steam engines pumped water from the mines, and hauled out men and coal. Railway trains were drawn by steam engines on wheels.

From 1700, steam engines were used to pump water out of mines. But they were slow and used a lot of coal. In the 1770s and 1780s, **James Watt**, a Scotsman, invented a much better engine. It needed less coal, and it could do more than just work a pump. Watt's engine could also turn a wheel, which meant that it could drive machines.

Watt's engines were made in Birmingham at **Matthew Boulton's** workshop. They were made one at a time at first — there were not enough skilled engineers to make the parts for more. By 1800 a few hundred were in use, in mines, cotton mills, and iron works.

The spread of steam power took place mainly after 1800. As more factories were built, more steam engines were needed. More workmen became skilled in making boilers and pistons. New firms followed Boulton's lead, supplying engines to all parts of Britain and selling them abroad.

Now try Exercise 39.3.

Source 39d

i The steam engine was used in a wide range of industries. Before the railway age, though, it was important only in cotton, iron, and mining.
ii Costs fell in British industry, and this made it easier to sell British goods abroad.

Adapted from a book written by Miss Phyllis Deane in 1965. The 'railway age' began in 1825.

Source 39c

Steam engines built 40 years ago are still in use. How many horses would have been worn out doing the same amount of work? How much corn would they have eaten? Steam engines use coal, so they give work to miners. And they help to mine the coal – draining water from the pits, and hauling up the coal. They drive engines in cotton mills and iron-works, and on railways. They are cheap to run, so the goods which they help to make are cheap. Because of this, we sell more abroad, and we are all better off.

Adapted from a book written by Andrew Ure in 1835.

Exercise 39.3

Read **Section C** and **Sources 39c** and **39d**.

a In a group, discuss what, if anything, the two sources say about
  i horses,
  ii which industries used steam engines.
  iii exports.

b Make a group display (with drawings and written work) showing the links between steam engines and i horses, ii industry, and iii exports.

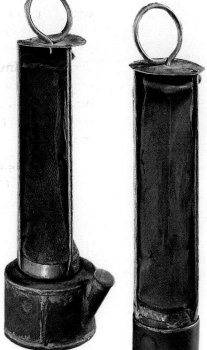

Two Davy lamps. The fine mesh round the flame stopped the methane gas in the mine from exploding.

D Coal-mining

Ironworks and steam engines needed coal. As they spread, the demand for coal grew. So more mines were opened, and deeper shafts were sunk. Deeper pits meant more danger for the miners, above all from water and gas. An explosion at Felling pit on Tyneside in 1812 killed 92 men and boys.

Inventors tackled the problems, but only partly solved them. The steam engine helped with the pumping. Using two or more shafts produced a flow of air and better ventilation. **Sir Humphry Davy's** safety lamp (invented in 1815) reduced the risk from gas.

In Scotland the mine-owners employed women and girls as well as men and boys. (Their wages were lower than men's.) Inspectors in the 1830s found pits where boys and girls of four or five sat for hours in the dark, opening and closing trap-doors. Their report shocked the public. In 1842 Parliament passed a law which said that girls, women, and boys under ten could not work underground.

Now try Exercise 39.4.

Causes and Results

Causes come **before** results. Causes are the answer to the questions: **Why** did it happen? **Why** was it like that?
Results comes **after** causes.
We may say: 'Because of Cort's inventions, iron became cheap and popular.' In that case, 'Cort's inventions' is the **cause** and 'iron became cheap and popular' is the **result**.

A pithead with steam winding gear in about 1820

Exercise 39.4

Read **Section D** and the note on 'Causes and Results'. Then make notes on:

a The causes of **i** deeper mines being sunk, and **ii** some mine-owners employing women and children.
b The results of **i** mines becoming deeper, and **ii** inspectors going down mines in the 1830s.

40 The Industrial Revolution — Textiles

A From cottage to mill

Since the Middle Ages, making **woollen** cloth had been England's main industry. Most of the work was done by country people in their own homes. Labourers' wives would spin and weave when they had time to spare. Their husbands helped when there was no work for them on the farm.

Rich **clothiers** bought the raw wool, employed the spinners and weavers, and sold the finished cloth. Most of the time, they could sell all the cloth that was made. So they were glad when inventors came up with machines that could spin and weave more quickly.

From the mid-eighteenth century, inventors brought about a massive change. **John Kay's** 'flying shuttle' made weaving much faster. Then **James Hargreaves**, with his 'spinning jenny', gave the spinner the power to work sixteen spindles at once. By and large, though, spinners and weavers still worked in their own homes, making woollen cloth.

Weavers in England had made cloth that was part-cotton and part linen for some time. (The yarn was not strong enough for pure cotton cloth.) But **Richard Arkwright's** 'water frame' spun strong cotton yarn. And the 'water frame' was driven by a **waterwheel**, not by hand or foot. Arkwright and a partner started a water-driven **cotton-mill** near Derby in 1771.

Samuel Crompton's 'mule' spun fine, smooth cotton yarn. Before long, British cotton cloth was the best in the world. It was also the cheapest, because the spinning was done on machines, in **mills**. The power in the mills at first was water. In the 1790s, though, came the first cotton-mills with machines that were worked by **steam**.

Now try Exercise 40.1.

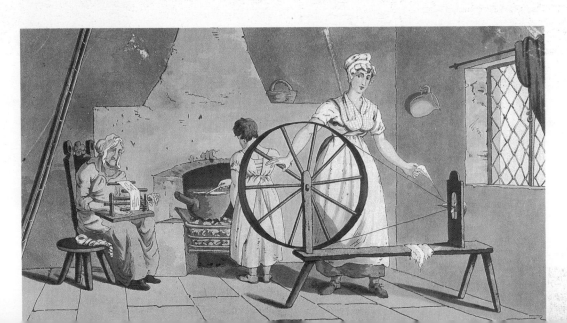

Source 40a

A woman spinning by hand in her own home in the eighteenth century

Centuries

The **eighteenth** century was the hundred years from 1701 to 1800. The **nineteenth** century was the hundred years from 1801 to 1900. The **twentieth** century is the hundred years from 1901 to 2000. We call the years 1701 to 1730 the **early eighteenth century**. We call the years 1731 to 1770 the **mid-eighteenth century**. We call the years 1771 to 1800 the **late eighteenth century**.

Exercise 40.1

Read **Section A** and the note on 'Centuries'. Then write out the sentences, replacing the dates with 'the _____ _____ century'. The first missing word should be 'early', 'mid', or 'late'. The second missing word should be 'eighteenth' or 'nineteenth'. The first one has been done for you.

a In **1750** woollen cloth was made by country people in their own homes.
Answer: In **the mid-eighteenth century** woollen cloth was made by country people in their own homes.
b James Hargreaves invented the 'spinning jenny' **in about 1765**.
c In **1779** Samuel Crompton invented the 'mule'.
d In **the 1780s** most cotton-mills used water power.
e By **1820** a lot of cotton-mills were using steam engines.
f Cotton cloth was Britain's main export in **1850**.
g The price of cotton cloth fell in **the 1880s**.

B 'King cotton'

Cotton mills spread through **Lancashire** in the first years of the nineteenth century. (A second, smaller cotton district grew up in Scotland.) At first, as many of the mills had water-wheels as steam engines. But by 1840 nearly all were driven by steam.

Soon after 1800, Britain was making as much cotton cloth as wool. By 1830, cotton was miles ahead. Cotton was popular because it was fine, light in weight, and easy to wash. Above all, it was cheap — the new machines, and low wages in the mills, meant that the prices steadily fell.

Until 1820, cotton exports went mainly to Europe and the U.S.A. After that, though, much more went to India and the Far East. By 1850, cotton cloth was Britain's biggest export, and India was her biggest market. Cotton was 'king' in Lancashire. The port of **Liverpool** thrived, importing raw cotton from the U.S.A., and exporting finished cloth.

Until the 1830s, most of the weaving was done by **handloom weavers**, working at home or in their workshops. They were well paid — in 1805 they got 23 shillings (£1.15) a week. Then, after 1830, power looms and weaving mills began to take over. Handloom weavers' wages crashed to six shillings (30p) a week.

The woollen industry also changed to machines and mills. But here the changes came later. Until 1830, most of the spinning and weaving was still done by hand. By 1850, though, spinning was done mainly in the west Yorkshire mills. Weaving took another 20 years to follow suit.

Now try Exercise 40.2.

Source 40b

Spinning with 'mules' in a Lancashire cotton mill in 1834. The boy in the bottom right of the picture is sweeping beneath the machine while it is working.

'The Dinner Hour' – factory girls outside a mill in Wigan in 1874

Exercise 40.2

Read **Section B**, and look at **Sources 40a** and **40b**.
Write out the notes, filling in the blank spaces.

Things that changed between 1750 and 1850:

a _____ was done on a wheel in 1750, and on a 'mule' in 1850.

b _____ engines were used to drive machines in cotton mills.

c The _____ of cotton cloth fell.

d _____ became Britain's main market for cotton cloth.

e The wages of _____ _____ fell to almost nothing.

Things that did not change between 1750 and 1850:

f Britain continued to make a lot of _____ cloth.

g Most _____ of woollen cloth was still done by hand.

C Factory children

Mill owners said that they had to keep their prices down. That was why workers' hours had to be long, and wages low. Women and children got lower wages than men, so the owners employed a lot of women and children. (Look at the **cartoon**.)

Children as young as six or seven worked up to fourteen hours a day in the mills. Their pay was about three shillings (15p.) a week. Many were killed or injured by the moving parts of the machines they had to clean. Others were maimed by a foreman's fist or strap. Sadly, many of them were forced to work by their own parents. Their fathers were out of work, and the family needed the few shillings that they could earn.

Some decent employers paid their workers a fair wage. Some even built good houses for them, and ran schools for their children. Some mill-owners took part in a movement for factory reform. Most mill-owners were against the reformers, though. They said that shorter hours for children would put up their costs, and bring them to ruin.

Mill-owners did not obey Parliament's first acts cutting mill hours. But an act passed in 1833 said that inspectors would enforce the law. The act banned all children under nine from cotton mills. Children over nine were allowed to work, but there were strict controls on their hours. By 1847, ten hours per day was the limit for boys and all female workers.

Now try Exercises 40.3 and 40.4.

Women and children working in a cotton mill

Source **40c**

Don't come to me with the old tale that the rich know nothing about the hard life of the poor. If they don't know they ought to know. We are their slaves as long as we can work. We pile up their fortunes with the sweat of our brows. Yet we live as separate as if we were in two worlds.

Words spoken by a character called John Barton in the novel *Mary Barton*, written by Elizabeth Gaskell in 1848.

Source 40d

As you enter the factory, the whirring of a million hissing wheels hits your ears. Then you see the hundreds of helpless children. They have lost all trace of health, joy, and youth. Lean and crooked limbs, pale and sunken cheeks, dim and hollow eyes make them look old before their time. Neither these little slaves nor the whirling spindles they serve ever stop — the foremen, straps in hand, are watching all the time.

Adapted from a novel, *Michael Armstrong*, written by Mrs. Trollope in 1840.

Source 40e

There are now 145 men, 217 women, and 795 children employed at New Lanark mills. The children are well fed — they get oatmeal porridge with milk twice a day, barley broth for dinner, and either beef or cheese. They begin work at six in the morning, and stop at seven at night. Those under nine years old do not work at all. There is a school for the children — those under nine attend in the day-time, and the others after work.

Adapted from an account written by William Lockhart in 1795.

The division of workers in cotton mills in 1835

Children under 14 years old.

Young people between the ages of 14 and 18.

Men over the age of 18.

Women over the age of 18.

Exercise 40.3

Read **Section C** and **Sources 40c, 40d, and 40e**. Ask these questions about each of the sources. Make the answers into a chart.

a Who wrote it?
b When was it written?
c What kind of book or paper does it come from? Do you know the title?
d Is it fact or fiction?

Exercise 40.4

Discuss these questions in a group:

a What do **Sources 40b, 40c, 40d, and 40e** tell us about factory conditions?
b What do the sources tell us about the opinions of workers and bosses?
c Can you think of any reasons for saying that **i** these sources give us a good idea of factory life; **ii** they may give a false impression?

Either give your answers as talks to the class, or make a group tape.

41 Canals and Roads

A collier unloading coal in the Thames near Deptford. A painting by Samuel Scott.

A Colliers and barges

As industries grew, more heavy loads of iron and coal had to be moved from place to place. As towns grew, they had to have more food and fuel. Moving heavy loads in horse-drawn wagons on bad roads was slow and expensive. It was much cheaper to send them by **water**.

Hundreds of small ships with cargoes of corn and wool sailed from port to port along the coasts. Ships called **colliers** carried coal from the Tyne to London. As London grew, so the number of colliers grew as well. Other loads went by river. Gangs of men worked on the Trent, Severn, and Thames, making them deep enough to take barges of iron and cloth.

It was a short step from rivers to **canals**. England's first canal was the **Sankey Cut**, from St. Helens to the River Mersey. It was opened in 1757, to let barges carry coal from the Lancashire mines to Liverpool.

A canal from the **Duke of Bridgewater's** coal-mine at Worsley to Manchester (seven miles away) was opened in 1761. Its engineer, **James Brindley**, became famous, and his canal was the engineering wonder of its day. Part of it ran in a tunnel into the mine, and part was on an **aqueduct** over the River Irwell. Barges on the canal carried the duke's coal cheaply to Manchester — the price of coal there was cut by half.

Now try Exercise 41.1.

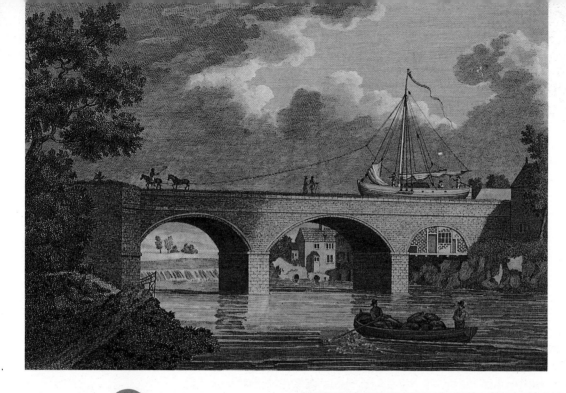

Source **41a**

The Barton Aqueduct in 1794

Source **41b**

The canal passes over the River Irwell at Barton bridge. It is carried by a strong, thick, stone bridge, consisting of three arches. The centre arch is 63 feet wide and 38 feet above the surface of the water. The bridge is high enough to let the largest barges on the Irwell go through with their masts and sails standing.

Adapted from a book written by John Aikin in 1795.

Exercise 41.1

Read **Section A** and **Source 41b**, and look at **Source 41a**.

a Make notes on the Barton aqueduct?

  i   Which details can we learn from **Source 41a**, but not from **Source 41b**?
  ii Which details can we learn from **Source 41b**, but not from **Source 41a**?
  iii Which details can we learn from both sources?

b Draw a picture of the Barton aqueduct.

A canal joins the River Severn at Stourport

B Canal mania

After 1770, canals began to snake their way through much of England. (Look at the **map**.) Engineers like Brindley planned the routes, with all their locks and tunnels. Men with picks and shovels did the digging. They were called 'navigators' (or 'navvies') because they dug the 'navigations'. The work was hard, but the wages were good.

Canals were expensive to build. The men who **invested** money in them had to be rich. They hoped that canals would make them big profits, and some of them were right. The profits came from the tolls paid by the firms whose barges used the canals. For many investors, canals also meant cheap transport for their own goods (e.g. coal, cloth, or corn).

Owners of coal-mines, cotton-mills, and iron-works used canals because they were far cheaper than the roads. (One horse could pull a canal barge loaded with 50 tons of coal. A horse could draw only two tons of coal by road.) The great potter **Josiah Wedgwood** was both a canal-user and an investor. (Smooth canals were far better for his wares then bumpy roads.)

In the 1790s there was a mad rush to invest in new canals. It was the time of 'canal-mania'. Too many canals were built, and a lot of investors lost money. But good schemes still made profits. The Leeds to Liverpool canal, finished in 1816, was a great success. Then traffic began to decline as the railways spread in the 1830s and 1840s. In some areas, though, canal barges continued to carry coal until well after 1900.

Now try Exercises 41.2 and 41.3.

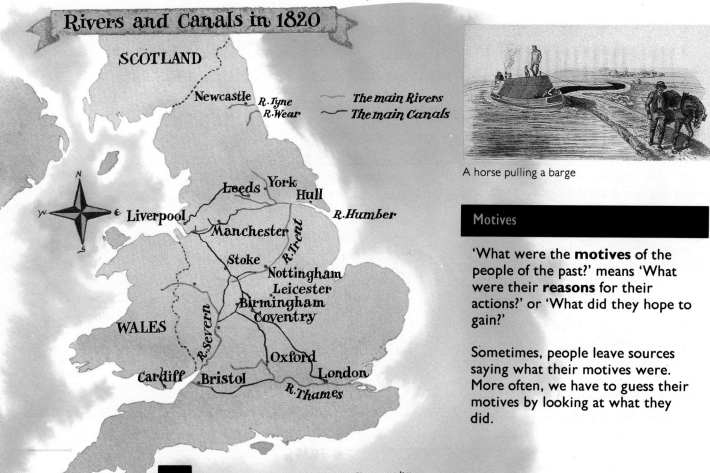

Rivers and Canals in 1820

SCOTLAND

Newcastle
R. Tyne
R. Wear

— The main Rivers
~ The main Canals

Leeds
York
Hull
Liverpool
R. Humber
Manchester
R. Trent
Stoke
Nottingham
Leicester
Birmingham
Coventry
R. Severn
WALES
Oxford
Cardiff
Bristol
London
R. Thames

0   50   100 Km

A horse pulling a barge

Motives

'What were the **motives** of the people of the past?' means 'What were their **reasons** for their actions?' or 'What did they hope to gain?'

Sometimes, people leave sources saying what their motives were. More often, we have to guess their motives by looking at what they did.

Exercise 41.2

Read **Section B** and the note on 'Motives'. Think of suitable ways to complete the sentences. Write out the whole sentences.

a The motive of the 'navvies' was probably _____ .

b All investors in canals wanted to make _____ .

c Many investors also got cheap _____ .

d Owners of coal mines used canals because _____ .

e Josiah Wedgwood's motives were _____ .

Exercise 41.3

Write out the sentences. Fill in the blank spaces (two in each sentence) with words from this list:

early   mid-   late   eighteenth   nineteenth   twentieth

a James Brindley built the Bridgewater canal in the _____ _____ century.

b A lot of canals were built in the _____ _____ century.

c There was a period of 'canal mania' in the _____ _____ century.

d The Leeds to Liverpool canal was completed in the _____ _____ century.

e Canals began to decline in the _____ _____ century.

f Some canals were still used in the _____ _____ century.

C Turnpikes and stage coaches

Canals were built partly because the roads were so bad. Most roads were just tracks, with huge ruts and pot-holes. When it rained, coach wheels sank in the mud. Before 1700, no-one built new roads. It was the job of each parish to mend its roads, but not much work was ever done.

In the eighteenth century, Parliament passed laws to set up **turnpike trusts**. Each trust had the right to take charge of a stretch of road. It could charge tolls at toll-gates, and was supposed to repair and improve the road. Some trusts bought land, and built completely new roads.

By 1830, about 20,000 miles of Britain's roads belonged to turnpike trusts. (More than 120,000 miles were still in the hands of the parishes.) Not all the trusts did good work — some just collected tolls and left the roads as bad

as before. But some trusts employed engineers to plan and build new roads and bridges.

Two famous road-builders were **Thomas Telford** and **John Macadam**. Telford used the same methods as the Romans — firm foundations and packed layers of stone and gravel. Macadam's roads were simpler — he relied on the weight of the traffic to press stones and chips into a solid surface.

Through the work of Telford, Macadam, and others, some roads were much improved. Regular **stage-coach** services became possible. (The coaches changed horses at coaching-inns after each eight or ten-mile 'stage'.) By 1832, the coach from London to Edinburgh took only two days. In 1754, the same journey took ten days.

Now try Exercises 41.4 and 41.5.

213

Canals and Roads

Source 41c

From Preston to Wigan (in Lancashire) there is a turnpike, but I do not know words that can describe this road. I warn travellers to avoid it like the devil. They are almost bound to break their necks or their limbs on it. They will find ruts four feet deep, full of mud after a wet summer. The only mending it gets is when they throw in some rough stones.

Written by Arthur Young in 1770.

Source 41d

The turnpike from Salisbury to Romsey (in Wiltshire and Hampshire) is the best I ever saw. The trustees of that road look after it really well. The surface is smooth, and there are no loose stones, ruts or pools of water. It is wide enough for three coaches to pass each other, it is straight, and it has an even grass verge the whole way.

Written by Arthur Young in 1768.

Source 41e

The turnpike from Tyburn through Uxbridge (in Middlesex) has more heavy wagons on it than any road in England. Yet all last winter there was only one decent track on it. That was less than six feet wide, and eight inches deep in mud. The rest of the road was at least a foot deep in mud. It was crowded with broad-wheeled wagons, drawn by as many as ten horses.

Written by John Middleton in 1798.

A stage-coach

Exercise 41.4

Read Section C and **Sources 41c**, **41d**, and **41e**. Write out the sentences, and write TRUE or FALSE after each of them.

a All turnpike trusts built new roads.
b All turnpike trusts charged tolls, but some did not improve the roads.
c The only bad turnpikes were in the north of England.
d Arthur Young must have travelled round England.
e Arthur Young liked the Salisbury to Romsey road.
f All the roads leading out of London were good.
g The Tyburn to Uxbridge road was so bad that no-one used it.

Exercise 41.5

Write sentences to show that you know what these words and terms mean:

colliers   aqueduct   navvies   investors
canal-mania   potholes   turnpike trust   toll-gate
road engineers   stage-coaches

42 Railways and Ships

Euston station in London in 1837

The opening of the Canterbury and Whitstable railway, 1830

A The first railways

Before the year 1700, trucks ran on wooden rails in the Cornish tin mines. On Tyneside, truck-loads of coal ran on wooden or stone tracks. By the late eighteenth century, in some places, the rails were iron. All the trucks on these 'waggonways', of course, were drawn by horses.

By 1800, fixed steam engines were working at many coal-mines, pumping and winding. The next step was to make a locomotive – a moving steam engine that would pull trucks of coal. Many men worked on the idea. The most successful was a Tyneside mine engineer, George Stephenson. An engine which he built in 1814 pulled coal trucks to and from the docks.

The first railway which carried passengers as well as coal was opened in 1825. It linked Stockton and Darlington and its engineer was Stephenson. He used locomotives, but not for the whole route. For part of the way, fixed engines pulled the trucks with cables.

More important was the Liverpool to Manchester railway. George Stephenson was its engineer. At an engine trial in 1829, he had proved that steam locomotives worked, and that his were the best. And when the railway opened in 1830, the people were thrilled by its speed and comfort. In its first year, 400,000 passengers used it.

Now try Exercise 42.1.

Source 42a

The Liverpool to Manchester railway was opened on Wednesday last. They say that the trains will be able to travel at sixteen to eighteen miles an hour. That would cut by half the time the journey takes. The people here talk of having breakfast at home, travelling each way by train, and getting home for dinner. Before long we shall have railroads all over England.

Adapted from *The Observer* newspaper, 19 September 1830.

Source 42b

What will happen to men who have put money into turnpikes? What will become of the coach-makers, coachmen, and inn-keepers? What about the men who breed horses and the harness-makers? Do you realise how much smoke and noise these railway engines will make, rushing past at ten or twelve miles an hour? They will frighten the cattle grazing in the fields. They will destroy the peace and quiet of gentlemen's estates.

Part of a speech made in the House of Commons in the 1830s.

Exercise 42.1

Read **Section A** and **Sources 42a** and **42b**, then answer the questions.

a Was the author of **Source 42a** in favour of railways or against them?

b According to **Source 42a**, what was the best thing about railways?

c Was the author of **Source 42a** right about the future of railways?

d Was the author of **Source 42b** in favour of railways or against them?

e The author of **Source 42b** said that which people would lose their jobs?

f According to **Source 42b**, what was the worst thing about railways?

g Who do you think wrote **Source 42b** – a landowner, a mill-owner, or a merchant?

Source 42c

Building the Britannia Bridge over the Menai Straits (between North Wales and Anglesey) in 1849

B The railway age

After 1830, there was a rush to build railways. London and Birmingham were linked in 1838. By 1850, all the main cities were connected. 'Navvies' did the work, laying track, building bridges, digging tunnels. In twenty years or so, the face of Britain was changed.

In the 1840s, investors rushed to buy shares in railways. (It was just like the 'canal mania' of the 1790s.) Once again, not all the plans were wise, and some fortunes were lost. And there were crooks — **George Hudson**, the 'railway king', swindled lords and bankers out of vast sums.

Most of the railways used the '**standard gauge**' — the lines were 4 feet $8\frac{1}{2}$

inches (1.43 metres) apart. But the Great Western Railway's engineer, **Isambard Kingdom Brunel**, used the '**wide gauge**' of seven feet (2.13 metres). He said it gave passengers a smoother and safer ride. A law passed in 1847 made all new lines use the standard gauge. But the Great Western did not change until 1892.

The railways took a lot of trade from the canals, and killed the stage-coaches. Busy coaching-inns became quiet country pubs. Strangely, though, the spread of railways led to more demand for horses. The horses pulled the coaches and carts that took people and goods to the stations.

Railways had a huge effect on jobs. As well as the 'navvies' who built them, there were the drivers, guards, porters, etc. who ran them. Then there were the engineers who made the locomotives and coaches. (New towns, such as Swindon and Crewe, grew up around the railway works.) Thousands of men worked making the iron for the track, bridges, and rolling-stock. And thousands of miners were employed digging the coal that the railways used.

Now try Exercises 42.2 and 42.3.

Source 42d

I began work on the railways when I was nine. My first job was greasing wagons, then I drove horses. After that, I was a navvy on the London to York line. I got 2s.9d. (14p) a day there, but only four days' work a week. Then the work stopped, and I was sacked. I got jobs on other lines, but last March I was paid off again. I sold all my tools to buy food, and now I don't know what to do. I'm only twenty-seven, but I'm dead beat.

The words of a navvy, reported by Henry Mayhew in 1861.

Source 42e

Men came from all over to work as navvies. They were experts in digging ditches, sinking wells, and boring tunnels. Each gang of men agreed the price for a job with the boss before they started. They could work twelve or sixteen hours at a stretch, with only short stops for meals. Danger meant nothing — the bigger the risk the keener they were to do the job.

Adapted from a book written in 1861 by Samuel Smiles, who would have seen navvies at work.

Source 42f

Navvies at work on the Liverpool to Manchester railway

Primary and secondary sources

Letters and books written by people who were present when events happened are called **primary sources**. Words spoken by people who took part in events are also primary sources. So are drawings made at the time.

Papers and books written by people who were **not** present are called **secondary sources**. The authors of secondary sources must have heard about the events from someone else, or read about them in books.

Exercise 42.2

Read **Section B** and **Sources 42d** and **42e**, and look at **Sources 42c** and **42f**. Read the note on 'primary and secondary sources'.
Write two sentences about each of the sources:

a Say what the source tells us or shows us.
b Say whether it is a primary or a secondary source.

Exercise 42.3

Write a short essay about **Sources 42d** and **42e**.

a What do they tell us about navvies and the kind of life they led?
b What differences are there between what the two sources say?
c Why do you think that **Sources 42d** and **42e** give different pictures of the navvies' lives? (Try to think of more than one reason.)

Right: A souvenir postcard of a steamer at Helensburgh in Scotland in the 1880s

Below: The famous clipper, the 'Cutty Sark'

C Sailing ships and steamships

The first boats with engines were **paddle-steamers**. The engine drove two paddles, one on each side of the boat. In the early days, they worked only on rivers and lakes. But in the 1820s steamers were running between England and France. Experts agreed, though, that steamers could not make long voyages — there would be no room for all the coal they would need.

A steam paddle-boat did cross the Atlantic in 1819. But this was not a real victory for steam, as the boat used sails for most of the way. **Brunel** (see **Section B**) began a steamer service from Bristol to New York in 1838, but his ships also used sails as well as steam.

Sailing ships took a long time to die. In the mid-nineteenth century, the **clippers** were fast and cheap to run. Each year, they raced to bring the new

Brunel's 'Great Eastern' in 1858

season's crop of tea from China to England. After 1869, when steamers took over the China trade, clippers still carried wool from Australia. Even in 1900, a fifth of British ships still used sails.

From the 1850s, Britain began building ships of iron, and later steel. Iron ships could be bigger — Brunel's 'Great Eastern', built in 1858, was 19,000 tons, five times as large as the biggest wooden ships. Iron ships with steam engines began to take charge of the world's trade. Most of them were built in British yards. By 1900, Britain had a big lead as the world's first shipping and shipbuilding nation.

Now try Exercise 42.4

Exercise 42.4

Find out the dates of the events below. (They are all in this chapter.) Write the dates and events in the right places on a time chart. The chart should be divided into two sections, 'Railways' and 'Ships'.

Stephenson made the first successful locomotive.
Opening of Stockton to Darlington railway.
Opening of Liverpool to Manchester railway.
Opening of London to Birmingham railway.
Law saying that new lines had to use the standard gauge.
Great Western Railway changed to standard gauge.
First paddle steamer crossed the Atlantic.
Brunel began steamer service from Bristol to New York.
Brunel's 'Great Eastern' launched.
Steamers took over the China trade.

Draw a picture of either an early locomotive or an early steamboat.

43 Britain and the French Revolution

Marie Antoinette, the queen of France, on her way to the guillotine in 1793

Source 43a

The execution of King Louis XVI of France, January 1793

A Guillotines in London?

In the eighteenth century, the king of **France** was the real ruler of his country. There was no parliament to help make the laws. Many Frenchmen thought that this was wrong. In the **Revolution** which broke out in 1789 they demanded a share of power and fair rights for the people.

Men and women in Britain were shocked by the violence of the French Revolution. But some of them (called the 'radicals') were on the side of the French reformers. They thought that Britain also needed a good deal more freedom. They said that rule by king, lords, and gentry was unfair. They wanted all men to have the right to vote.

By 1792 most towns in Britain had radical clubs. But the news in 1793 turned the British people against the French. The king and queen of France were put to death in public on the **guillotine** in Paris. Hundreds of nobles and ordinary men and women came to the same end. Horror swept through Britain. Radicals, it was said, were the friends of murderers.

The outbreak of war with France in 1793 made things worse for the radicals. Now their enemies called them traitors as well. The government banned radical meetings, closed down their clubs, and arrested their leaders. They said that those who took the radicals' side wanted guillotines in the streets of London.

Now try Exercise 43.1 and 43.2.

Exercise 43.1

Read **Section A**, then copy and complete the sentences.

a The French reformers wanted _____ .

b People in Britain who took the side of the French reformers were called _____ .

c British radicals wanted _____ .

d British people turned against the French when they heard that _____ .

e Radicals were accused of being traitors when _____ .

f The British government attacked the radicals by _____ .

Source 43b

Last night in a London coffee-house, a foreigner jumped up and started to make a speech. He called the king (of England) a tyrant, and the people slaves. He said that in nine months' time the Jacobins of Paris would bring freedom to London. At this, an English gentleman seized him, gave him a horse-whipping, and kicked him out of the house.

Adapted from *The Observer* newspaper, 27 May 1792. [Mass executions took place in France when the 'Jacobin' party took power.]

Source 43c

Yesterday morning King Louis XVI was put to death in the Square of the Revolution in Paris. The scaffold was high for all to see, and the houses round the square were full of women, looking out of the windows. The king took leave of his priest, but was not allowed to make a speech. His head was cut off straight away, and the blood-thirsty Jacobins waved their hats in the air, shouting 'God save the nation!'

Adapted from *The Observer* newspaper, 27 January 1793.

Exercise 43.2

Read **Sources 43b** and **43c**, and look at **Source 43a**. Write out the sentences, and write either TRUE or FALSE after each.

a   There were foreigners in London in 1792.
b   The French hoped that a revolution would break out in Britain.
c   Well-off English gentlemen were on the side of the French Revolution.
d   Executions took place in public in Paris.
e   Soldiers were on guard round the guillotine.
f   French people did not show much interest in the execution of the king.
g   Those about to die were allowed to make speeches.
h   Jacobins were against all kings.

B The threat of invasion

In 1793, France was at war with most of the countries of western Europe. Her enemies planned to march into France, take Paris, and bring the Revolution to an end. But the French fought hard and drove the invaders out. Then they went on the attack themselves. Britain sent an army to Holland to help the Dutch, but it too was beaten.

One by one, the nations of Europe made peace with the French. Britain did not have to give in, for she had the sea and her navy to protect her. At sea, the Royal Navy won a string of victories. The bold and clever Admiral **Nelson** became a national hero.

Britain's trade made her rich enough to afford the world's strongest navy. She was also able to give money to other states to pay for their armies. But on land the French always beat them. One reason was that they had the best generals. The ablest of them was **Napoleon Bonaparte**. In 1804, he made himself **Emperor** of France.

Bonaparte crossing the Alps

In 1805 Napoleon gathered a huge army and a fleet of boats on the north coast of France. He tried to trick the Royal Navy into leaving the Channel clear. But the plan failed. And a few months later Nelson crushed the fleets of France and Spain (France's ally) in the Battle of **Trafalgar**. Nelson was killed in the battle, but Britain was safe from invasion.

Now try Exercises 43.3 and 43.4.

Source 43e

A British cartoon from 1805 – John Bull (standing for Britain) challenges 'Boney' (Napoleon Bonaparte) to try to invade

Taking Sides

People often take sides – they are for one party, or they support one team. Men and women in the past took sides as well. The author of **Source 37c** (page 191) was for enclosures, but the women in **Source 37b** were against them. **Sources 42a** and **42b** (page 216) give two different views of railways. Artists could take sides also, as you will see if you look at **Sources 43d** and **43e**.

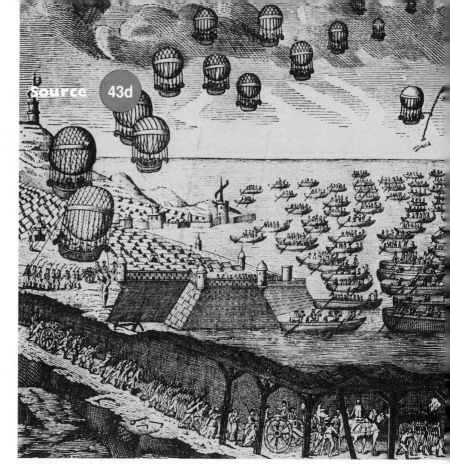

A French cartoon from 1804 – invasion of Britain by sea, by air, and through a tunnel

Source 43f

'John Bull goes to war' – a set of cartoons drawn in 1793

Exercise 43.3

Read **Section B** and the note on 'Taking Sides'. Study **Sources 43d** and **43e**. Write two paragraphs, answering these questions:

a How can you tell that **Source 43d** was drawn by a French artist?
b How can you tell that **Source 43e** was drawn by a British artist?

Exercise 43.4

Study **Source 43f**, then answer the questions in sentences.

a Who do you think 'John Bull' is meant to be?
b When did these events occur?
c What happened to John Bull?
d What happened to John Bull's family?
e What do you think were the artist's opinions? (Write more than one sentence if you can.)

C Napoleon and Wellington

Between 1805 and 1807, Napoleon's armies again crushed the great powers – Austria, Prussia, and Russia. He took land from them to add to his French empire. (Look at the map on page 224.) He made one of his own brothers King of Holland, and another King of Spain.

Napoleon tried to beat Britain by cutting her trade. He passed a law which said that the parts of Europe controlled by France must not trade with Britain. Since most of Europe was under French rule, this would have cut Britain's merchants off from their markets. But smugglers got round the law, so it did not do Britain much harm.

The French invaded **Portugal** to make her obey the trade law. But the British sent an army to help the Portuguese. In 1812, the British troops, led by the **Duke of Wellington**, advanced from Portugal to **Spain**. In the next year, they and the Spanish drove the French out of Spain as well.

Also in 1812, Napoleon fell out with the Tsar (emperor) of **Russia**. He sent a huge army (500,000 men) to teach the Tsar a lesson. The Russian army did not beat the French, but the Russian winter did. Hundreds of thousands of Frenchmen died in the cold on the long retreat from Moscow.

Now all of Europe rose against Napoleon. He was beaten, and had to give up his throne. The allies sent him to the island of **Elba**. But he escaped and returned to France. In a last battle at **Waterloo**, in 1815, the Duke of Wellington, with Prussian help, beat the French. Napoleon spent the rest of his life as a prisoner on the island of **St. Helena** in the South Atlantic.

Now try Exercise 43.5.

Napoleon's Empire in 1812

Ruled by Napoleon

Allies controlled by Napoleon

0 200 400 600 800 1000 Km

Atlantic Ocean

Moscow

North Sea

UNITED KINGDOM

London

Paris

FRANCE

PORTUGAL

Madrid

SPAIN

PRUSSIA

CONFEDERATION OF THE RHINE

GRAND DUCHY OF WARSAW

RUSSIA

Vienna

AUSTRIA

ITALY

Rome

NAPLES

TURKISH EMPIRE

Mediterranean Sea

THE CAUSES OF NAPOLEON'S DEFEAT

Britain had command of the ----. Nelson won Battle of -------- .

Napoleon quarrelled with the ---- of Russia.

The Spanish rebelled when Napoleon made his ----- King of Spain.

French tried to cut off Britain's ----- with rest of Europe.

Napoleon lost nearly 500,000 men when he invaded ------ .

War in ---- and Spain (British led by Duke of ------).

Napoleon forced to surrender in 1814. Escaped and beaten at -------- in 1815.

Exercise 43.5

Read **Section C**. Then copy out the chart on the causes of Napoleon's defeat, with or without the cartoons. Fill in the blank spaces in the boxes.

44 The Reform of Parliament

A Rule by property-owners

The polling booth – an election in the eighteenth century

In the eighteenth century, Britain was ruled by its great landowners. Most of them were nobles — members of the **House of Lords**. The leaders of the gentry (smaller landowners) sat in the **House of Commons**. They were less important than the lords, and often followed their lead.

The members of the House of Commons (M.P.s) were elected, but not by all the people. On the whole, only better-off men had the right to vote. (All the men could vote in a few towns.) No women could vote. And voting was in public. So landlords often **told** their tenants who to vote for. Men who could not be forced to vote the right way would be bribed.

Each **county** and **borough** in England had two M.P.s. Boroughs were supposed to be the most important towns. But some of them were 'rotten boroughs' – villages with only a few voters. These voters obeyed their landlords. So it was the landlords who chose the M.P.s. On the other hand, some large towns, such as Birmingham, did not have their own M.P.s.

The **radicals** (see Chapter 43) wanted to get rid of rotten boroughs, and to give all men the vote. But the lords and gentry said that only men who owned property should be able to vote. And the lords and gentry were in control. During the wars with France (1793 to 1815) they said that the radicals were no better than the French Jacobins.

Now try Exercise 44.1.

B The 1832 Reform Act

The radicals were just a small group. The main parties were the **Tories** and the **Whigs**. The Tories were a party of lords and gentry, and strongly against the reform of Parliament. The Whigs were a mixture of landlords and businessmen. They thought that **some** reform would be wise. But until 1830 the Tories were in power, so Parliament stayed unchanged.

At last, in 1830, the Whigs formed a government. In 1831, they brought in a bill to abolish some rotten boroughs and give more men the vote. The Tories voted against it. But the people wanted reform – there were riots in London and Bristol in favour of the bill. In the end, it was passed and became the **1832 Reform Act** (i.e. a new law).

The Reform Act abolished 56 rotten boroughs and gave towns such as Birmingham, Manchester, and Leeds the right to have their own M.P.s. It

Exercise 44.1

Read **Section A**, then copy and answer the questions.

a Which group of men ruled Britain in the eighteenth century? _____

b Who had the right to vote in the eighteenth century? _____

c Why was there so much bribery in elections? _____

d How many M.P.s did each English county have? _____

e Boroughs were supposed to be what? _____

f Which two things did radicals want? _____ and _____

g The lords and gentry thought that which people ought to have the right to vote? _____

gave middle-class men in towns and the richer tenant-farmers the right to vote. But there were no votes for the working class.

The Reform Act gave the vote to about half a million men. Now, one man in every five could vote. But there was no secret ballot. So men could still be forced or bribed to vote as their landlords wished. The landowners still had more power than anyone else.

Now try Exercises 44.2 and 44.3.

Lord Grey (The Whig Prime Minister) sweeping away the rotten boroughs

Source 44a

The middle class have grown richer and stronger. Now they want the House of Commons to be reformed, so that they can have a share of the power that the nobles have at present. If we are wise, we will give in to their just demands before it is too late. If we do not, there will be riots and revolution, as there were in France.

From a speech made in the House of Commons by Thomas Macaulay in 1831.

Source 44b

The present House of Commons could not be improved. Its members are all men of property, and most of them own land. I think that is as it should be. So I am against any kind of reform. And so long as I am a member of the government, I will oppose reforms which other men propose.

Adapted from a speech made by the Duke of Wellington in the House of Lords in 1830. The Duke of Wellington was Prime Minister at the time.

Exercise 44.2

Read **Section B**, and read again the note on 'Motives' on page 212. Read **Sources 44a** and **44b**.

a Which of the speakers (Thomas Macaulay and the Duke of Wellington) do you think voted in favour of the Reform Bill, and which voted against it? (Write two sentences.)

b What do you think were Thomas Macaulay's motives for saying what he did? (Choose two sentences from the list below.)

c What do you think were the Duke of Wellington's motives for saying what he did? (Choose two sentences from the list below.)

   i He thought that the House of Commons was perfect.

   ii He wanted to avoid riots and revolution in England.

   iii He wanted to give votes to the working class as soon as possible.

   iv He thought that most M.P.s should be landowners.

   v He wanted to give the rich middle class a share of power.

Source 44c

Source 44d

Fizkin's side have got 33 voters in the lock-up coach-house at the White Hart Inn. They keep them locked up there till they want them (to vote). That stops us getting at them. And even if we could, it would be no use, for they keep them very drunk. Smart fellow, Fizkin's agent.

Adapted from *Pickwick Papers*, a novel written by Charles Dickens in 1837.

An election in Tonbridge in Kent, December 1832

Fact and fiction

Fiction sources (novels and stories) do not describe events that actually happened. But that does not mean that they are useless to the student of history. Descriptions of events and places in novels often tell us a great deal about how things were in the past.

Exercise 44.3

Read the note on 'Fact and fiction' and **Source 44d**, and look at **Source 44c**.

a Write notes on **Sources 44a, 44b, 44c** and **44d**. Say who spoke, wrote, or drew them, and when. Which sources are fact, and which is fiction?

b What do **Sources 44c** and **44d** tell us about elections in the 1830s? (Write a paragraph.)

c Is the fiction source useful to the historian? Can you find anything in **Sections A** and **B** to make you think that you should believe the fiction source? (Write a paragraph.)

C Rule by the people

Not everyone was happy with the Reform Act. The **Chartists** (see Chapter 49) wanted votes for all men. Later, the trade unions took up the same call. By 1866, the leaders of the main parties agreed. The **Conservatives** (who had been called Tories) passed a second Reform Act in 1867. The **Liberals** (formerly Whigs) passed a third one in 1884.

The 1867 Act gave the vote to working-class men in the towns. Farm labourers had to wait until 1884. But after the third Reform Act, most men could vote. (Women could not vote until 1918.) Also, from 1872 voting was secret. This meant that voters no longer had to follow the orders of their landlords or employers.

The Reform Acts took Britain well on the way to **democracy** – rule by the people. Some of the lords and gentry

Signing a petition in favour of votes for working men

were alarmed and afraid. They thought that working men were too ignorant to have the vote. They expected wild men with crazy ideas to be elected as M.P.s. They said that rich men's property would be taken away.

In fact, the working men voted for Conservatives or Liberals, and there was no revolution. (There were very few working-class M.P.s at first, though.) The biggest change was that after 1832 the House of Commons was more important than the House of Lords. The party that won most seats in the Commons formed the government. So after the Reform Acts, the **people** chose their government.

Now try Exercises 44.4 and 44.5.

Source 44e

We, the working classes of Britain, are denied our basic rights. We pay most of the taxes, but we are not allowed a share in choosing those who fix the taxes. We obey the laws, but we do not elect the men who make the laws. So let us join together to demand votes for all men, and the secret ballot. Let us respect the law and march forward to our freedom.

From a speech by Edmund Beales, president of the Reform League, in 1865.

Exercise 44.4

Read **Section C** and **Source 44e**. Answer the questions in sentences.

a Which two 'basic rights' did the speaker in **Source 44e** demand?
b The speaker said that people who pay taxes deserve what?
c He said that people who obey the law are entitled to what?
d Did he urge his audience to riot and break the law?
e Is **Source 44e** a primary or a secondary source? Give a reason for your opinion. (If you are not sure, look again at the note on page 218.)

Exercise 44.5

Write sentences to show that you know what these words and terms mean:

nobles	gentry	bribe	rotten borough
Tories	Whigs	act	secret ballot	democracy

45 The Move to the Towns, 1750-1900

A The growth of population

The first **census** (official count of people) in Britain took place in 1801. After that, there was a census every ten years. For the years before 1801, experts have made **estimates**. They have studied the records of births and deaths that are kept in churches. Put together, their results and the census figures give the graph which you see on page 231.

The graph shows that the population of England and Wales began to rise in the mid-eighteenth century. By 1901, it was six times as large as in 1750. What the graph does not show is that the rise was much faster in some places than others. In Lancashire, west Yorkshire, and the west Midlands, the population grew very fast indeed. In other words, it grew fastest in regions where there was a lot of **industry**.

Historians agree that the population grew. But they do not agree on **why** it grew. Some say that the main cause was that more babies were born. Some think that the main cause was that people lived longer. Most experts think that it was a mixture of the two. What is clear is that the rise in population took place at the same time as the growth of industry.

Now try Exercises 45.1 and 45.2.

Between 1815 and 1860, seven million people *emigrated* from the British Isles. Most of them went to the USA, Canada, and Australia. Cartoons like this told them that they would have a better life abroad.

HERE AND THERE;
Oᴿ, EMIGRATION A REMEDY.

Exercise 45.1

Read **Section A** and study the **graph**. Then draw a timeline from 1750 to 1900. Divide the timeline into centuries and parts of centuries (early, mid, late). Mark the following on the time-line:

i Population of England and Wales began to grow.
ii The first census.
iii Population of England and Wales reached 10 million.
iv Population of England and Wales reached 15 million.
v Population of England and Wales reached 20 million.
vi Population of England and Wales reached 30 million.

Source 45a

After 1740 people lived longer, so the population grew. This was because:

i *Farmers could keep more cattle, because they had turnips to feed them on in winter. The result was more meat for people to eat.*

ii *People were more healthy because they ate bread made from wheat, not from a mixture of wheat, barley, and rye.*

iii *People washed more, partly because soap became cheaper.*

iv *Cotton became cheap, and cotton clothes are easy to wash.*

v *New houses were warmer and healthier. They were built of brick or stone, not wood and clay. Their roofs were tiled, not thatched.*

vi *Doctors became more skilled, and there were more hospitals.*

Ideas adapted from a book written by Professor T. S. Ashton in 1947.

Source 45b

After 1740 the population grew.

i *There was not so much disease about, because:*

  a *Houses were more healthy. They were built of brick instead of wood and clay, and had tiled roofs instead of thatch.*

  b *Brown rats drove the black rats out of the towns and cities. Plague germs were carried by black rats' fleas.*

  c *It may be true that people washed more.*

ii *Fewer people died of hunger – harvests were good, so bread was cheap.*

iii *In the towns, there were more jobs and higher wages. So young men and women got married earlier and had more children than before.*

iv *Doctors learned more, but very few people could afford doctors. Hospitals were more likely to spread disease than cure it.*

Ideas adapted from a book written by Miss P. M. Deane in 1965.

Growth of population in England and Wales

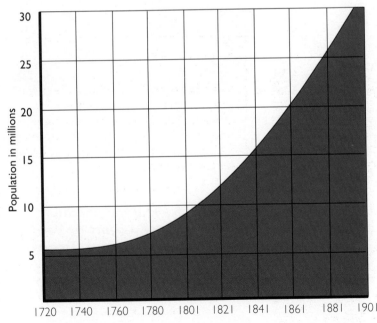

Exercise 45.2

Read **Sources 45a** and **45b**. Each source gives a list of reasons why the population grew, but the two lists are not the same. Write notes to show:

a Which ideas appear in both lists. (The words are not exactly the same.)

b Which ideas appear in **Source 45a**, but not in **Source 45b**.

c Which ideas appear in **Source 45b**, but not in **Source 45a**.

d Which point the two sources disagree about.

B Towns and cities

With the spread of industry, Britain's towns and cities got bigger. London and the great ports continued to grow. Mill towns like Oldham and Rochdale appeared from nothing. In 1800, two-thirds of the population still lived in the countryside. By 1850, the figure was down to a half. By the 1890s, three-quarters of Britain's people lived in towns.

The first reason for this change was that men and women moved from the country into the towns. They came to work in the factories and mills. The wages were low, but better than labourers could get on the farms. The second reason was that families were large. It was a good thing to have a lot of children if five and six-year-olds could earn money in the mills.

Workers' houses were thrown up quickly and cheaply. A lot of them were two or three-roomed 'back-to-backs'. They stood in rows in narrow streets or clustered round gloomy courtyards. Many families lived in a single room. Most streets were not paved, and the only sewer was an open drain. Water was piped from the river to a pump in the street or yard.

Bad housing and impure water led to disease, of course. People died much younger in the towns than in the countryside. **Cholera** was common — an outbreak in London in 1849 killed 13,000 people. **Typhoid fever** threatened not only the poor in the slums — it killed Prince Albert, Queen Victoria's husband, in 1861.

Now try Exercise 45.3.

Source 45c

The street was unpaved. A gutter ran down the middle, with pools every now and then. Women from their doors tossed household slops into the gutter. The slops ran into the pools, and lay there, stagnating. Passers-by had to step on the heaps of ashes to keep their feet clean.

Adapted from the novel *Mary Barton*, written by Elizabeth Gaskell in 1848.

Source 45d

Dudley Street in the Seven Dials district of London in 1872

Source 45e

Houses were built back-to-back along narrow alleys, or round the four sides of a court or yard. The only entry to the court was a tunnel. Towns grew too fast for these houses to be connected with the water-supply. So the people had to buy from the water-carriers, who sold water by the pail.

Adapted from a book written by Professor J. D. Chambers in 1961.

Spectators looking at the gas lights in Pall Mall in 1809

You need to be careful when you are using history sources. You should ask questions about the people who wrote or made them. For example: Did the author who wrote the source (or the artist who drew it) know how things really were? Did he write about (or draw things) that he had seen himself? Did he read lots of sources and look at all kinds of evidence? Did he have any reason for not telling the truth?

Exercise 45.3

Read **Section B** and **Sources 45c** and **45e**. Look at **Sources 45d** and **45f**. Read the note 'Can we believe the sources?' Then discuss these questions in a group:

a What do the sources tell us about town streets in the nineteenth century? (And why is **Source 45f** so different from **Source 45d**?)
b What reasons are there for **i** believing, and **ii** not believing what each of the sources tells us?
Either give short talks telling the rest of the class what you think, **or** make a group tape

C Health in the towns

Before 1830, the government did not think that the state of the towns was its business. Local councils could improve things or not, as they wished. In fact, some did so. Birmingham and Manchester had some paved streets by 1800. Glasgow and London had gas street-lights by 1815.

The first big change was an act to reform the **councils** in 1835. It said that they had to be elected by the men who paid the rates. And it gave them the power to provide water supplies and systems of sewers if they wished. In some places, big improvements followed. In others they did not – ratepayers did not like councillors who spent a lot of money.

By the 1840s, people knew that there was a connection between bad sanitation and disease. And the government in London was growing

Charles Pierce, one of the first Metropolitan policemen, in 1850

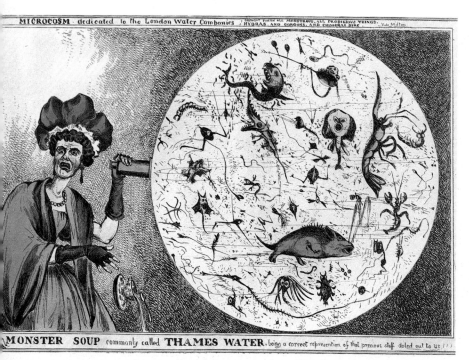

MICROCOSM dedicated to the London Water Companies) BRINGS FORTH ALL MONSTROUS, ALL PRODIGIOUS THINGS,) HYDRAS AND GORGONS, AND CHIMERAS DIRE. Vide Milton.

MONSTER SOUP commonly called THAMES WATER, being a correct representation of that precious stuff doled out to us !!!

A cartoonist's view of London water in the mid-nineteenth century. People in London and elsewhere were forced to drink untreated water which led to the spread of disease.

A new block of flats built to replace some of London's slums

more and more alarmed about people's health in towns. From 1848, it passed a string of acts urging the councils to take action. In the end, it said that they had to pave and light their streets, provide sewers, and see that new houses had proper water supplies.

The nation's health slowly improved. But there was not much change in housing. An act passed in 1875 said that councils could buy slums, pull them down, and build new houses for the people. Birmingham council made good use of the act, but not many others followed its lead. In 1900 far too many working people still lived in slums.

Now try Exercise 45.4.

Exercise 45.4

Read **Section C**. Copy the sentences and write TRUE or FALSE after each one.

a Before 1830, the government took no interest in improving towns.

_____

b No town councils made any improvements before 1830.

_____

c The way local councils were elected was reformed in 1835.

_____

d After 1835 all councils laid on supplies of pure water.

_____

e In 1840 doctors knew that open sewers were a danger to health.

_____

f After 1848 the government tried to improve the people's health.

_____

g In 1875 the government forced councils to pull down slums.

_____

h All town councils built better houses for the people.

_____

46 Making Ends Meet, 1750-1900

Source 46a

A The standard of living – the evidence

'The Harvest Home'. At the end of the harvest, the farmer leads his workers home to a celebration feast.

The '**standard of living**' of a family depended on how much money came in and how high the prices were. If father got a pay rise, they could afford better food, clothes, and shoes. In other words, the standard of living rose. If father lost his job, the standard of living fell.

We do not know enough about the standard of living in the past. We know how high the wages were in some trades, but not all. We know about the rise and fall in the price of bread. But we do not know enough about the price of clothes, or rent. We know that wages were high in some parts of Britain, and low in others. We know that the unemployed suffered, but not who was unemployed, or for how long.

The **weather** had a lot to do with the standard of living. If it was good, there was a good harvest, and the price of **bread** was low. A bad harvest meant a shortage, and a high price. Bread was working people's main food — they sometimes had cheese with it, but seldom got meat.

The things that working people bought are clues to their standard of living. By the year 1850, their bread was made from pure wheat, not the cheaper mixture of wheat, barley, and rye that they had eaten before. Also, tea and sugar sales had greatly increased. (In the early eighteenth century, only the rich could afford tea and sugar.) By 1875, working people were spending far more on bacon, jam, chocolate, and beer.

Even at a time when the standard of living was rising, there were years of bad harvest and high unemployment. Food riots in 1795, 1812, and 1830 tell us a lot about the farm labourers' standard of living in those years. High unemployment in the late 1830s was the chief reason why so many working people backed the Chartists. (See Chapter 49.)

Now try Exercises 46.1 and 46.2.

Deductions from evidence

The **evidence** (what we know about the past) does not always tell us everything we would like to know. But we can often **make deductions** from the evidence (work things out from the clues we have). For example:
Corn prices were very high in the 1790s. **Therefore**, there must have been a shortage of corn.
Therefore, the harvests must have been bad. **Therefore**, the weather must have been bad.

Exercise 46.1

Read **Section A**, then copy out the following sentences and use these words to fill in the blanks:

fell   higher   price   rent   rose
unemployed   wages

a If wages _____ the standard of living improved.
b If prices rose, the standard of living _____ .
c We do not know how high the _____ were in all trades.
d We have some information about the _____ of bread.
e Wages were _____ in some areas than others.
f We do not know how much _____ people paid for their homes.
g We do not know how many people were _____ .

Exercise 46.2

Read the note 'Deductions from evidence', and use paragraphs 3, 4, and 5 of **Section A**. Look at **Sources 46a** and **46b**. Then copy and complete the sentences.

a Harvests were important for the standard of living, because _____ .
b The fact that people changed to pure wheat bread tells us that _____ .
c If working families could afford tea and sugar, _____ .
d People do not spend money on jam and chocolate if _____ .
e The food riots in 1830 tell us that _____ .
f In **Source 46a**, we can tell that it had been a good harvest, because _____ .
g The villagers in **Source 46b** must have done so much knitting because _____ .

Source

The Wensleydale knitters (1814). Men, women and children in Wensleydale in Yorkshire spent every spare moment knitting stockings. They needed the extra money because farm workers' wages were so low.

B The rising standard of living, 1750-1875

Working people's standard of living rose between 1750 and 1793. Harvests were mainly good, so bread prices were fairly low. Labourers had money to spare for new clothes, as well as food. And from the 1780s, the new cotton mills were making cheap cloth.

During the long wars with France (1793 to 1815) it became harder to make ends meet. Britain imported less wheat from abroad, and prices rose. Also, there were bad harvests in the mid-1790s and in 1811-12. On the other hand, wages were quite high at this time, and unemployment was rare.

From 1815 to 1850, wages fell, but prices fell even more, so people were better off. Some were not so lucky, though. The wages of **handloom-weavers** (see Chapter 40) fell far more than prices. And there were spells of unemployment that hit most trades. Since no work meant no pay at all, unemployment brought great hardship.

From 1850 to 1875, prices were rising, but wages were rising faster. New factories, mills, mines, and ship-yards were taking on people. Thousands of workers left the land, where wages were low, and took better-paid jobs in the growing towns. Standards of living were higher than ever before.

Now try Exercise 46.3.

Not everyone was prosperous in this period. On the left is a family of match-box makers in London in 1871. Below is a poor family of cotton workers in Manchester in 1862.

Exercise 46.3

Read **Section B**. The notes below refer to four different periods of time. Write the notes in the right order, and add the dates.

a Prices and wages both fell, and there were spells of unemployment.
b Prices and wages both rose, and most working people were quite well off.
c Wages were high, but so were prices, and the standard of living did not rise.
d Harvests were good, prices were low, and the standard of living was rising.

C The Poor Law

Before 1900 there were no old-age pensions or free health service in Britain. And there were no state payments for those too sick to work or for the unemployed. Instead, there was the **Poor Law**. This was meant just for the very poor — the old, the sick, and the starving.

Each **parish** had an 'overseer of the poor'. His job was to collect **rates** from the heads of households (most men in the parish). He used the money to help those in need. (But he had to be careful not to give out too much!) If they wished, parishes could join together, build **workhouses**, and make the old, the sick, and orphans live in them.

The parish of **Speenhamland** in Berkshire began 'topping-up' the wages of low-paid farm workers in 1795. This 'system' soon spread through most of southern England. It had two very bad effects — the farmers paid even lower wages than before, and the poor rates had to go up to meet the cost.

The act which Parliament passed in 1834 was meant to make the Poor Law cheaper. It said that groups of parishes had to build workhouses. In future, 'able-bodied' poor would get help only if they came into the workhouses. And workhouses were made unpleasant, to discourage idlers. The food was poor, discipline was strict, and families were split up.

Poor rates were cut by half after the 1834 act, and rate-payers were pleased. But poor people hated the workhouses. And the new law did not really work. In times of slump and high unemployment, there was no room in the workhouses for all those who needed help. So they were given 'out-relief' — they got Poor Law money while they stayed at home.

Now try Exercise 46.4.

Husbands and wives were separated in the workhouse

Source 46c

The mill-owner got the children, at the ages of six, seven, and eight, from the workhouses of Edinburgh. It was his duty to feed, clothe, and educate them, and he spared no expense in doing this. Their rooms were clean and airy, and there was plenty of food. But to meet the costs of all this, he had to make the children work in the mill from six in the morning to seven at night. Their schooling began when they had finished work.

Written by Robert Owen about New Lanark mill in about 1800. [When they were old enough, workhouse orphans were apprenticed to tradesmen.]

Source 46d

When she was ten years old, her mother died. As there was no-one among her friends that was rich enough to save her from the workhouse, to the workhouse she went. Three months later, she and many others were sent as apprentices to Deep Valley factory. They were supposed to go there to learn a good trade, but in truth they went as slaves.

Adapted from the novel *Michael Armstrong*, written by Mrs. Trollope in 1840.

Source 46e

A notice was pasted on the outside of the gate next morning. It offered a reward of five pounds to anybody who would take Oliver Twist off the hands of the parish. In other words, five pounds and Oliver Twist were offered to any man or woman who wanted an apprentice...
... Mr. Gamfield, the chimney-sweep, smiled as he read the notice. Five pounds was just the sum he wanted. As to the boy, Mr. Gamfield knew that a workhouse boy would not need much to eat.

Adapted from the novel *Oliver Twist*, written by Charles Dickens in 1839.

Exercise 46.4

Read **Section C** and **Sources 46c, 46d**, and **46e**.
Write short paragraphs, answering the questions below.

a   What were supposed to be the duties of employers who took on workhouse orphans as apprentices?
b   Why were some employers quite keen to take on workhouse orphans?
c   What do you think about the education mentioned in **Source 46c**?
d   Which of the sources are fact, and which are fiction? Should we believe what the fiction sources say? If so, why?

47 Free Trade

A Tariffs and Corn Laws

All governments need to collect **taxes**. Some are on the wages people earn (income-tax), and some on what they buy. For most of the eighteenth century, the government's money came mainly from **tariffs** (customs duties). These were taxes on imports, such as tea, silk, and brandy. But **Adam Smith** said that tariffs reduced trade, and so harmed Britain. He was in favour of **free trade**.

In the 1780s, the government did reduce some tariffs. But during the wars with France, from 1793 to 1815, it needed more money, so tariffs went up again. Then in the 1820s they were cut once more, but Britain was still a long way from free trade in 1830.

There were always tariffs on corn imports in the eighteenth century. But the **Corn Laws** passed in 1815 **banned** imports if the price of corn in Britain was less than £4 per quarter. The **motive** was to keep the farmers' pro-fits up, so that they could pay high rents to the landowners.

Merchants and mill-owners did not like the Corn Laws. In 1838 a group of them formed the **Anti-Corn Law League**. They said that the Corn Laws put up the price of bread, and that if they were **repealed** (abolished), the price of bread would fall. Workers' wages could then be reduced, so British-made goods would be cheaper, and there would be more trade.

The government did not give in straight away. But in 1842, **Sir Robert Peel**, who was then Prime Minister, made a big cut in tariffs. (He brought in an income-tax at the same time.) Then in 1846 came famine in Ireland. (See Chapter 50.) The Irish needed cheap food, so Peel **repealed the Corn Laws**. The move split Peel's party, the Conservatives, but it made Britain a free trade nation.

Now try Exercises 47.1 and 47.2.

Workers and mill-owners versus farmers and landowners

Source 47a

The aim of the Anti-Corn Law League is to abolish the Corn Law. This law is a tax on corn, a tax to help the land-owners. If we can get rid of it, all the other taxes on trade will follow. We will then have Free Trade, which will make all nations better off. Not only that, but it will also lead to peace and goodwill, and an end to war and conquest.

Adapted from a speech made by Richard Cobden in 1840. Cobden was one of the leaders of the Anti-Corn Law League.

Source 47b

When news reached Ashton-under-Lyne that the Corn Laws were repealed, flags were raised in all parts of the town. The flags had slogans on them, such as 'Free trade for ever', and 'Free trade with all the world'. Outside a barber's shop was a flag saying 'No supporters of the Corn Laws shaved here'. Some of the mill-owners have held feasts for their workers.

Adapted from a report in *The Times* newspaper, 3 July 1846.

Exercise 47.1

Read **Section A** and **Sources 47a** and **47b**, then copy and answer the questions.

a 'Tariffs' is another name for what? _____ _____

b Adam Smith was in favour of what? _____ _____

c What happened to tariffs in the 1820s? _____

d **Source 47a** says that the Corn Laws were meant to help whom? _____

e **Source 47a** says that free trade will end what? _____

f Which new tax did Sir Robert Peel start in 1842? _____

g When were the Corn Laws repealed? _____

h Who were the main employers in Ashton-under-Lyne (**Source 47b**)? _____

i Why do you think the people of Ashton-under-Lyne were so pleased about the repeal of the Corn Laws? _____

John Bright and Richard Cobden (left and centre) were the leaders of the Anti-Corn Law League

Exercise 47.2

Answer these questions about **Sources 47a, 47b, 47c,** and **47d**.

a Who wrote it (or said it)?
b When was it written or said?
c Is it a primary or a secondary source?

Write your answers out in a chart.

B The 'workshop of the world'

By 1860 there were hardly any tariffs left, and free trade was almost complete. Even though bread prices did not fall, the years after 1850 were a time of success for Britain. In 1873 her exports were worth £240 million a year, nearly five times what they were in 1842.

Britain, with her mills and factories, produced far more goods, and much more cheaply, than any other nation. Britain invented railways, and was the first country to have a railway system. By the 1850s, she was exporting railway lines and engines to the rest of the world. She was right to call herself the 'workshop of the world'.

But Britain's **imports** grew also. Her population had grown so fast that she needed to import a lot of her food. Most of her raw cotton came from the U.S.A. A growing share of the wool and iron ore she used was coming from abroad. By 1870, Britain was paying more for her imports than she was earning from her exports.

A large part of the difference was made up by the money earned by the **merchant navy**. After 1850, trade was growing all over the world. More than half of it was carried in British ships. By 1890, Britain's merchant navy was as big as all other merchant fleets combined.

Now try Exercise 47.3.

Miners in 1871 cutting coal by hand. They are using Davy lamps. You can also see a pit-pony and a boy employed to look after it down the mine.

Source 47c

The typical Englishman was still a farm-hand in 1831. And most of those who worked in industry in 1831 were employed in small workshops, not factories. By 1851, more people lived in towns. ... But still only a quarter of the workers were employed in factories and mines.

Adapted from a book written by Professor J. D. Chambers in 1960.

Do they agree or disagree?

Authors sometimes **appear** to disagree with each other, when in fact they do not. If we read what they say carefully, we can see that they may **both** be right. The authors of **Sources 47c** and **47d** **appear** to disagree about Britain in the mid-nineteenth century. But is that really the case?

Source 47d

By 1830 Britain was mining 75 per cent of Europe's coal, and making more than half of its cotton goods. By 1860 she was producing 54 per cent of the world's iron and steel. The volume of her trade was going up all the time. ... She truly deserved to be called 'the workshop of the world.'

Adapted from a book written by Martin Roberts in 1972.

Exercise 47.3

Read **Section B**. Read the note 'Do they agree or disagree?' and read **Sources 47c** and **47d very carefully**.
Then discuss these questions in a group.

a Does **Source 47c** say that Britain was **not** producing a lot of coal, cotton, and iron?
b Does **Source 47d** say that **most** British workers were employed in mines, mills, and factories?
c Does **Source 47c** make you think that the number employed in factories and mines was growing?
d What does **Source 47d** tell us about industry in other countries?
e Do the two sources disagree with each other?
f What do the two sources together tell us?
Either give talks, telling the rest of the class what you think, or make a group tape.

C The Great Exhibition

It was **Prince Albert's** idea to hold a festival of arts and science in London, and he played an important part in the planning. On 1 May 1851, the **Great Exhibition** was opened by Queen Victoria. It took place in the **Crystal Palace**, a huge structure of iron girders and glass plates, built for this one event in Kensington Gardens. The 'palace' was 550 metres long, and more than 40 metres high.

The first aim of Prince Albert and the planners was to display the arts and

The outside of the Crystal Palace

Queen Victoria opening The Great Exhibition in the Crystal Palace on 1 May 1851

industry of all nations. Out of this came their second aim, to show that Britain's industry was the best. This, they hoped, would prove the value of free trade. And free trade, as Richard Cobden said, brought world peace. (See **Source 47a**). Lastly, it would be a great show to entertain and inform the public.

Entries came from all over the world. Visitors liked the chinaware from France and the lace from Spain. But it was British industry that impressed them most. Never had there been such a show of human skill. British workers, it was said, were the 'working bees of the world's hive'.

The exhibition was open for five months. In that time, 6,000,000 visitors saw it. Thousands came up to London on special trains. A trip to the Crystal Palace was everyone's idea of a day out in 1851. Queen Victoria was so thrilled that she came back 30 times.

Now try Exercise 47.4.

Some of the exhibits in The Great Exhibition

Exercise 47.4

Read **Section C**.

a Plan an essay on 'The motives of the men who planned the Great Exhibition of 1851'. Write brief notes saying what each paragraph would be about – one paragraph for each motive.
b Draw a picture of the outside of the Crystal Palace.

48 The End of British Prosperity?

A The decline of agriculture

A quarter of all British men were farm workers in 1850. Britain's **agriculture** was still her most important trade. But industry was growing all the time. And after 1875, farming hit bad times.

Food from abroad was the main cause of the decline of agriculture. As her population grew, Britain had to import more of her food. And by the 1880s, imported **wheat** (mainly from the U.S.A.) was cheaper than wheat grown in England. British farmers could not get a decent price for the crops they grew.

Why was wheat from the U.S.A. cheaper to buy in London than wheat grown 20 miles away in Essex? The first answer is that land was very cheap on the American prairies. (English

farmers had to pay rent.) Secondly, there were more machines (e.g. binders and steam ploughs) in the U.S.A., so they did not need so many men. And thirdly, with railways and steamships, transport costs were low.

Low prices meant low profits for farmers. Landlords had to charge lower rents, so they were worse off too. Many farmers stopped growing wheat, and kept cattle and sheep instead. Then, in the 1880s and 1890s, frozen mutton and beef began to arrive from abroad, and meat prices fell as well. A lot of farmers went out of business. Those who did not needed fewer labourers. Farm workers and their families made for the towns.

Now try Exercise 48.1.

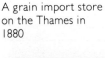
A grain import store on the Thames in 1880

The End of British Prosperity?

Source 48a

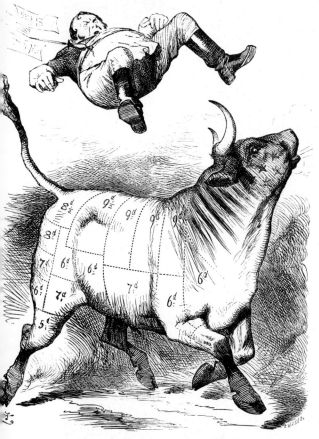

'John Bull and American beef' – John Bull (the English butcher) is trying to sell English beef at 15d (15 old pence, or 6 new pence) a pound. The most expensive cut of American beef is only 9½d (4 new pence) a pound.

Source 48b

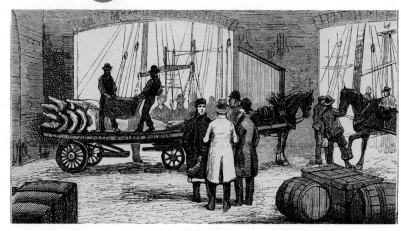

Unloading a cargo of American meat at Liverpool in 1877

Exercise 48.1

Read **Section A**, and study **Sources 48a** and **48b**.
Write TRUE or FALSE after each of the sentences.

a Coal-mining was Britain's most important trade in 1850.
b The decline of British farming took place after 1875.
c Cheap wheat from America made prices fall in Britain.
d American farmers did not have to pay high rents for land.
e British landlords did not suffer from the decline in farming.
f **Source 48b** shows a cargo of frozen meat from America.
g **Source 48a** shows the British butcher suffering from American competition.
h In **Source 48a**, John Bull is being 'thrown' because his meat prices are too high.

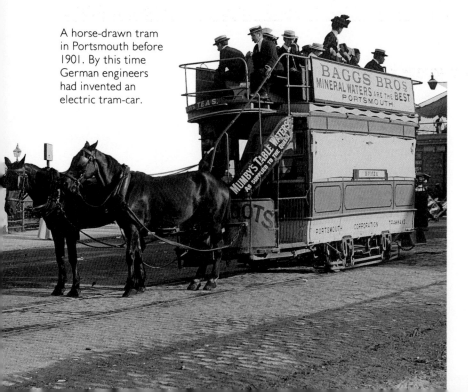

A horse-drawn tram in Portsmouth before 1901. By this time German engineers had invented an electric tram-car.

B Good news and bad

Low food prices were good news for most workers. For those with jobs, the standard of living rose between 1870 and 1900. But not everyone had a job. And spells of unemployment brought hunger and misery.

It was the age of coal. Steam engines drove machines in factories and mills. Every home had a coal fire. Railways, with steam engines, were the main form of transport. Towns and cities were blackened with smoke. All this was good for miners and mine-owners

– coal output almost doubled between 1870 and 1900.

A lot of coal was sold abroad, but the chief export was still cotton cloth. Britain, though, was no longer the only country with cotton mills. Now there were **competitors** in Europe and the U.S.A. And most of these foreign makers of cotton were using new machines. The British mills kept to their old machines, which were starting to become out-of-date.

A worse sign was that Britain no longer led the world with new inventions and ideas. The **Germans** were the leaders in the **chemical** industry (making dyes for textiles, for example). And it was a German who invented the **petrol engine** and the first **car**. Until 1896 cars were allowed on British roads only if a man with a red flag walked in front.

In the late nineteenth century, inventors found ways of making **steel** in large amounts. Steel took over from iron in machines, bridge girders, and ships. Some of the steel-making inventions were British. But more steel was made in Germany and the U.S.A. than in Britain.

Now try Exercise 48.2

An early car in the 1890s

Exercise 48.2

Read **Section B**. then copy the sentences and fill in the blanks.

a For workers who had _____ the standard of living rose after 1870.

b Industry's main fuel in the nineteenth century was _____

c The numbers of jobs for _____ nearly doubled between 1870 and 1900.

d _____ _____ remained Britain's main export.

e Mills in _____ and the _____ were now making cotton cloth.

f A _____ invented the petrol engine and made the first car.

g Both Germany and the U.S.A. were making more _____ than Britain.

Now draw a picture of a car of the 1890s.

C Why did Britain lose her lead?

Britain had been the world's leader in industry and trade. Why did she let Germany and the U.S.A. catch up? Part of the answer is that she could not stop them. The U.S.A. is far bigger and richer than Britain. In the end, it was almost bound to take the lead.

At the same time, some British firms were badly **managed**. By the 1880s and 1890s, a lot of them were run by the sons and grandsons of the men who set them up. And the sons and grandsons, too often, never went near the mills and factories. They just lived off the profits.

To keep up with their rivals, firms need to **invest** money. (For example, they have to buy more up-to-date machines.) The money comes from the firm's own profits or from well-off **investors**. But after 1870, British investors put more money into foreign railways and mines than they put into British factories and mills. They got good **dividends**, but they did not help British industry. In fact, they helped foreign firms to grow.

British firms which sold machines abroad also helped Britain's rivals. Foreign mills, full of British-made machines, made good, cheap cloth. Then they sold it to customers who, 30 years before, had bought from Britain.

On top of this, Britain stuck to free trade, while most other countries did not. The French and Germans put **tariffs** on imports to **protect** their own industries. French tariffs on imported cloth made British-made cloth expensive in France. So French people bought French-made cloth instead.

Lastly, British inventors were falling behind. Had this something to do with education? German schools and universities led the world in science and engineering. But young men in Britain's 'public schools' studied Latin and Greek and not much else. Most of them knew no science at all.

Now try Exercises 48.3 and 48.4.

Source 48c

A British cartoon in 1885 against free trade. The combination of British free trade and foreign tariffs on British imports is helping our competitors and crushing British industry and workers.

Exercise 48.3

Read **Section C**.
Divide a page into two halves, left and right. In the left-hand half, write down the five causes below.

a Some British owners did not visit their mills and factories.
b Not enough money was invested in British factories and mills.
c British firms supplied machines for foreign cotton mills.
d Many countries put tariffs on exports from Britain.
e Pupils in British schools did not learn much science.

In the right-hand half, write down a **result** opposite each cause.

Source 48d

A depression began in about 1875. By 'depression' we mean that profits fell and unemployment rose. There were three main causes:
1 *Our factories and mills produced more than they could sell.*
2 *Foreign countries brought in tariffs and ended free trade.*
3 *Foreign competition made it harder to sell our goods, at home and abroad.*

Adapted from the report of a Royal Commission on trade, 1886.

Source 48e

India is the most important market for our cotton cloth. So long as we keep control of the seas, the 250 million people there will be ready to take our produce. At present we sell them cottons to the value of two shillings (10p.) per head per year. This could easily be increased to six shillings. If we did that, it would be very good for the British working man.

Adapted from a speech made by Sir Richard Temple, M.P. in 1887.

Source 48f

You will find that your clothes, and your wife's, are made from cloth that was woven in Germany. Your children's toys and dolls were made there too. Your newspaper is printed on paper that came from Germany. Go where you like in your house and you will see the same "Made in Germany" mark. It is on the piano in your drawing room and the mug on your kitchen dresser. It is even on your drain-pipes and the poker for your fire.

Adapted from a book written by E. E. Williams in 1896.

Exercise 48.4

Read **Sources 48d**, **48e**, and **48f**, and look at **Source 48c**.

a **Source 48c** – i Describe what you can see in the cartoon. ii What were the artist's **opinions** about free trade and tariffs?
b **Source 48d** – i What did the authors mean by 'depression'? ii In their **opinion**, what were the causes of the depression?
c **Source 48e** – i Note down any **facts** in this source. ii What were the author's **opinions**?
d **Source 48f** – i Note down at least six 'Made in Germany' items. ii What do you think the author's **opinions** were?

49 Working Class Movements

A From Luddites to Chartists

The British working class did not care about revolutions. Sometimes they took part in protests, but only when they were hungry or unemployed. The things that concerned them were jobs, wages, and the price of bread.

Source 49a

Soldiers break up a meeting at St Peter's Field in Manchester in 1819. This event came to be called the 'Peterloo massacre'.

The 'Luddites' who smashed knitting and spinning machines in 1811 did not want to cut the king's head off. They were afraid of losing their jobs — they said that the machines put them out of work. The crowds who listened to **Henry Hunt** between 1816 and 1819 cheered when he said that all men should have votes. But what they really cared about were unemployment and high taxes. When trade improved after 1820, the troubles ceased.

The leaders of the **Chartists** were angry that the 1832 Reform Act did not go far enough. Their 'People's Charter', which they drew up in 1838, asked for votes for all men (but not women), a secret ballot, and elections every year. Between 1838 and 1848,

Cut them down, doan't be afraid, they are not Armed, courage my boys, and you shall have a vote of thanks, & he that Kills most shall be made a Knight errant, and your exploits shall live for ever, in a Song, or second Chivey Chace!

None but the brave deserve the Fair.

Cut him down, Cut him down,

Oh pray Sir, doan't Kill mammy, she only came to see Mr Hunt.

Shame, Shame, murder, murder, Massacre.

Shame

Shame

Reformers

Peculators

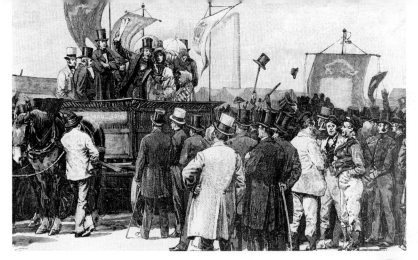

A Chartist demonstration at Kennington Common in London in April 1848

the Chartists got massive support from the working people. Thousands took part in their meetings and strikes. Millions signed their petitions to Parliament.

But it was jobs, wages, and prices that were the main worries of the working class. There were trade slumps in the 1830s and 1840s, and workers knew that if you lost your job there was nowhere to go but the dreaded workhouse. This was what made them follow the Chartists.

Britain's rulers did not give in to Luddites, radicals, and Chartists. They said that machine-breakers would be hanged. They cut down the freedom of the press. They banned meetings, and sent troops to break them up. These tactics worked — mill-hands could not take on the army. The last Chartist protest, in 1848, was a dismal flop.

Now try Exercises 49.1 and 49.2.

Source **49b**

A crowd of 60,000 men and women gathered in St. Peter's Field, Manchester. When Henry Hunt (the radical) arrived, he brought them to silence, and began to speak. Just then, a platoon of cavalry was seen making for the platform. To get through the mass of people, they drew their swords and struck out to right and left. A company of hussars came to their aid. The crowd panicked and fled, chased by the soldiers with drawn swords. Eleven persons were killed, and several hundred injured.

Exercise 49.1

Read **Section A**. What do you think were the **motives** of the following? (What did they want, or say they wanted?) Write your answers as notes.

a The Luddites.
b Henry Hunt.
c The people who attended Henry Hunt's meetings.
d The Chartist leaders.
e The people who followed the Chartists.

Exercise 49.2

Read **Source 49b** and study **Source 49a**.
Copy out the sentences and fill in the blanks. (Use words from the list below.)

dressed   eleven   large   panicked   **Source 49a**
Source 49b   swords   trampled

a _____ shows us that a man tried to make a speech, but does not tell us anything about him.

b Only _____ says that the speaker was a radical.

c Only **Source 49b** tells us how _____ the crowd was.

d Only **Source 49a** shows us how the soldiers were _____ .

e Both sources tell us that the soldiers drew their _____ .

f Both sources tell us that the crowd _____ .

g Only **Source 49a** shows us that some people were _____ by the horses.

h Only **Source 49b** tells us that _____ people were killed.

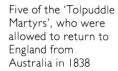
Five of the 'Tolpuddle Martyrs', who were allowed to return to England from Australia in 1838

B Early trade unions

The first trade unions were set up between 1700 and 1750. Most of them were like the guilds of the Middle Ages. Members paid in a few pence a week, and got help if they were unemployed or ill. Strikes were rare, but they were not unknown. The miners of Tyneside went on strike in 1765.

Employers did not like the unions. Some used **lock-outs** to try to smash them. (They closed their works, and gave the men their jobs back only if they left the union.) And the government took the employers' side. In 1799, during the wars with France, all unions were banned by law.

In spite of the ban, some unions kept going, often in secret. When the ban was lifted, in 1824, new unions were set up. Most of them soon failed, though – employers locked the men out, and brought in non-union workers. And wages were low, so not many men could afford union fees.

Robert Owen tried to set up a union for all trades and for the whole of England in 1834. But it lasted only a few months. It collapsed when six farm workers from Tolpuddle in Dorset were charged with taking a secret oath when they joined it. They were found guilty and sentenced to seven years' transportation to Australia.

News of the 'Tolpuddle Martyrs' killed Owen's union. Workers did not want to risk transportation for themselves and ruin for their families. For the 'martyrs', though, the outcome was not all bad. Fair-minded people wrote letters and signed protests, saying that they had been wrongly treated. After four years, the 'martyrs' were brought home.

Now try Exercise 49.3

A meeting of 50–60,000 Trade Unionists at Copenhagen Fields in 1834, to carry a petition to the king, asking for the release of the Tolpuddle Martyrs

A lock-out against the union

Exercise 49.3

Read **Section B**. Then draw a timeline from 1700 to 1850. Mark these events in the correct places on the timeline, with dates if you know them.

a Robert Owen's union was set up.
b War with France began. (See Chapter 43.)
c War with France ended. (See Chapter 43.)
d Tyneside miners went on strike.
e The 'Tolpuddle Martyrs' were allowed to return home.
f The first trade unions were set up.
g The last Chartist protest took place. (See Section A of this chapter.)
h Trade unions were banned by law.
i The end of the ban on trade unions.

C 'New unions'

The unions of the 1840s were small, and most of them did not last long. But in the 1850s the first of the 'new unions' were set up. Like the early unions, they were for **skilled** workers, such as engineers, iron founders, and joiners. They were 'new' in that they were **national** — their members came from all parts of Britain.

The new unions helped their members when they were ill or unemployed. They looked after former members' widows and orphans. They tried to **persuade** employers to pay higher wages. They tried to get the government to give more rights to unions and their members. They had some success — the 1867 Reform Act gave the vote to working men in towns. And an act in 1875 said that **strikes** were legal, so long as **pickets** were peaceful.

By the 1870s, most skilled trades had unions. The next step was unions for **unskilled** workers. And there were strikes for better wages. The London match girls won their strike in 1888, and so did the London dockers in 1889. But a miners' lock-out in south Wales in 1898 ended in defeat.

In 1874, for the first time, two working men took their seats in the House of Commons — as **Liberal** M.P.s. The first independent **Labour** member was elected in 1892. But it was only in 1900 that the trade unions decided to set up their own party. Even then, it did not become the **Labour Party** until 1906.

Now try Exercise 49.4.

The girls who worked in Bryant and May's match factory in London went on strike in 1888. The public supported them and they won their case.

Source 49c

Until the 1890s, trade unions were content to follow the Liberals. But in the 1890s this changed when the Liberals would not pick working men to stand for Parliament. At the same time, some employers were banding together to fight the unions. And the law courts took the employers' side. Also, more and more workers wanted someone to speak for them. All of these things were causes of the birth of the Labour Party.

Ideas taken from a book written by Professor W. Ashworth in 1960. [Not Professor Ashworth's words.]

The banner of the Amalgamated Society of Engineers, 1852

Source 49d

In the last ten years of the nineteenth century trade was bad. At the same time, employers, with the help of the law courts, were trying to reduce the rights of the unions. For these reasons, workers began to say that there should be a party to take the side of the working class.

Adapted from a book written by Martin Roberts in 1972.

Exercise 49.4

Read **Section C** and **Sources 49c** and **49d**. Answer the questions in sentences.

a The first working men in Parliament belonged to which party?
b Which source tells us why the union leaders became unhappy with the Liberals?
c Why did the unions fall out with the Liberals?
d Which source tells us that trade was bad? When was trade bad?
e What do both sources say about the courts?
f What else were employers doing to fight the unions?
g What did workers begin to say in the 1890s?
h Which source mentions the birth of the Labour Party?

Protestant landlords owned most of the land in Ireland. They lived very comfortably on the rents paid by their Irish tenants.

Inside the house of a quite prosperous Irish tenant farmer

A The Act of Union

In 1750, three-quarters of the people in Ireland were **Catholics**. But the **Protestants** (who were partly English) had all the power. They owned most of the land. Only they could hold the top jobs in the state. Only they could vote, or be members of the Irish Parliament, which met in Dublin. In any case, the Irish Parliament was forced to take orders from the government in London.

Irish Catholics got the right to vote in 1793. But they still complained that they were treated unfairly. In 1796, when Britain and France were at war, the Irish rose in revolt. (**Wolfe Tone**, their leader, was a Protestant.) The French tried to help, but storms at sea broke up their fleet. By 1798, British troops had crushed the rebels.

In 1800, Parliament passed an **Act of Union**. The act closed the Irish Parliament. Instead, Ireland was to have 100 M.P.s in the House of Commons in London. **William Pitt**, the Prime Minister, wanted to give Catholics equal rights to Protestants. But the king, George III, would not agree. So Ireland lost its Parliament, and did not get much in return.

In the 1820s, a great public speaker called **Daniel O'Connell** was the Irish leader. He said that there should be equal rights for Catholics. He meant that they should be free to be M.P.s, mayors of towns, judges, etc. The people were soon all behind him. It was clear that, if Britain did not give way, there would be civil war in Ireland. So in 1829 a **Catholic Relief Act** was passed, giving O'Connell most of what he asked for.

Now try Exercise 50.1.

Starving Irish children at the time of the Great Famine

Exercise 50.1

Read **Section A**, then answer the questions.

a What was the religion of most people in Ireland?
b Could Catholics be members of the Irish Parliament?
c Who led the Irish revolt in 1796?
d Who tried to help the Irish rebels?
e Which act closed down the Irish Parliament?
f Which king refused to let Catholics have equal rights?
g Who led the Irish protests in the 1820s?
h When did Parliament pass an act allowing Catholics to be M.P.s?

B The Great Famine

Ireland was a farming country. It had fertile parts, where landlords and tenants grew corn and raised cattle. But in the barren west, the peasants lived in rough cabins on tiny plots of land. The men worked on the landlords' land — the wages they earned paid the rent. On their own plots, they grew **potatoes**, which were their main food, and often their **only** food.

In the autumn of 1845, disaster struck. When the peasants dug up the potatoes, they found a black, stinking mess. **Potato blight**, a fungus disease, had destroyed the tubers below the ground. Half the crop was lost in 1845. The whole crop was destroyed in 1846, and 1848 was just as bad.

Over a million peasants died of hunger or the fever which went with it. In large parts of the west and south-west of Ireland, starving people lived off raw turnips, berries, and nettles.

They had no money to pay the rent for their homes and land. Some landlords let them off, but some **evicted** those who could not pay.

The government set men to work on the roads to earn money for food. It opened soup kitchens. It cancelled the Corn Laws (see Chapter 47) and brought in cheap foreign corn and maize. But the problem was too big — there were not enough jobs or places in the workhouses. The government said that there was not enough money to pay for all the schemes.

Families left their homes and took to the roads in despair. Over a million hungry, evicted people **emigrated** (left their homes for good). Some made their way to England. But many braved the 'coffin ships' that crossed the Atlantic, and started new lives in the U.S.A.

Now try Exercises 50.2 and 50.3.

Source 50a

An eviction. Soldiers stand by as peasants are thrown out and their cabin is pulled down.

Source 50b

I am not easily moved, but I have to say that I was sickened by what I saw today. Crowds of women and children were scattered over the turnip fields like a flock of crows. They were eating the raw turnips, shivering in the snow and sleet. The children were screaming with hunger.

Adapted from a letter written by Captain Wynne, an English officer on duty in the west of Ireland in 1846.

Source 50c

In one place I was surprised to find the village street empty. I entered one of the cabins to find the cause, and saw six starving skeletons huddled in a corner on some filthy straw. Their only covering was a ragged cloth. As I approached, I heard a low moaning sound. They were alive, but all of them were ill with fever — four children, a woman, and a man.

Adapted from a letter written by an Irish magistrate in December 1846.

Source 50d

After the potatoes failed in 1846, the government gave eight million pounds. We hoped that the money would see the Irish through the crisis, and that they would find some other kind of food. But they just planted potatoes again. And now the potatoes have failed again. How can you help people like that? We cannot give them any more money – the result would be just the same.

From a letter written by Lord John Russell, the Prime Minister, in 1848.

Source 50e

The sheriff arrived with a strong force of police and some men with crowbars. The sheriff gave a signal, and the work began. The men dragged the miserable peasants out of their cabin. They tore the thatched roof down, and battered in the earth walls. I was only twelve at the time, but I will never forget the sight. I can still see the screaming women and the half-naked children.

An account of the events of 1848 written by Sir William Butler.

Exercise 50.2

Read **Section B** and **Sources 50b, 50c,** and **50d**.
Answer the questions in sentences. (Use your own words.)

a What sickened Captain Wynne (**Source 50b**)?
b Why were the women and children in **Source 50b** so hungry?
c Why was the village street empty in **Source 50c**?
d What were the feelings of the magistrate in **Source 50c**?
e What did Lord John Russell (**Source 50d**) think about the Irish?
f Can you think of any reasons why Lord John Russell's feelings were so different from the feelings of Captain Wynne and the magistrate? (Write more than one sentence if you can.)

Source 50f

After the eviction. A peasant family takes refuge in a ditch.

Exercise 50.3

Read **Source 50e**, and look at **Sources 50a** and **50f**.
Then write three paragraphs:

a Do **Sources 50a** and **50e** tell the same story about an eviction? Are there any differences?
b Describe **Source 50f**. What do you think has happened?
c What do you think were the opinions of the author of **Source 50e** and the artist who drew **Sources 50a** and **50f**?

C Parnell and Gladstone

The English were not to blame for the potato blight. But the Irish blamed them for not helping more during the famine. And English landlords who evicted poor peasants were hated. In the 1870s, evictions were the main cause of trouble between England and Ireland.

The Irish 'Land League' tried to protect the peasants. It organized protests and attacks on the stock and property of landlords who evicted. At the same time, Charles Stewart Parnell formed a Home Rule party. He wanted Ireland to have its own Parliament again. In the 1880s, Parnell's party won most of Ireland's seats in the House of Commons.

In England, the great Liberal Prime Minister William Gladstone tried to solve Ireland's problems. He got Parliament to pass acts which made it hard for landlords to evict peasants. He made sure that rents were not too high. But Parnell and his party were not satisfied. In the end, Gladstone decided that Ireland must have Home Rule. But not all of the Liberals agreed, and he failed to get a Home Rule bill passed.

By 1900, Parnell and Gladstone were dead. Most Irishmen still wanted Home Rule, and most of the English were against it. But there was now the question of Ulster as well. A large part of the population of north-east Ireland was Protestant. They said they were British, not Irish, and did not want Home Rule.

Now try Exercise 50.4.

Parliament rejects Gladstone's Home Rule Bill

Exercise 50.4

Read **Section C**. Find words and names in **Section C** to fit the following:

a A fungus disease which attacks potatoes.
b Peasants being put out of their homes by their landlords.
c An organization that tried to protect Irish peasants.
d A party that wanted Ireland to govern itself.
e The leader of the party that wanted Ireland to govern itself.
f A great Liberal Prime Minister of the late nineteenth century.
g A part of Ireland where a large part of the population was Protestant.

51 The British Empire in the Nineteenth Century

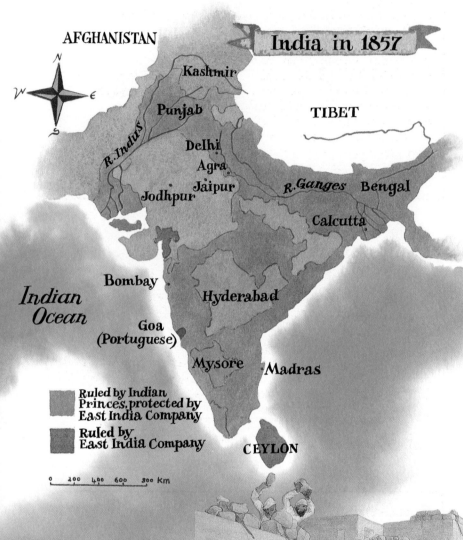

India in 1857

- AFGHANISTAN
- Kashmir
- Punjab
- TIBET
- R. Indus
- Delhi
- Agra
- Jaipur
- Jodhpur
- R. Ganges
- Bengal
- Calcutta
- Indian Ocean
- Bombay
- Hyderabad
- Goa (Portuguese)
- Mysore
- Madras
- CEYLON

Ruled by Indian Princes, protected by East India Company

Ruled by East India Company

0 200 400 600 800 Km

British troops and Indian sepoys loyal to the British retake Delhi during the Indian Mutiny

A India

The **East India Company** (see Chapter 38) was a company with an empire. It had its own army, with British officers and Indian 'sepoy' soldiers. And by 1850, it controlled most of India. (Look at the **Map**.) Even the parts that still had rajahs and nawabs were 'protected' by Britain.

The British thought that they had brought law and order and progress to India. So they were appalled in May 1857 when the sepoy soldiers revolted and took Delhi and other towns in the north. But the British fought back, and within a year they were in control again. Both sides were guilty of many savage crimes (See **Sources 51a** and **51b**.)

The British called it a 'mutiny'. They said that the main cause was that the sepoys did not like the new greased cartridges which they had to use. (This was to do with religion. Hindu soldiers said that the grease was beef fat, and cows are sacred to Hindus. Muslims thought that it was pork fat, and Muslims are not allowed to eat pork.)

Indians called it a **rebellion** against foreign rule. They had a long list of complaints. The British had taken away the lands of the rajahs and nawabs. No Indians were employed as judges, army officers, or in other senior jobs. The British did not respect Indian customs and laws. And imports of British cotton cloth had damaged Indian trade.

The rebellion (or mutiny) failed. But the British learned lessons from it. They ended the rule of the East India Company. In future, a **viceroy** ruled India in the name of the queen. They went on using Indian troops, but the number of British soldiers in India was greatly increased.

Now try Exercises 51.1 and 51.2.

Source 51a

If I told you about all the things the rebels have done you would not believe me. Such awful crimes have never been known before. You in England will not hear the worst, for the worst is so bad that the papers would not dare publish it. The British soldiers here are furious. They say very little, but every face shows that when the time comes they will show no mercy to those who have shown none themselves.

Letter from a journalist in India to an English newspaper in 1857.

Exercise 51.1

Read **Section A**, then answer the questions. You can find the right answers, and some wrong ones, in the list below.
a i Which words mean the same as 'rebellion'?
   ii Which words mean the same as 'mutiny'?
b According to the British, what was the main cause of the mutiny?
c According to Indians, what were the causes of the rebellion? (More than one answer.)

- The British brought law and order to India.
- A revolt by soldiers or sailors against their officers.
- The British did not understand or respect Indian ways.
- The viceroy ruled India in the name of the queen.
- Imported British goods harmed Indian trade.
- The British took land that belonged to Indian princes.
- A war against a foreign ruler.
- No Indians were employed in top jobs.
- Sepoys had to use greased cartridges.

Source 51b

It was a savage war. Both sides were guilty of dreadful crimes. At Cawnpore, Nana Sahib had all his British prisoners put to death. He did not even spare the women and children. But when the British took Delhi back, all the houses, shops, and stores were ransacked. The people in them were killed – men, women and children. Every British soldier became rich.

Adapted from a book written by D. P. Singhal, an Indian historian, in 1983.

Exercise 51.2

Read **Sources 51a and 51b**. The write out and complete the sentences.

a The author of **Source 51a** was shocked by _____ .
b **Source 51a** says that some of the crimes were so bad that _____ .
c **Source 51a** says that the British soldiers were _____ .
d **Source 51b** calls the mutiny a _____ .
e **Source 51b** says that the Indians murdered British _____ .
f **Source 51b** says that the British soldiers _____ .
g The two sources say different things because _____ .

The British brought industrial technology to India, e.g. by building railways. This is Victoria railway station in Bombay.

B The dominions

Britain did not treat her **white** subjects overseas in the same way as her black and Asian ones. The loss of the American colonies (see Chapter 38) taught her a lesson. She learned that it was wiser to share power with the colonists than to fight them. Before 1900, though, noone in Britain thought that the same was true of subjects who were not white.

Canada was in two parts, one British and one French. Each of them got the right to govern itself in 1791. But after a revolt in 1837, the two parts were joined together. And an act passed in 1867 made Canada a **dominion**. This meant that it was almost free from British control. (The Queen of England was still Queen of Canada.)

The British government took over from the East India Company as ruler of India after the Mutiny. In 1876, Parliament gave Queen Victoria the title 'Empress of India'.

Britain began sending convicts to **Australia** in 1787. But far more settlers went there of their own free will than in chains. Some went to look for gold, but most of them went as sheep-farmers. The wool they sent home kept the Yorkshire mills running. In 1850, there were 265,000 people in New South Wales, and **thirteen million** sheep!

The colonies in Australia got the right to govern themselves between 1856 and 1861. But it was not until the 1890s that they talked about joining together. In the end, they did so, and became a dominion, like Canada, in 1901. (**New Zealand** became a single state with the right to rule itself in 1876.)

Now try Exercise 51.3.

Exercise 51.3

Read **Section B**. Draw a timeline from 1750 to 1901, and mark the following in the right places:

a Canada became a dominion.
b Australia became a dominion.
c New Zealand got the right to rule itself.
d The two parts of Canada got the right to govern themselves.
e The first settlement for convicts was set up in Australia.
f Revolt in Canada.
g Australian colonies got the right to elect their own governments.

C Empire-building

The trade in black slaves made some English merchants rich in the eighteenth century. But Parliament banned the slave trade in 1807. And in 1833 it ordered that the slaves should all be set free. In the **West Indies**, the freed slaves worked for wages on the sugar plantations. But the wages were low, partly because the price of sugar took a sharp fall.

The first white settlers at the **Cape of Good Hope** (see the **Map** below) were Dutch (or **Boers**). In 1815, the Cape became British. For the rest of the nineteenth century, there was a long string of quarrels between the British and the Boers. Britain lost the first **Boer War** in 1881. And the second Boer War (1899–1902) began badly as well.

The second half of the nineteenth century was a time of great growth in the British Empire. The reasons were mainly to do with trade. And trade with India and the Far East meant that the **Suez Canal**, which was built in 1869, was vital to Britain. So when there was disorder in **Egypt** in 1882, Britain used it as an excuse to send in troops and take over.

From the 1880s, a '**Scramble for Africa**' took place, as the states of western Europe rushed to carve up the continent. They were all looking for new markets for the goods their industries produced. Soldiers came in with the traders, and the map of Africa was drawn to suit the statesmen of Europe. (Look at the **Map** below.)

Now try Exercise 51.4.

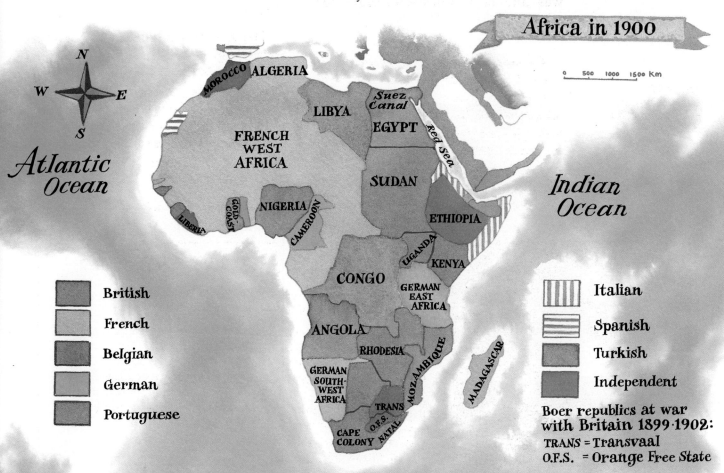

Africa in 1900

0 500 1000 1500 Km

Atlantic Ocean

Indian Ocean

N W E S

MOROCCO ALGERIA
LIBYA
Suez Canal
EGYPT
Red Sea
FRENCH WEST AFRICA
SUDAN
LIBERIA
GOLD COAST
NIGERIA
CAMEROON
ETHIOPIA
UGANDA
KENYA
CONGO
GERMAN EAST AFRICA
ANGOLA
RHODESIA
MOZAMBIQUE
MADAGASCAR
GERMAN SOUTH-WEST AFRICA
TRANS
O.F.S.
CAPE COLONY
NATAL

British
French
Belgian
German
Portuguese

Italian
Spanish
Turkish
Independent

Boer republics at war with Britain 1899-1902:
TRANS = Transvaal
O.F.S. = Orange Free State

263

Troops leaving Southampton Dock to go and fight in the Boer War

Source 51c

At a time when people are demanding that our forces should attack Egypt, we have to ask the reason why. A few years ago, our government and the French began to interfere in Egypt, without having any right to do so. The result was that the National Party was formed. Its slogan was 'Egypt for the Egyptians'. If Englishmen cried 'England for the English' we would praise them. So why should we condemn Egyptians for doing the same?

Report of a meeting of the Workmen's Peace Association, 24 June 1882.

Source 51d

At last, the world has been taught what happens if England is defied and its subjects are killed. We regret the damage to Alexandria and its people. But in fact what has happened was good both for Egypt and for England. Egypt has been freed from the rule of the National Party tyrants. And the massacre of Englishmen has been avenged.

Amended from *The Observer* newspaper, 16 July 1882. (When Englishmen were killed in riots in Alexandria, the Royal Navy shelled the city.)

Explorers, such as David Livingstone, helped to spread the British Empire in Africa. This picture shows Livingstone on the River Shire in Malawi in 1859.

Exercise 51.4

Read **Section C** and **Sources 51c** and **51d**.

Write a short essay which answers these questions:

a What did the two sources think about the Egyptian National Party?
b What did the two sources think about using force against Egypt?
c Do you think that all British people were proud of the Empire? Do you think that they all had the same opinion?

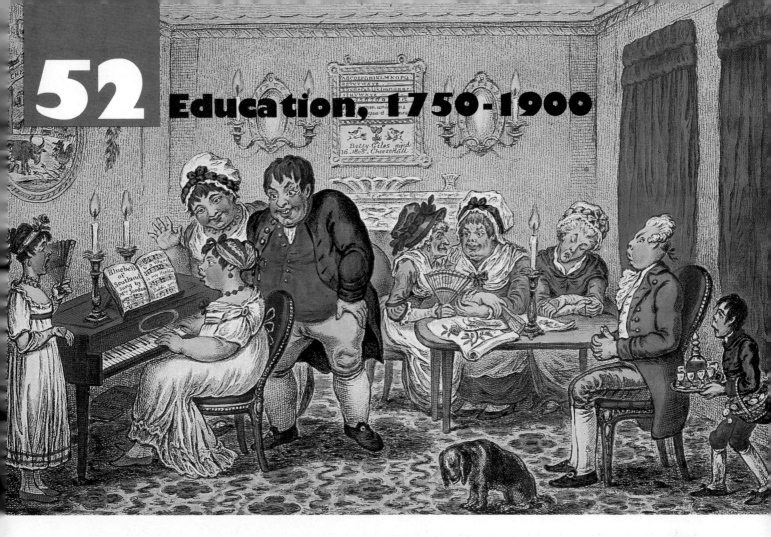

52 Education, 1750-1900

A Public schools and private schools

Most of the great 'public' schools of England took boarders and charged fees. They were for the **sons** of the rich, and were not **public** at all. They taught their pupils Latin and Greek, but not much mathematics, and no science, history, or French. Rich men's **daughters** stayed at home. They were taught by their mothers, or perhaps a governess.

Dissenters (Protestants who did not belong to the Church of England) had their own schools. They were the best in England. Only they taught science, commerce, French, and German. Many of the businessmen and inventors of the Industrial Revolution had been to dissenters' schools.

The very poor did not send their children to school, because they could not afford the fees. Also, they needed the wages that their children earned. But men and women who had just a little money sent their sons and daughters to **private** schools. Some of these were really awful. They had no proper books, desks, or classrooms, and the teachers were ignorant, greedy, and cruel.

Charities ran schools for the poor in some towns, but there were not enough of them. Then, in 1780, **Robert Raikes** opened his first **Sunday school** in Gloucester. His aim was to occupy the children of the poor, who worked in factories on week-days. (See **Source 52b**.) Some of the children learned to read and write. All of them were taught to obey 'their betters'.

Now try Exercise 52.1.

Farmer Giles and his wife show off their daughter, Betty, to their neighbours. Betty has just returned from a private school, where she has learned to play the piano and sing.

Source 52b

On Sundays the streets of Minchinhampton have always been full of half-naked, half-starved little brutes. But last Sunday I was pleased to see that the streets were empty. The children were all in the Sunday School. I found 300 of them there, all busy, some learning their letters, some learning to spell, and some reading the Bible. There was silence and good order, and all seemed happy and contented.

From the *Gloucester Journal* newspaper, 15 November 1784.

Exercise 52.1

Read **Section A** and **Source 52b**, and look at **Source 52a**.
Write four short paragraphs:

a What **facts** does **Source 52b** contain?

b What were the **opinions** of the author of **Source 52b**?

c Describe what you can see in **Source 52a**.

d In **Source 52a**, what do you think were the **opinions** of **i** Farmer Giles, and his wife, **ii** Betty, **iii** Betty's younger sister, **iv** the neighbours, **v** the servant, **vi** the dog?

B Public money for schools

The biggest problem about schooling for the poor was money — the cost of teachers, books, etc. Soon after 1800, **Andrew Bell** and **Joseph Lancaster** found what seemed to be an answer. (See **Sources 16c** and **16d**.) They used **monitors**, and this was cheap — one person could teach a very large class.

Bell's and Lancaster's schools were run by societies which were linked to the Churches. And it was to these Church schools that the first grants of **public money** were made. In 1833, Parliament gave £20,000 to help with schooling for the poor. (Even in 1833, this was quite a small amount.)

The government gave more and more money to the Church schools during the next thirty years. By 1860, some people said that it was giving too much. So new rules, brought out in 1862, said that only schools which were doing a good job would get support. Inspectors went round, testing the pupils. Schools got so much for each pupil who passed the test. This was called '**payment by results**'.

Source 52c

By 1860, about half the children in England and Wales were getting some kind of schooling. But most of them left school before the age of twelve. Schools in Scotland were much better. And in many parts of Europe, education was **compulsory**.

People began to say that the state should take charge of schools in England and Wales as well. It should **force** parents to make their children attend. And state schools should be **free**. Some said that if the workers were not educated, British industry would fall behind its rivals. Others said that now that working men had the right to vote, they needed to be able to read and write. (See **Source 52g**.)

Now try Exercises 52.2 and 52.3.

Source **52d**

The cheapest way of teaching a large number of pupils is to use monitors. The teacher chooses the best pupils as monitors. He teaches them himself, then makes them pass on what they have learned to the rest of the pupils. In this way, the teacher gets a set of assistants, and does not need to pay them wages. Using this method, I have taught a class of 225 pupils.

Adapted from an article published in the *Quarterly Review* in 1831.

One of Joseph Lancaster's schools in the East End of London in 1839. The older boys acted as monitors, passing on knowledge to the younger boys. The toys hanging from the ceiling were given as rewards for good work and behaviour. The artist drew what he saw for himself, but we do not know his name.

A 'ragged school' in 1853. This was a kind of charity school where poor children learned practical skills and moral values. The artist would have seen a ragged school, but his name is not known.

Source 52f

We know that there will always be some crime. But we should try to stop crime at its source. To do that we must teach children the difference between right and wrong, and make them learn God's laws. We must get them into the habit of obeying rules and orders. If we do that, when they become men they will obey the laws and keep order in our society.

From a speech made by Lord Palmerston, the Prime Minister, in 1860.

Source 52g

I suppose that we will now have to educate our masters. You have placed the government of this country in the hands of the masses. So you will now have to give them education. I used to be against education for all, but I am now ready to accept it.

Adapted from a speech made by Robert Lowe, M.P. in 1867, just after Parliament had given the vote to working men.

Exercise 52.2

Read **Section B** and **Sources 52d, 52f**, and **52g**. Look at **Sources 52c** and **52e**. Answer these questions about each of the sources:

a Who wrote or drew it? (Write 'not known' if you do not know.)
b When was it written or drawn?
c Is it a primary or a secondary source? (Look again at the note on page 218.)

Put your answers to questions **a, b**, and **c** above in a table, with columns for 'Source', 'Author or artist', 'Date', and 'Primary or secondary'.

Exercise 52.3

What were the **motives** of the authors of **Sources 52b, 52d, 52f**, and **52g**? – **Why** were they in favour of schools for the children of the working class? Discuss these questions in a group. Then make a group display:

a Write out the sources.
b Write paragraphs saying what the motives of the authors of the sources were.
c Draw cartoons to go with the written work.

Divide up these jobs among the members of the group.

C Board schools

An act passed in 1870 started a state system of schooling in England and Wales. But to save money, it did not go as far as many people would have liked. The act said that where there were church schools, they would continue to get public money. New schools would be built only where there were no church schools. The new schools would be called 'board schools'.

The 1870 act did not make it **compulsory** to go to school. From 1880, though, parents were **compelled** to send children up to ten years old to school. By 1900, full-time schooling was compulsory up to the age of twelve. The 1870 act did not make education **free**, either. Parents had to pay nine old pence (about 4p.) a week for each child. (Board schools became free in 1891.)

Board schools, as a rule, were solid, dismal buildings, red brick outside and stone corridors and stairs inside. Iron railings round the concrete yards made them look even more like prisons. Most of them had no science labs, art or craft rooms, or gyms. P.E., which was called 'drill', was done outdoors, in the yard.

Classes were huge (sixty was common), and lessons were dull. The children were taught to read, write, and do simple sums, and they learned a lot of scripture. Sometimes, there was singing or drawing for a change. Boys and girls were shouted at for most of the time, and caned when they were slow to learn.

Now try Exercise 52.4

Exercise 52.4

Read **Section C**. Copy the sentences and write TRUE or FALSE after each one.

a After 1870, Church schools got no more public money. _____

b Board schools were built after the 1870 Education act. _____

c After 1880, education was compulsory for children up to the age of ten. _____

d Parents still had to pay nine pence per week for each child at school in 1900. _____

e Board schools were made to look attractive to the pupils. _____

f Most board schools had no playing fields. _____

g In board schools, classes were large and lessons were dull. _____

h Boys could be caned in board schools, but girls could not. _____

Boys' drill in a board school yard in around 1900

53 Arts and Leisure, 1750-1900

Source 53a

A Architecture and painting

West Wycombe Park, a country house built in Buckinghamshire between 1735 and 1765 in the Roman and Greek style

Only the rich can afford to hire architects. And 'the rich' in the 1750s meant the landowners. They paid architects to design their country houses. And the architects of the time copied **Greek** and **Roman** styles, with columns and **grand doorways**. (Look at **Source 53a.**) Before long, the Greek and Roman style reached the towns as well. The finest streets and squares of Bath and London were built between 1760 and 1820. (Look at **Source 53b.**)

In the nineteenth century, though, big companies and town councils hired the architects. Some fine country houses were still being built. But the chief buildings of the years 1860 to 1900 were town halls and railway stations. At the same time, there was a change in style. The Greeks and Romans were out, and the **Middle Ages** were in. That is why St. Pancras Station in London looks like a cathedral. (Look at **Source 53d.**)

270

Regent Street in London as it was when first built in 1811

The Royal Pavilion in Brighton, designed for the Prince Regent (later King George IV) by his architect John Nash. It was completed in 1823. The design copies the palaces and temples of India.

St. Pancras Station in London, which was built between 1868 and 1874

The great artists of the mid-eighteenth century painted **portraits**. By 1800, though, 'romantic' **land-scapes** were much more popular. (Look at **Source 53e**). Fifty years later, the public wanted pictures that told a **story**. So artists gave them scenes from history or the Bible, or views of modern craftsmen at work. (Look at **Source 53f**.)

Now try Exercise 53.1.

Source 53e

'Crossing the Brook', a landscape by J. M. W. Turner. The artist lived from 1775 to 1851.

Source 53f

'Iron and Coal', painted by William Bell Scott in 1861

Exercise 53.1

Read **Section A**. Look at **Sources 53a, 53b, 53c, 53d, 53e**, and **53f**. Draw a timeline from 1750 to 1900. Mark on it 'mid-eighteenth century', 'late eighteenth century', 'early nineteenth century', etc.

Mark the following at the right points on the time line:

a West Wycombe Park was completed.
b Regent Street was built.
c The Royal Pavilion, Brighton was completed.
d St. Pancras Station was completed.
e J. M. W. Turner was born.
f W. B. Scott painted 'Iron and Coal'.

B Fashion

In clothes, also, fashions were set by the rich. They could afford a lot of new clothes, and could keep up with the changing styles. Fashion did not mean much to the poor, except when they could get hold of rich men's and women's cast-offs. For that reason, poor people's fashions were a few years behind the styles of the rich.

Women's dresses were always long, but their shape changed. Hooped petticoats in the mid-eighteenth century gave way to the straight 'Empire line' of 1800. (Look at **Sources 53g** and **53h**.) By the 1850s, metal supports were back with the **'crinoline'**. And this in turn was replaced by the **'bustle'** in the 1870s. (Look at **Sources 53i** and **53j**.)

Between 1750 and 1900, men's fashions changed much more than women's. They stopped wearing wigs before 1800. By the mid-nineteenth century, they were wearing **trousers**, not breeches. And **suits**, not very different from those that are worn today, had appeared by the 1880s. All this time, men's clothes had been growing less colourful – no men dressed in pale blue or yellow by 1900.

Now try Exercise 53.2.

Source 53g

Fashionable dress in the 1760s. The man wears a silk, embroidered coat, a flowered silk waistcoat, knee breeches, and white stockings. The woman wears a cream satin gown with a hooped skirt. Both wear powdered wigs.

Source 53h

Fashion in 1800. The woman wears an 'Empire line' gown in the Greek style, with no hoops and only one petticoat. The man still wears knee breeches, but the coat is cut in a different style, and he has a 'Beaver' top hat, and black leather boots.

Source 53i

Fashion in the 1850s. The man wears a black silk top hat, a frock coat, and trousers. The woman wears a ball dress of white crinoline with a taffeta bodice and overskirt.

Source 53j

A lady of the 1870s. She wears a dark brown silk afternoon dress with a bustle skirt.

Source 53k

Men's fashion in the 1880s. He wears a brown tweed suit and a black bowler hat.

Women's tennis outfit in the 1890s. She plays tennis in a striped blouse, a long serge skirt, a black belt and tie, with black canvas shoes, and a straw hat.

Exercise 53.2

Read **Section B**. Look at **Sources 53g, 53h, 53i, 53j,** and **53k.** Write a short essay, describing

either a the changes in women's fashion between 1750 and 1880.

or **b** the changes in men's fashion between 1750 and 1880.

Draw at least one picture to go with your essay.

C Sport and entertainment

To the upper classes, 'sport' meant killing birds and animals — **shooting** and **fox-hunting**. The landlord's hounds could chase the fox through his tenant's crops. And no-one but the landlord could take his 'game'. The laws against **poaching** were severe.

Many a young man 'of good family' lost his money and land gambling on cards, dice, or horses. After 1800, though, **racing** became more honest and fair. It also became a sport for all classes, not just the rich. After 1850, a trip to Epsom on Derby Day was a treat for thousands of London families.

In 1750, **cricket** was a game played on the village green. **Football** was more like a war between rival sides. The nineteenth century saw both games turned into formal sports, with fixed rules. By the 1890s, large crowds were turning out to watch professional players in cup-ties and test-matches. **Lawn-tennis**, on the other hand, was a new sport. It was invented in the 1870s as a pastime for people with big houses and gardens.

The **theatre** was popular in London in 1750. Soon after 1800, most of the large towns outside London had theatres too. But the theatre was for people with some money. After 1850, the middle class went to the **music-hall**, where they could drink, watch the acts, and join in the songs. For working-class men, and some women, there was the **public house**.

Before 1850, working people did not take **holidays**. But the railways made travel quick and cheap. And the rising standard of living meant that there was more money to spend. So some people could take day-trips to the seaside. And by 1900, more and more could look forward to a week each year at Blackpool or Margate.

Now try Exercises 53.3 and 53.4.

An F.A. Cup tie between Notts County and Blackburn Rovers in 1891

Exercise 53.3

Read **Section C**, and look at the illustrations connected with sport. Write notes (in your own words) on the following:

a The favourite sports of the gentry.
b The changes in football and cricket.
c Sporting clothes in the 1890s.
d Theatres and music-halls.
e Holidays.

Source 53l

A street musician in 1877

Source 53m

To many people, street music is a great nuisance, but there are far more who enjoy it. The upper class can afford to go to the opera and the best concerts. The middle class and the tradesmen have their music halls. But the working class can not afford even the music halls. The street bands and organs are their entertainment. The noise they make is sometimes awful, but a big crowd gathers whenever a band begins to play.

Adapted from *The Observer* newspaper, 3 July 1864.

Exercise 53.4

Read **Source 53m** and look at **Source 53l**.
Then fill in the blank spaces in the sentences.

a The people who objected to music in the street could probably afford to go to the _____ or _____ hall.
b Working-class people must have liked street bands, because big _____ gathered to listen to them.
c The words 'there are far more who enjoy it' in **Source 53m** tell us that the _____ class must have been bigger than the other classes.
d Opera and concert tickets must have been _____ in the 1860s.
e Music halls must have been _____ expensive than the opera house.
f The street musician in **Source 53l** is playing a _____.
g **Sources 53l** and **53m** both say that people _____ street music in working-class districts.

54 Religion, 1750-1900

A The Church of England

In 1750, the great majority of people in Britain were Christians. And well over half of those in England and Wales belonged to the **Church of England**. But the Church of England was more suited to the past than to the future.

Each village or group of villages formed a **parish**. And each parish had its church and parson. With the Industrial Revolution, some villages grew into towns. But still there was one parish church, and one parson. In the new towns, there was often no church near to where the people lived. And there was no parson to visit them when they needed help or comfort.

Some parsons worked very hard. But too many, especially in the country districts, took life easily. They were more keen to be on good terms with the local gentry than working among the poor. The **bishops** should have given them a lead. But too many bishops were more bothered about their own careers than the clergy they should have led and guided.

One group within the Church of England saw that all was not well. The **evangelicals** were keen to preach the Christian message in the new towns. They wanted people to read the Bible for themselves, so they were in favour of schools for the poor. But they were shocked by what they saw in the factories and mills. This is what led them to press for changes in the law. (See **Section C**.)

Now try Exercise 54.1

Source 54a

Churches were often full on Sundays in the mid-eighteenth century, even if some of the congregation fell asleep!

Source 54b

The bishops are worried about a planned inquiry into their incomes. They are afraid that the government might take some of their money away.

Exercise 54.1

Read **Section A**, and look at **Sources 54a** and **54b**. Copy and complete the sentences.

a In 1750, most people in England and Wales belonged to _____ .

b The church in **Source 54a** was _____ .

c In many new towns, there were too few _____ .

d A lot of country parsons _____ .

e The bishops in **Source 54b** were worried because _____ .

f Bishops were supposed to _____ .

g Evangelicals were keen on education because _____ .

John Wesley preaching from his father's tomb

B The Methodists

John Wesley was a Church of England parson and a great preacher. Crowds flocked to hear him as he travelled round the country. Between 1738 and 1791, it is reckoned that he travelled 224,000 miles on horseback, and preached 40,000 sermons. The men and women who followed his lead were called '**Methodists**'.

Wesley said that he had been 'converted' suddenly, one day in May 1738. In a flash, he had seen that God loved him, and that he was 'saved'. He spent the rest of his life – another 53 years – touring England and Wales, begging people to let God 'save' them too.

In a lot of places, Wesley was not allowed to preach in the church. In a good many places, there was no church to preach in. So he did a great deal of his preaching in the open air. This suited him well – he could reach a bigger audience that way. Men and women came to his meetings in thousands. And they did not just listen in silence – they sang, cried out, wept, danced, and jumped for joy.

Wesley and other Methodist preachers won a huge following, mainly among working people, both in the towns and on the land. By 1791, there were over a million Methodists. In one important sense, though, Wesley failed. He wanted Methodists to remain in the Church of England. But soon after his death, the Methodists and the Church of England split apart for good.

Now try Exercise 54.2.

William Wilberforce

Source **54c**

Joseph Rawlins, who was known as the 'pit preacher', died not long ago in Staffordshire. He got his nickname because he acted for many years as a Methodist minister for the miners in those parts. He first became a Methodist after he heard John Wesley preach in 1749. Rawlins was blind, but he worked on week-days as a miner. He gave most of his wages away to the sick and the poor.

From the *Bristol Journal* newspaper, 11 June 1791.

Exercise 54.2

Read **Section B** and **Source 54c.** Which of the statements below do you think is true? Write out the sentences which you think are true.

a All Methodist ministers were Church of England parsons.
b John Wesley preached in Staffordshire in 1749.
c Most Church of England parsons did not approve of John Wesley.
d A lot of miners in Staffordshire were Methodists.
e Joseph Rawlins died in 1793.
f Some Methodist ministers had week-day jobs as well as preaching on Sundays.
g John Wesley would have been sad if he had known that the Methodists left the Church of England.
h Working people had no interest in religion.
i Methodists believed in giving money to the sick and poor.

C The Churches and reform

Between 1750 and 1900, trade and industry made Britain rich and strong. She became the 'workshop of the world', she gained a great empire, and her navy ruled the seas. But there was a dark side to all this success. This was the suffering of the black slaves and the children in the mills. It was the women in the mines and the crowded families in the filthy slums.

Evangelicals, such as **William Wilberforce**, tried to put right these wrongs. Wilberforce spent his life

fighting for the rights of slaves. In 1807, he and his friends got Parliament to ban the **trade** in slaves. But it was not until 1833, the year of his death, that all the slaves in the British Empire were freed.

Lord Shaftesbury was troubled by the 'slaves' in the mills and mines. He was the leader of the 'Ten Hours Movement'. This was a group of evangelicals in Parliament, who wanted to shorten the working day to no more than ten hours. They had some success

— Factory Acts passed in the 1830s and 1840s cut children's hours of work and banned women from the mines. In the end, they led to shorter hours for men as well.

After 1870, reformers turned to **housing** for the poor. **Cardinal Manning**, the leading Catholic, tried to improve the state of London's slums. Some charities put up new blocks of flats. But the best work in this field was done by **George Cadbury**, a Quaker, and the head of a chocolate firm. At Bournville, near Birmingham, he housed his workers in a brand new town.

Now try Exercises 54.3 and 54.4.

Exercise 54.3

Read **Section C**. Find words or phrases in **Section C** which mean the same as the following:

a Black workers who were owned by their employers. _____

b Dirty, overcrowded, badly-built housing. _____

c Members of the Church of England who were in favour of reform. _____

d M.P.s who wanted to cut the working day. _____

e A new law to do with hours and conditions in factories. _____

f Organizations which collect money and try to help those in need. _____

g A new town for workers in a chocolate factory. _____

Lord Shaftesbury inspecting conditions in a coal mine

Source 54d

Pass through Edinburgh on a Sunday morning and you will not meet a soul. The streets are silent and empty. But the moment prayers are over, they pour out of the churches in crowds. After spending some time at home, they go back to church again. But at five o-clock prayers are over for the day, and they begin to amuse themselves. The young ones go for walks in the meadows. The older folks meet in groups to discuss the scandal of the town.

Adapted from a book written by Captain Topham in 1776. The Scots people belonged to the Church of Scotland, which was different from the Church of England. It had no bishops, the minister did not read the service from a prayer book, and the sermons were longer.

Source 54e

In Birmingham there is one fine large church. There are also three chapels and eight meeting houses for Dissenters. But the great mass of people do not care about religion. They seldom, if ever, go to church, and spend Sundays in their working clothes, amusing themselves.

Adapted from W. Thompson's *A Tour of England and Scotland*, written in 1788. The 'fine large church' would belong to the Church of England. 'Dissenters' were Protestants who did not belong to the Church of England. Methodists would count as 'Dissenters'.

Exercise 54.4

Read **Sources 54d** and **54e** and the notes which go with them.
Write an essay with the title 'Sunday in Edinburgh and Birmingham'. Your essay should answer these questions:

a Who wrote these sources? Which source was written first? How many years were there between them?
b How were Sundays different in Edinburgh and Birmingham?
c Which Church did the people of Edinburgh belong to?
d Were the people of Edinburgh all devout Christians?
e What kind of churches were there in Birmingham?
f Can you think of any reasons why most people in Birmingham did not go to church?

Sunday in Edinburgh, according to **Source 54d**.

Sunday in Birmingham, according to **Source 54e**.

Criteria grid

Key Elements and corresponding exercises (those printed in bold type are particularly relevant)

Chapters	1	2	3	4	5	6	7	8	9	10	11	12	13	14	15	16	17	18

Key Element 1: Chronological knowledge and understanding

		1	2	3	4	5	6	7	8	9	10	11	12	13	14	15	16	17	18
a	Historical knowledge	1.1 1.2	2.1 2.3	3.3	4.2 4.3	5.1 5.3	6.1 6.3	7.1 7.2	8.2 8.3	9.2 9.3	10.2	11.1 11.2	12.1	13.1 13.4	14.1 14.3	15.3 15.4	16.2	17.1 17.3	18.3
b	Concepts and technology	1.3			4.2	5.1	6.2				10.1		12.3		14.2			17.2	18.1
c	Chronology – dates and sequence		2.2						**8.1**		10.2			13.1					
d	Chronology – conventions			**3.2**				**7.3**		9.1	10.5					15.3			

Key Element 2: Range and depth of historical knowledge and understanding

		1	2	3	4	5	6	7	8	9	10	11	12	13	14	15	16	17	18
a	Cause and consequence			**3.5**		**5.3**			8.3			11.2	12.4			15.4		17.3	
b	Motivation	1.1				**5.4**		7.2						13.4			16.5		
c	Continuity and change		2.5		4.3		6.3				10.4		12.1		14.3	15.3	16.2		18.3
d	Different features of situations		2.6		**4.5**	5.6		7.5	8.4	9.5				13.5		15.2	16.6	17.4	18.3

Key Element 3: Awareness and understanding of interpretations of history

		1	2	3	4	5	6	7	8	9	10	11	12	13	14	15	16	17	18
a	Distinguishing fact and fiction			3.1						9.4								17.5	18.5
b	Different versions of events and topics	1.5		3.1					8.4		10.3	11.1	12.2	13.5					18.4
c	Recognizing fact and opinion		**2.4**	3.4								11.3			14.4				
d	Different interpretations						**6.4**	7.4	8.5			11.3	12.5	13.3			16.4		
e	Reasons for different interpretations							**7.4**	8.5					13.3					

Key Element 4: Knowledge and understanding of the processes of historical enquiry

		1	2	3	4	5	6	7	8	9	10	11	12	13	14	15	16	17	18
a	Acquiring information	1.1	2.1	3.3	4.1	5.2	6.1	7.1	8.2	9.3	10.2	11.5	12.1	13.1	14.1	15.1	16.3	17.3	
b	Sources – authorship and dates	**1.4**		3.1		5.5	6.5								14.5	15.5			
c	Primary and secondary sources				**4.4**	5.5							12.4		14.5				
d	Making deductions from sources							7.6	8.6			11.4		13.2				17.5	
e	Using different kinds of source	1.5	2.3		4.1			7.1	8.2	9.5		11.5	12.1	13.5	14.1	15.3	16.2	17.1	
f	Value and reliability of evidence						**6.5**		8.6	9.2					14.5	15.5	16.1		18.2

Most of the exercises seek to develop organisational and communication skills (**Key Element 5**).

Criteria grid

Chapters	19	20	21	22	23	24	25	26	27	28	29	30	31	32	33	34	35	36

Key Element 1: Chronological knowledge and understanding

		19	20	21	22	23	24	25	26	27	28	29	30	31	32	33	34	35	36
a	Historical knowledge	19.1 19.3	20.1 20.4	21.4	22.2 22.3	23.1 23.2	24.1	25.1 25.4	26.2 26.5	27.1	28.1 28.4	29.2	30.1 30.5	31.1 31.2	32.1	33.2 33.4	34.2	35.3 35.4	36.1
b	Concepts and terminology		20.3	21.1					26.4		28.3	29.1						35.1	36.3
c	Chronology – dates and sequence			21.3	22.1	23.2											34.3		
d	Chronology – conventions	**19.4**						25.3									34.3		

Key Element 2: Range and depth of historical knowledge and understanding

		19	20	21	22	23	24	25	26	27	28	29	30	31	32	33	34	35	36
a	Cause and consequence		**20.4** **20.5**				24.3		26.2		28.5								36.1
b	Motivation							**25.5**		27.4				31.1	32.2				
c	Continuity and change							25.4				29.3		31.4		33.2	34.2	35.4	36.2
d	Different features of situations	19.5				23.5				27.3			30.3	31.3			34.5		36.4

Key Element 3: Awareness and understanding of interpretations of history

		19	20	21	22	23	24	25	26	27	28	29	30	31	32	33	34	35	36
a	Distinguishing fact and fiction															33.1		35.5	36.5
b	Different versions of events and topics		20.2		22.5	23.3					28.1	29.5							
c	Recognizing fact and opinion			**21.5**						27.2			30.2			33.3	34.4		
d	Different interpretations			**21.2**			24.4	25.2	26.3	27.5			30.4	31.2			34.1		
e	Reasons for different interpretations									**27.6**			30.4	31.2			34.1		

Key Element 4: Knowledge and understanding of the processes of historical enquiry

		19	20	21	22	23	24	25	26	27	28	29	30	31	32	33	34	35	36
a	Acquiring information	19.3	20.1	21.4	22.2	23.1	24.1	25.1		27.1	28.4	29.2	30.1	31.4	32.1	33.4	34.2	35.3	36.5
b	Sources – authorship and dates	**19.2**	20.2						26.3			29.4				33.1			
c	Primary and secondary sources				**22.4**	23.3			26.3			29.4					34.5	35.2	
d	Making deductions from sources	19.5					24.5		26.1	27.3	28.2				32.3			35.2	
e	Using different kinds of source			21.5			24.2		26.5		28.1	29.4		31.5	32.3				36.4
f	Value and reliability of evidence				22.5	**23.4**								31.5		33.5			

Most of the exercises seek to develop organisational and communication skills (**Key Element 5**).

Criteria grid

Key Elements and corresponding exercises (those printed in bold type are particularly relevant)

Key Element 1: Chronological knowledge and understanding

	Chapters	37	38	39	40	41	42	43	44	45	46	47	48	49	50	51	52	53	54
a	Historical knowledge	37.1 37.3	38.1	39.1 39.4	40.1	41.2	42.4	43.1	44.1	45.1	46.3 46.4	47.1	48.1	49.3	50.1	51.1 51.4	52.4	53.1 53.3	54.1
b	Concepts and terminology	37.5				41.5			44.5						50.4				54.3
c	Chronology dates and sequence		38.2				42.4				46.3			49.3		51.3		53.1	
d	Chronology – conventions				**40.1**	41.3				45.1								53.1	

Key Element 2: Range and depth of historical knowledge and understanding

		37	38	39	40	41	42	43	44	45	46	47	48	49	50	51	52	53	54
a	Cause and consequence			**39.4**				43.5					48.3			51.1			
b	Motivation					**41.2**			44.2			47.4		49.1			52.3		
c	Continuity and change			39.1	40.2					45.4			48.2					53.2	
d	Different features of situations	37.2					42.1	**43.3**							50.2	51.4			

Key Element 3: Awareness and understanding of interpretations of history

		37	38	39	40	41	42	43	44	45	46	47	48	49	50	51	52	53	54
a	Distinguishing fact and fiction				40.3				**44.3**		46.4								
b	Different versions of events and topics		38.3			41.4	42.3												54.4
c	Recognizing fact and opinion	**37.4**						43.4					48.4		50.3		52.1		
d	Different intrerpretations			39.3						45.2		**47.3**		49.4		51.2			
e	Reasons for different intrerpretations		**38.3**			41.4	42.3									51.2			54.4

Key Element 4: Knowledge and understanding of the processes of historical enquiry

		37	38	39	40	41	42	43	44	45	46	47	48	49	50	51	52	53	54
a	Acquiring information	37.3		39.2				43.4	44.4		46.4							53.3	54.2
b	Sources – authorship and dates				40.3				44.3			47.2					52.2		
c	Primary and secondary sources						**42.2**		44.4			47.2					52.2		
d	Making deductions from sources			39.2				43.2			**46.2**		48.4					53.4	54.2
e	Using different kinds of source		38.4			41.1		43.2		45.3					50.3		52.1		
f	Value and reliability of evidence				40.4					**45.3**	46.1			49.2					

Most of the exercises seek to develop organisational and communication skills (**Key Element 5**).

Index

Index of Teaching Notes